Little Gypsy

Little Gypsy

ROXY FREEMAN

SIMON &
SCHUSTER

London · New York · Sydney · Toronto

A CBS COMPANY

First published in Great Britain by Simon & Schuster UK Ltd, 2011
A CBS Company

1 3 5 7 9 10 8 6 4 2

Simon & Schuster UK Ltd
1st Floor
222 Gray's Inn Road
London WC1X 8HB

www.simonandschuster.co.uk

Simon & Schuster Australia
Sydney

A CIP catalogue record for this book is available
from the British Library.

ISBN: 978-1-84983-344-8

Typeset by Hewer Text UK Ltd, Edinburgh
Printed in Great Britain by CPI Cox & Wyman Ltd, Reading, Berkshire

To my Mama and Papa with love

Contents

CHAPTER I

Travelling Genes

I close my eyes and the memory of dewy berries and fresh damp leaves fills my mind. My heart skips a beat as my senses are transported back to the days of my childhood. Sitting in my artificially lit study, surrounded by radiators and home comforts, I think back to the endless battle with nature, trying to stay warm and dry as a youngster. The permanently wet feet and knotted hair of the traveller's life are engraved into my being and will always be part of me. It doesn't matter how often I shower or get my hair done, I still imagine myself to be a scruffy little gypsy girl in a world of clean, civilised people.

Some days come back to me as if they were only yesterday. One place rolls into the next in my mind and I'm left with the overwhelming smell of the spongy peat, mixed with the aroma of the goats and wood smoke, the sound of the wind whistling across the marshes and the sight of my pregnant mother kneading bread dough and working tirelessly. One summer day, I think it was around 1984, my brother Rollin and my cousins Jerry and Ome and I set off across the bog to play. We'd finished our chores and were keen to get out of sight before someone found more work for us to do. We were living in Tipperary then, on a disused train track known as the Loony Line, where various families camped up. When it was a working railway line, the trains dropped people off at the lunatic asylum in Clonmel, hence the name. My father Dik's brother Bob and his family live there so we spent a fair amount of time with them when I was very young, camped on the side of the bogland.

We were really close as cousins back then. At that stage there were four children in our family and four children in theirs: Uncle Bob's eldest daughter Simone was, at ten, a year or so older than my elder sister Essie; a son Jerry who was my seven-year-old brother Rollin's close friend; another daughter, Ome, who was six; and a wee girl called Karen who was slightly younger than my three-and-a-half-year-old little sister Perly. I was five. Ome was my best friend and ally – we were a pair of mischievous little girls, always getting into things we shouldn't and causing trouble. She had an angelic look about her, with big brown eyes and a round face. I had dark curly hair and a cheeky spirit. We did everything together and thought we would be close forever.

We ran, filled with a sense of freedom and excitement, feelings I can now only conjure up when remembering that exact time and place; feelings that can only be felt by carefree children at one with nature and the elements. We didn't mind that the wind was howling, or that our clothes were damp. We didn't care that we had bare feet and had to watch the ground as we ran to avoid the thistles and splinters. We set out across the bog jumping the ditches as we went. They seemed vast and deep to a short-legged five-year-old, and I struggled to keep up with the older children, approaching each one with trepidation but nonetheless leaping without pausing, praying that I wouldn't find myself neck-deep in the brown peaty water below. Every so often one of us would lose our footing and end up falling in. Sometimes, if the weather was warm, we would all jump in too, not to rescue the wet person, but to mess around in the swampy bog.

Always, in the background, we could hear the roar of the Bord na Móna digger chugging away as the digger men turned the black ground into turf and briquettes for fuel. We knew not to go onto that land as the turfed ground was precarious and potentially lethal.

Instead we headed off through the swathes of bracken and gorse to the wide-open marshland. The soil here was dark and had little or no mineral wealth. Its only commercial use was for fuel. Many parts of Tipperary were still uncut in the early 1980s and offered expansive tracts of bleak terrain, empty but for wild life – and adventurous children.

After an hour or two running about in the marshes, the abundance of peppery watercress told us that we were getting closer to the wetland. Our feet started to sink further and further into the ground. Rollin looked around and saw me pausing on one foot.

'Don't stand still, Roxy!' he shouted. 'It's quicksand! You'll disappear if you don't keep moving.'

Was he teasing? I couldn't tell, but I wasn't going to hang around to find out. I pulled my foot out of the soil and kept on running, still trailing far behind.

Up ahead, Rollin, Jerry and Ome were standing in a circle discussing something. Rollin was a strong, wiry little boy with brown hair and chocolate brown eyes. He was protective of me if often belittling of my efforts. But bickering and constant competing aside, we adored each other.

'You were lucky to get out of there alive, Rox,' Rollin said jovially as I approached. 'If you can't keep up you should've stayed at the camp and helped Dixey cook or somefink.'

'I can keep up. I'm here, aren't I?' I replied indignantly.

Jerry pointed towards the digger that was slowly working through the land to our left and said, 'I fink it's Con. Let's go and see him.'

Con worked for Bord na Móna, clearing the bog and preparing the land ready for turfing. We'd made friends with him over the past couple of weeks and enjoyed chatting to him. We knew he'd keep an eye out for us. Some days he'd let us pile into the shovel of his machine, before slowly driving us around the turfland. Dik and Bob would go spare if they knew, but we were far away from the camp and well out of sight.

'All right, kids?' Con shouted over the engine as we approached. He gestured us to come over. 'What are you scallywags up to today?'

'Just messing about,' Jerry replied.

'Keeping out the way so we don't have to work, more like,' I piped up.

Con ruffled my curls and said, 'I'd better get on, I've got to clear all these elder trees so the turf cutters can start their work on this section of the bog. I've a long day ahead.' He told us how he was going to rip up the trees by their roots and push them into the ditch that ran along the side of the field.

We all looked at him in astonishment. 'But you can't!' we cried. 'They're elders! It's bad luck!'

To us, the elder was a sacred tree – every part of it could be used for food, drink or medicine. We believed the tree warded off evil and bad luck. A twig tied into knots and kept in your pocket guarded against illness. The flowers and berries could be used to make cordial or tea, which was delicious sweetened with a bit of honey.

Con chuckled and said, 'I don't know where you kids get your hocus pocus ideas from, but if them trees aren't gone by morning, I won't have a job.'

'Can't you jus' move 'em without killin' 'em?' I asked, looking up with my eyes wide.

'I s'pose I could, but where would I move them to?' said Con. He could see our shock and fear.

'Bring 'em over to our camp,' Ome suggested.

'All right, but I haven't got time to replant them. You'll have to go an' sort it out with your ma and pa,' Con said grudgingly.

We hared off, just a bunch of scruffy children, full of the delirious joys of a life without structure. No schooling, no toys or telly, it was a free existence. We got out of bed when we woke, we had no idea of time, days or dates, we ate when the food was hot and stopped when the pan was empty, we fell to sleep when our bodies could take no more and our natural playground was lit by just the sun and the moon.

We got back to the camp to find Con with all the trees standing topsy-turvy in his shovel. He plonked them down on the ground, and began digging a hole big enough to house them all. We got to work settling them in and prayed for their survival while Dik tried to explain to Con why he must never kill an elder tree or dig up a birch and the importance of the oaks to the air and the natural world. Con looked on, nodding in bemusement.

'There's enough trees round here. I don't think we'll be running out of oxygen any time soon. Sure, I'm glad to oblige, but I better get on with my work.'

He turned and bade us all goodbye.

I looked to Dik for approval for saving the trees, hoping he'd be pleased with me. Instead his face darkened as he turned to us kids.

'Where've you lot been? There's jobs to do.'

My dad, Dik Freeman, was a gypsy by choice. He and Uncle Bob were brought up by their mother, Edith Smith, in an ordinary house in Faversham in Kent – a childhood in one place with four walls around them and a roof over their heads. But Edith's family, for generations back, were nomadic horse breeders. Dik's great-grandfather, Daniel Smith, had been the last in a long line of relations to live the travelling life as they moved from place to place working horses for the gentry of the area. That way of life had come to an end when Daniel was kicked in the head by a client's stallion leaving him permanently damaged. The client felt so bad about the injuries his horse had caused, he offered Daniel and his family a cottage on his land, and so the roaming Smiths were grounded.

In Dik, though, the gypsy genes remained strong. Edith kept

a strict Catholic home and Dik had always chafed under its restrictions. His father moved out when he was a boy, leaving Edith for another woman. As time went on he regretted his decision, but Edith was a proud lady and never let him back into the family home. Dik was a wild boy and left home at the first opportunity, taking any job that came his way, travelling where the mood took him.

He got a job working on a fishing trawler and made friends with a worldly chap named Tony Bird. Tony was a fair bit older than Dik, but they bonded and became good friends; perhaps he was the older brother Dik never had. Tony took great pride in showing him the ropes on the vessel. A while later, Dik moved out of town into a caravan with his younger brother Bob; they travelled a bit, but always stayed in the Kent area. Tony visited from time to time bringing freshwater trout or the odd mackerel for the brothers. He was their only connection with Faversham, apart from the occasional phone call to their mother Edie to let her know they were okay. She had little time for them and was disappointed that they had left her alone and gone to live on the road.

Dik and Bob were living in a caravan outside Ashford when my mum, Dixey, entered Dik's life. Dixey was a beautiful but naive seventeen-year-old American girl touring Britain. Initially Dik was struck by her beauty, but as he got to know her it was her calm, loving personality that won him over. Dixey was a child of privilege. She had grown up in a Boston mansion filled with fine furniture, collectible artwork, and every creature comfort. Her parents, Esther and Peter Brooks, made sure she and her brother and sisters had everything they could wish for

– private educations, abundant extra-curricular activities and extensive travel – but Dik's type of travelling was not the kind they'd had in mind. Yet, despite their wildly contrasting backgrounds, Dik and Dixey hit it off.

It was the early 1970s, and Dik dreamed of living the 'free life' in Ireland – he'd tell Dixey all about it as they sat round the fire outside his caravan. So, shortly after they got together, he and Dixey bought a van in Wales and headed over the Irish Sea. In Ireland, Dik ignited his passion for horses and invested in a hairy-legged, long-maned gypsy cob and his first horse-drawn bow-top wagon. Horse breeding was in Dik's bones and he took to it like a duck to water. Together, Dik and Dixey were constantly on the move, taking their wagon from place to place with the horse strapped between the shafts and soon there were goats tied to the back and chickens in baskets strung underneath. Dik trained and proudly combed his horse on a daily basis. His long fetlocks and shiny mane were a constant source of inspiration and adoration.

In Ireland, Dik and Dixey's lives had the serenity they had hoped for; they were rarely bothered by the state and lived outside of the system. But it was often less calm between the two of them. Dik suffered with black moods that would take over his entire being and possess his body like a dark cloud; sometimes they would quickly lift but other times they lingered for days on end. He wasn't a violent man but he had spirit and with spirit comes a temper. Such extreme changes in temperament were new to Dixey – a contented, passive person by nature – and she felt helpless and sad when Dik's moods descended. He would lie in bed hidden under his hair, groaning and distressed but he never voiced the reasons for his anxiety and got irritated if she questioned him on the cause of his unhappiness.

To us kids, Dixey was the soft touch and Dik was the grumpy, strict one. If you asked Dik (we always called our parents by their names) for anything his first answer was always 'no'. Then he might mull it over and occasionally, if we asked again, he would come back with a conditional 'yes'. But he had another side to him, one we didn't get to see enough when I was young: he was intelligent and had a sharp sense of humour. He often cracked jokes, although the jokes were at the expense of someone else. Dik's cutting wit rubbed off on Rollin and all of us to some degree. There was a lot of practical joking and teasing around the camp fire. It meant that we grew up to be pretty hardy, physically and emotionally.

I respected Dik wholeheartedly, but I wished he'd relax and show us his happy side more often. On occasions when the moods hadn't taken hold of him, he'd sing, his powerful voice echoing around the camp, or he'd grab Dixey and dance with her round the camp, while she beamed from ear to ear. I didn't recognise the songs he chose then, as we didn't have a radio or a cassette player, but I now know they were blues songs and those of soul and rock and roll artists like Little Richard and Sam Cooke. Occasionally Dik would smoke a pipe with marijuana in it and he'd be particularly laid-back and easy-going. We quickly learnt to wait until he got stoned before we asked anything of him because it was the only time we'd get a positive response. Sometimes he'd go months without having a pipe; during these periods the things we wanted from our father would mount up.

★　★　★

'Go and help your mother, Roxy,' Dik said now in his gruff voice. 'You two, get off home,' he said to Jerry and Ome.

I wanted to go and play, but knew better than to argue as his word was final. I saw Dixey chopping carrots on an upturned bucket. She was wearing a long colourful skirt and a loose-fitting top. I could see she was sitting on her haunches, perhaps to ease the strain on her back and pregnant tummy, and had a weary look about her, but her blue eyes still sparkled brightly, the same colour as the turquoise necklace hanging around her neck.

'All right, Roxy Riddle? Comin' to help me milk the goats?' Dixey asked.

'S'pose so,' I replied.

'I wondered where you'd got to. They'll get mastitis if we leave them much longer,' she added.

I picked up the milking bowl and skipped over to where the goats were grazing. They were tethered on the grassy verge just behind the wagon and fireplace. I knelt down next to the black goat, Ebony, holding her back legs as Dixey squatted down to milk. I looked forward to drinking a glass of warm milk fresh from the goats' udders; it was one of the few luxuries we had. We often queued up at milking time, eager to warm our tummies with the frothy goodness. Ebony thrashed and pulled but I hung on: a battle between a stubborn goat and an even more stubborn little girl that would continue for many years to come.

Dixey talked about what she was doing as she milked away. 'Squeeze the tit at the top and then pull your hand down, forcing the milk out. Wanna have a go, Rox?'

'Nah,' I replied, remembering how, the last time I'd milked, the goat had stuck her foot in the bowl, ruining the whole day's supply.

I looked at Dixey's pretty, delicate features and was filled with adoration. She was calm, kind and eternally loving, she let us do what we wanted and rarely raised her voice. I was her little assistant, fetching, chopping and carrying from as young as I can remember.

Now I try to imagine what it was like for my mother, shutting the door on the world of comfort in which she grew up. It can't have been an easy decision. The way of life Dik was used to, which felt as natural to him as breathing, was cold, difficult and often painful for Dixey. But she had always loved nature and enjoyed learning, so she adapted as quickly as possible: she never questioned having to lug the water from the pump, cook on the fire or any of the other hardships she endured. She learned what plants to pick and cook and how to build the fire according to the direction of the wind. Though we slept in the canvas-covered wagons, our lives were lived outside with no conveniences. Dik wasn't lazy, far from it, but there were certain tasks that he did and keeping home wasn't one of them.

Dixey told me about the first time she saw a gypsy. It was 1969, she was sixteen and living in Tuscany with her American family. She had woken early and quietly sneaked past her parents' bedroom, hovering for a moment outside her sister Melanie's door. All was still. She crept quietly down the stairs and out of the front door.

It was a bright spring morning. Dixey ambled through the empty lanes and hills, the sun on her back and the wind gently swaying in the cypress trees around her. Her walk took her over a picturesque stone bridge with a rushing river below. Dixey paused and took in a deep breath of fresh, warm air.

She could hear the sound of a woman's voice coming from beneath her. Straining to see where the unexpected sound was coming from, Dixey spotted a young woman kneeling by the water's edge, scrubbing clothes on a rock in the river.

The woman was much older than Dixey, perhaps in her early thirties, with long dark hair tumbling down her back. She looked tired but had a contented glow in her cheeks. Though her olive skin looked weathered and her clothes worn, there was something about the way she squatted on the side of the river that made her seem as if she had always been there. She was so absorbed and secure in what she was doing, that Dixey felt she was almost part of the landscape.

She was completely mesmerised. Where had the woman come from? Why was she washing her clothes in the river? In the privileged existence of the Brooks family, you threw your clothes in the basket outside the door and they miraculously reappeared washed, folded and ironed the very next day.

Something in this gypsy woman tapped into a deep longing Dixey felt — a need to escape her sheltered life and get in touch with nature, to live close to the soil and birds, without a maid or a cleaner, without the suffocation of her family. Returning to the villa, Dixey said nothing as she sat down for breakfast, nor did she ever see the woman again. Yet that image haunted her.

Dixey's upbringing was, for the 1950s and 1960s, quite jet-set. Peter and Esther loved Europe and spent much of their time in Italy. Esther had gone to high school in France as a girl and thought languages were an essential part of a cultured education.

When Dixey was fifteen, the family went to Florence with the idea of staying for a year. Dixey and her siblings attended school, while Peter pursued spiritual avenues. At the end of the year, Esther and Peter started to organise the family's move back to America but Dixey didn't want to go. After much debate it was agreed that Dixey would stay in Italy with family friends and study for her final exams.

As she approached the end of the school year, Dixey fell for a boy of African descent. They spent languid afternoons studying and chatting together, hatching plans to travel and explore the world. Dixey's mind was always set on adventure. But when Esther and Peter learned of the love affair they were horrified. They worried where the relationship might lead and what plans the African boy had for their lovely young daughter. Hoping to nip it in the bud, they immediately sent Dixey to Paris to stay with a trusted family friend. They did not even allow her to finish her final semester at school.

If they hoped to get Dixey back on a conventional path they could not have made a worse decision. The excitements of Paris more than made up for the upset of leaving her first love behind. Her parents' friend, a kind and eccentric American lady named Alida, was welcoming and Dixey made friends with one of her daughters, Beany, who was a year older. Tall and attractive with long dark hair and soulful eyes, Beany was a talented musician and artist who shared Dixey's dreams of escape.

The girls sat up late into the night discussing the opportunities that life could offer them. They started making plans to take a trip together; they had no idea where they wanted to go but were set on leaving in the spring shortly after Dixey's eighteenth birthday. Beany was keen to visit Ireland so they decided to backpack for a month. Dixey told her parents and agreed to meet them and her siblings in Corfu for a holiday before setting off. Dixey and Beany assured their parents that after their little adventure they would both return to Paris and enrol at a prestigious art school.

In Corfu, Esther and Peter begged Dixey to stay in Paris and pursue her education. Peter came from one of America's wealthiest families, who had made their fortune in the marine insurance trade and he had high hopes of Dixey succeeding in the art world. He was a thoughtful man, who spent his days writing in his journal and learning about other cultures and places; he did yoga, played the flute and enjoyed a wide array of music. Esther hoped Dixey would follow in her footsteps as a dancer: she was the artistic director of Cambridge School of Ballet in Boston, Massachusetts and had spotted Dixey's natural ear for rhythm and innate gracefulness early on. To her dismay Dixey had stopped dancing after just a couple of years of training.

As the holiday went on, Dixey brought up the subject of her expedition at every opportunity, but was met with frosty silence. Esther and Peter declined to discuss the matter in the hope that she would change her mind.

She didn't. A month later, in the summer of 1970, Dixey and Beany arrived in Ireland on a cold, damp morning. They had no hotels booked and hitchhiked around the country, sleeping when and where they found shelter. For the first time they were free: no parents to restrict their movements or siblings to hinder their plans, no elder friends or relatives to keep a watchful eye, and they were full of the joys of life. Dixey was charmed by the wild greenness of the countryside and the misty rolling mountains. As they travelled, she sketched in preparation for her interview at the art school the following month.

But after three weeks the girls' spirits were slightly dampened by the continuous grey days of the Irish summer. With a week left before they were due to return to Paris, they decided to go to England and visit a couple they knew called Malcolm and Thea. Thea was from back home in Massachusetts and had visited Dixey's family a few years before with her new-found love Malcolm, an Englishman. Dixey had been struck by their description of the alternative life they were living somewhere in the south of England. The girls flew into London and hitchhiked to Kent to the address that Dixey had on a scrap of paper.

They found Malcolm and Thea living in an old purple touring caravan by the side of the road just outside a town called Ashford. Dixey could not get over how different and basic the caravan was compared to their lavish homes in the States, but Thea seemed very happy.

Over the next few days, Dixey and Beany spent afternoons walking through the barren fields and bracken-thick lanes and introduced themselves to two brothers, friends of Malcolm and Thea's, who lived in a beaten-up old caravan further down the lane. That week they often stopped at the little caravan nestled in the hedgerow to talk to the brothers and stroke the puppies that were sharing their home.

Dik and Bob looked alike, with their shock of coarse hair, but Dik was the darker and more striking. His left eye wandered off when he was speaking, making it hard to know where he was looking. It felt like he was keeping an eye on his surroundings while also looking and talking to you. Dik was wise and intelligent but also quite serious. When he talked of his dreams and experiences, it seemed to Dixey he was talking of a different world.

As the time approached for Dixey and Beany to leave, they headed down the lane to say goodbye to the brothers. Dik looked over the map with them and planned which roads they would hitchhike along to get to their destination while getting to see as much of Britain as possible. He said it would take four or five days, weather permitting, but why not go to the Isle of Wight before France as there was a big festival happening at the end of the month? Thea and Malcolm would be there and Jimi Hendrix and The Doors were playing. He warned them there was some bad weather on the horizon and that they might have to settle down for a while en route and let it pass so he leant them a lightweight tarpaulin in case they got caught up in the storms.

'You can give it back to me at the festival,' he said, grinning at Dixey in particular.

After a week of dodging the rain under the smelly tarpaulin, Beany had had enough. She announced that she wasn't interested in the festival, she was going to go straight back to Paris to prepare herself for university. Dixey, on the other hand, liked the idea of seeing Jimi Hendrix live and meeting up with Dik, so the friends agreed to meet up in a week or two and went their separate ways.

Dixey arrived at the Isle of Wight Festival on 26 August 1970 to find the festival in full swing. Europe was finally catching up with the Summer of Love. The festival that year was bigger than Woodstock, and packed with young, long-haired free spirits. She searched the crowds for Dik, Malcolm and Thea, filled with bemusement and intrigue: everyone she saw seemed to be intoxicated – a delirium induced by sun, drugs, alcohol, music and life. Dixey felt out of place, but relaxed and happy.

She found them later that day. They had pitched their tents on a putting green overlooking the main arena. Dik was lying sprawled under the shade of a tree.

'Cup of tea, Dix?' he said, as if they'd parted five minutes earlier.

Dixey made herself a cosy bed inside the tent, innocently thinking nothing of the fact that she was going to be snuggling up next to Dik for the rest of the weekend. During the next few days they sat up late into the night talking and laughing. Malcolm and Thea seemed to disappear into the festival throng as Dik and Dixey fell into their own little world. By the end of the festival they were mapping out their future together.

A few weeks later, Dixey called her parents to tell them she wasn't going to finish school, that she wasn't going to go to college, that she wasn't coming back. She had fallen in love with the most amazing man and she would be staying with him. She and Dik were picking potatoes in Kent and she was happier than she had ever been.

For Esther and Peter the shock was enormous. Their lives were soaked in wealth and culture, and they expected nothing less for their daughter. Who was this unwashed English hippy who had stolen their daughter's heart? Desperate to find a way of keeping Dixey close, they insisted on meeting him at once and bought the two of them flights to Italy. It was the first time Dik had encountered their world of cocktails and dinner parties.

For their part, Esther and Peter weren't much reassured by Dik's tatty appearance and lack of worldliness. Worse was his gruff nature and general lack of communication. Dik sat on the ground with his bare feet and alternative clothing, rarely contributing to their discussions. Yet they feared losing their daughter forever if they made too much of a fuss. Although they expressed regret at her choices, they kept quiet, hoping that Dixey would find the life too hard and return to them before too long.

But Dixey felt a deep sense of belonging and completeness when she was with Dik. They were as different as two people could possibly be, but it felt right and they fell deeply in love. Dixey didn't think about how her future would pan out, where they would live or how they would survive – she just knew that she had found her calling and it was by the side of a black-eyed gypsy man.

CHAPTER 2

Raised on the Bog

My earliest memories are of waking up in the wagon: it was always dark, no matter the season. A beam of light would shine through the corner of the door, where the wind blew the blanket that was hanging to stop the draught. I would lie in my bed – my first proper bed was a wooden bench so narrow that I had to stay completely still while I slept in order not to fall onto the stove below me – and listen to the breathing: Dik's heavy snores, mixed with Rollin and Essie's lighter breaths. They were all no more than three foot away from me but the only one within my view was Rollin. He lay opposite me on the other wooden bench, snuggled down in his doss-bag. Dixey and Dik slept with Perly, who was a baby then, in a double bed at the back of the wagon. Perly's soft cry, muffled by blankets, was enough to wake Dixey.

'Sshh,' she'd whisper under her breath.

At that time Essie slept stowed away under the double bed in a kind of cupboard which was actually the snuggest, most coveted sleeping place in the wagon. The cupboard bed had two painted wooden doors decorated with green scrolls and red flowers and a small brass flip-style catch on the outside. Once inside we had to pull the doors closed so that they didn't block the passageway to the main bed at the back. Essie had various stickers and decorations inside and a tiny torch hidden under her pillow, which meant she could stay awake after the candles had been blown out in the main part of the wagon. Even though Rollin loved to make us squeal by flipping over the brass catch on the outside and trapping us inside, I longed for her to outgrow the cosy cubbyhole bed so I could move in.

I itched to get out of bed and stretch my legs. Dixey sat up to sort Perly out, who was wiggling and whingeing.

'Morning love,' Dik said. His voice was soft and kind. I felt a wave of relief run through me: he was in a good mood this morning.

Below me was the Queenie, our small, ornate, cast-iron stove with intricate flowers moulded on the doors and devils' heads protruding from the sides, which heated our bow-top wagon. The wagon was no more than 12 foot long by about 6 foot wide inside. It swayed in the wind and we could hear every raindrop and bird tweet through the canvas but it was dry and when we were all snuggled up inside, with the Queenie burning, it was warm.

During the summer I was five, we experienced a rare hot spell in southern Ireland. We kids spent a lot of time splashing about in rivers and ditches. There were of course numerous residents in the water – leeches were a common problem, but they didn't faze us, we'd just pull them off and flick them away. There were also eels, which were my personal pet hate as well as frogs and toads.

We loved climbing to the top of the piles of turf that were covered in black plastic and sliding down the other side. One of the great things about the bog was how soft and forgiving it was: it provided the perfect landing for little bums, springing back like a warm, damp sponge when we landed on it.

One sunny afternoon we came across a pile of plastic. It had been discarded and had pools of water settled in it. I think it was Rollin, who always loved to make things with the stuff he found, who decided we should drag it back to the camp and make a swimming pool out of it. We lugged it back over our shoulders, tripping and giggling as we went. Rollin and Jerry had hold of a front corner each, while Ome and I tagged along behind making sure it didn't get caught or tangled on the gorse bushes.

Once we reached the camp, Jerry went to get Con and asked him to take a shovel of soil away with his digger so we could make a swimming pool. He happily obliged, piling the earth around the roots of the elder trees, which were settling in well to their new home, before going back to work. We spent the rest of the afternoon lining the hole with the plastic, securing it around the top with piles of soil, bales of hay and buckets of water. We looked proudly into the pool and wondered how we were going to fill it up.

'We could all get buckets of water from the pump on the road,' suggested Ome.

'Nah, will take forever, an' there ain't much water up there anyways,' said Jerry.

'We'll have to wait,' said Rollin. 'It'll rain soon.'

We didn't have long to wait – we lived in Ireland after all and the rain was never far off. When I woke up a few mornings later, the wagon was rocking in the wind, the door had blown open and Dik was fighting with the canvas that covered the door. He was dressed in just a shirt, his long dark hair hanging loose over his shoulders and his face dripping with water. It was almost daylight outside, but not time to get up just yet. I snuggled down under my duvet, trying to avoid the heavy pelts of rain making their way inside the wagon, pleased that our makeshift pool would be filling up.

It rained all day and all night. Wet weather was such a curse to our lives. We'd huddle up inside but we would all inevitably end up going outside and getting soaked. Chores still beckoned. We had to milk the goats, feed the horses and cook no matter what. Even when the jobs were done, we still had to go outside to have a wee in the bushes. One way or another we would end up drenched to the skin more than once and probably run out of dry clothes before the day was out.

But today we stood around the pool, holding plastic bags over our heads to protect us from the rain, gleefully watching it fill with water, dreaming of the day the sun would return. Parts of the plastic had started to fall in and the water was looking quite murky where the mounds of soil we had placed around the top had been washed into the pool, but it was as close to our own swimming pool as we were going to get.

A couple of days later, Dixey piled Perly and me onto the

back of the wooden flat-cart we used for shopping trips and announced that we were going into Thurles town to do the weekly shop. I loved going into town, looking in the windows of the shops and admiring all the pretty things, even if we rarely bought anything apart from sacks of brown rice and lentils. Dik appeared and backed a black-and-white horse between the shafts of the cart before jumping on board and off we went at a gentle trot. My face stung where the wind hit it and I held tightly on to Perly to keep us both warm and safe. The sound of the horse's hooves was irregular, as only three shoes had stayed in place: clip clop, clip, went the metal shoes as we plodded down the tarmac road.

Arriving in Thurles, Dik dropped us off near the shops and said he'd be back in an hour or so. I'd been so excited to get away from the camp but now I looked around at all the clean, smart people and felt even more grubby than normal. I could feel people staring at us, like they always did. I tried to wipe my face with the sleeve of my dress and pulled my hair out of my face.

I longed to spend a day in the life of one of these clean people, going through each day without the stares and sneers we always experienced. Dixey took Perly and me by the hand and ambled carelessly down the street, apparently oblivious to the looks we were getting. Our clothes and physical appearance were so little a priority for her I doubt she even noticed. Dixey was pregnant and dressed in her usual ethnic or Indian bright skirt and top and she wore her hair hanging loose around her shoulders. She always looked nice to me but, compared to everyone around us, she also was quite scruffy, yet she walked down the street with her head held high, humming a tune like she often did. As we headed towards the health food shop to buy some homeopathic remedies to treat ringworm, Dixey stopped for a moment to tuck Perly's shirt in and I wandered off towards the window of a shoe shop.

I pressed my face up against the glass, looking at all the bright, shiny leather shoes arranged in neat rows. In the middle was a pair of red patent leather shoes with little straps that clasped shut with a gold buckle.

'Dixey, Dixey, look! Aren't they beautiful?' I patted her side, ushering her towards the shoe shop.

'They're lovely, Rox,' she replied, walking on towards the health food shop. I lingered behind to get a last glance at the shoes, looking down at my muddy wellies and wiggling my toes. They were damp and touched the end of my boots. I imagined my feet in those shiny shoes.

We got back to the camp a few hours later to find Rollin and Jerry standing over the pool, grinning and dripping with water. It was ready!

'Wa'ers lovely, Rox. Get in an' try it!' Rollin shouted out to me.

I ran towards them, throwing my clothes off as I went, and jumped without a second thought into the murky pool of stagnant water. I couldn't swim, but my feet quickly found the floor and I didn't want to look too scared in front of the bigger kids. It was only a foot or two deep but to a five-year-old the mass of water seemed quite overwhelming, particularly when I looked up and could see several feet of black plastic between dry land and me. I wished one of them would jump in and join me. Why were they all standing around the edge giggling? Then I felt something slithering around my legs. Lots of things slithering around my legs. My heart missed a beat.

I was sharing the muddy pool with a family of eels.

'Help!' I gasped in absolute horror, and began to scramble for the edge as the slimy buggers wrapped themselves around me. I quickly lost my brave face and burst into tears as I tried to drag myself up the slippery sides, pieces of plastic tumbling down on top of me. Rollin waited until I was completely hysterical before reaching down with a stick and rescuing me. The other children were laughing fit to wet themselves. I stood on the edge of the pool, hiccuping and shivering with a mixture of fear, outrage and cold.

'We caught the eels in the river and thought we'd surprise you when you got home,' Jerry and Rollin told me, their faces dancing with delight.

'Didn't fink you'd scream that much,' Rollin said.

'Thought you were brave an' liked fish 'n stuff,' Jerry added. I desperately tried to pull myself together and recover from the trauma without losing face, but it was all too much. I withdrew, heading to the safety of the fireplace and Dixey's side and left the boys laughing.

A few weeks passed and Dixey was still using homeopathic remedies to treat the ringworm Rollin had on his arms. It was clearing up on Rollin but it had appeared on my scalp and it was getting worse and worse. I tried my best not to scratch the sores burning at the roots of my hair, but it was hard as they were so painful. Dixey had tried many different things to get rid of it:

she'd washed my hair in sage tea every day for a week in an attempt to dry out the sores; she'd made herbal tinctures and cold presses, but nothing was working. Finally I heard Dixey say she would have to take me to the doctor to get some cream to clear it up. I was surprised by the conversation, as I'd never been to a doctor in my life – generally our ailments were sorted out with the help of herbs, brews or tinctures.

The doctor prescribed a steroid cream and told Dixey to put it on the sores on my head twice a day. He was surprised by how angry and advanced the ringworm had got and told Dixey she was irresponsible for leaving it so long before she sought treatment. Dixey was dejected. She was used to sorting everything out in her own way without any assistance or interruption, and I could see the doctor's verdict had made her feel a failure. We put that cream on as soon as we got home, but instead of waking up next morning to an improved condition, I woke up in the night with my head burning. I woke Dik and Dixey up with my crying, and they were surprised to find that the condition had developed into something far worse than ringworm – my scalp was now oozing and irritated. I had developed an allergy to the steroid cream and my head was red raw.

'I'll 'ave to cut 'er hair off. No way we can sort it out with all them knots and tangles getting in the way,' Dik said. My tears escalated into hysteria as he went to get his scissors.

'Please don't cut it off, Dixey, please don't!' I begged her.

'It's the only way, love. We can't deal with it with all those curls in the way, it's just getting worse.'

Dik reappeared and promptly set to cutting my locks off. I looked at the ground where my tears mixed with my curls in a

26

damp pile and listened to my parents discussing the next move. When Dixey offered me a mirror, I covered my face.

'It's all right, Rox, you look even more beautiful. Everyone can see your pretty face now you aren't hiding behind that hair.' I refused even to look.

'C'mon, Rox, pull yourself together and go and do a wee in that pot, so I can wash your head,' Dixey said.

Things were going from bad to worse. I refused point-blank to have my head washed in my own urine and ran away to hide in my bed. I spent the following day avoiding my siblings and friends for fear of teasing over my new haircut.

But by the next evening the fierce allergy was now burning hotter than ever.

'Roxy love, I know it's hard for you but your pee will make it better, it's the only way,' Dixey coaxed, as I hid behind the wagon with a scarf wrapped around my head. Still I wouldn't budge. 'I won't force you,' she said, 'but we could come to a deal. If you let me try this every day for a week, I'll get you a treat next time we're in town. Is there something you need? Some clothes or shoes?'

I remembered the bright red shoes I had seen in the shop window that day in Thurles. I pictured the shiny gold buckles and how I'd thought they were the prettiest thing I'd ever seen in my life. I had no idea how much they cost or whether we could afford them, but I thought I could endure the humiliation of washing my hair in pee if I had those shoes on my feet. But we'd moved on, and Thurles was no longer our closest town. Still, I told Dixey I wanted the shoes more than anything in the world and if I had them I would try to be good and let her sort my head out.

Every morning I peed into a pot and stood in the hedgerow as Dixey poured it over my head catching it in a bowl and pouring it over again and again until we'd lost it all in the grass. It stung my scalp but I held back the tears and thought of the shoes. The sores quickly dried up and by the end of the week were flaking off. And Dixey was true to her word and made the extra long journey into Thurles to buy me the little red shoes. I didn't go with her but she measured my feet and came home with them neatly packaged in a box with tissue paper. She bought them a bit too big so they would last longer and told me not to get them wet.

They were the first pair of shoes I had ever chosen, my first red shoes and they felt so entirely different on my feet to the wellies I was used to. Those shoes sparked a lifelong obsession with footwear that would practically bankrupt me in later years, but at the tender age of five they made me feel like a princess. My hair quickly grew back, thicker and curlier than before and I had learnt that sometimes in life it is worth negotiating.

CHAPTER 3

The Loony Line

That year, Dik's old friend from Faversham, Tony Bird, came to visit us on the Loony Line. He wasn't related to us but we called him Uncle Tony nonetheless. I was very fond of him. He was a kind man, and seemed to have a lot more time on his hands than all the other adults around us, who were always busy. He came in a little campervan, ate all his meals around the fire with us and it was my job to make him cups of tea throughout the day. He drank a lot of tea; he liked big mugs and always took a lot of sugar. Sugar was forbidden in our family but I used the tea-making job as an opportunity to sneak the odd taste on the end of my finger. It seemed sweeter than honey but the texture didn't please me.

Tony can't have been more than fifteen years older than Dik but back then he looked twice his age; to me he seemed older than anyone else I had ever known apart from my granny Eddie who we saw from time to time. As far back as I can remember

Tony always looked the same: jowly, balding on top with wispy, greying hair around the sides and big thick glasses shielding his blue eyes. He wore heavy knitted pullovers and always had a cigarette in his hand. The smell of his scratchy, smoky jumpers rubbing on my face as he hugged me is more memorable than his actual appearance.

Everybody loved Uncle Tony. He had a friendly manner and many tales to tell of his times trawling the seas and working the land. He also knew more about nature than anyone else. He could tell you about the birds, squirrels, plants – the natural world that was so much part of our daily lives. Dik called him the Bird Man and not just because of his surname. He took me on walks and picked up leaves as we went, explaining how to recognise trees by their leaves. He'd teach me which mushrooms were safe to eat. We found ink caps growing in the fields; he picked a whole pile of them and showed me that the ones oozing black ink were past their best but the firm, closed ones were perfect to bring home for dinner. We gathered mushrooms and leaves and he promised me that he would teach me how to bake fairy cakes when we got back to his van.

He was there because he was Dik's old friend, but he soon became close to everyone he came into contact with, regardless of age or gender. He'd help Dik out with the horses from time to time, but more than any of the adults it was us kids he wanted to spend time with. That's what we liked best about him.

Dik never had a nine-to-five job but he was constantly busy. The horses – gypsy cobs with long hairy manes and fetlocks that were forever getting tangled with thistles – took up most of his time. He trained them, used them to pull the cart on shopping trips into town and to move the wagon from place to place. He usually had a dozen or so horses and in later years the herd was three times that size. Sometimes we'd keep the horses tethered close to the camp, but if we stayed in the same place for a while they'd soon eat their way through all the available grass and Rollin and Dik would have to tether them on other grassy areas on the bog. The further they were from home the more work we had to do to keep them, like carrying water to them and moving them regularly. When times were hard and there was no grass available on the verges or on the common land, Dik and the other men would take the horses out in the dead of night and let them loose in the fields of the local farmers. They'd wait until dawn broke before sneaking back to get them out before the farmers or landowners woke up. This was a common practice, known as 'sarking' and something Dik had picked up during the time he spent with the tinker families.

It took hours to check each and every horse. Some days I'd scurry along behind Dik, watching his every move while trying to avoid the back legs of these giant hairy beasts. In the afternoons he'd work on their harnesses, rubbing saddle soap into the leather and piercing holes with his awls to make the reins and blinkers fit particular horses. We rode as children, but we didn't have saddles. Instead, we'd use thick pieces of rope and sometimes attach a set of blinkers.

We kids had our jobs to do in the horse fields too – usually pulling up the ragwort so the horses didn't get poisoned, or breaking up the dried dung so the grass could keep growing. On a fine day I loved doing these jobs, a whole day wandering the fields, identifying flowers and gathering mushrooms as I went. On a bad day it would be more muddy feet and soaking hair.

But Dik's relationship with the horses was special. He could tell just by looking at a horse whether it was healthy or unwell. He'd know as soon as they were pregnant, or if they were going to give birth soon and he did everything for them, including trimming their hooves and shoeing them if they were going to venture out of the field. He wasn't scared of the cobs: he'd take hold of the hoof and grip it between his knees, each hoof as big as his head. Then he'd size up the shoes, get out his anvil and set to work, before taking hold of the hoof again and banging the nails in to hold the shoe on.

The horses trusted Dik. A horse has such a highly developed sense of smell – they can tell if you're scared. If you're calm and relaxed, they will be too. Dik could calm a wild stallion within moments by just talking to it, slowly coaxing it down, until it was nestling into his chest. In fact it seemed like he communicated better with them than with humans. The connection worked both ways: if he was in a bad mood, just a few minutes in the company of his horses and he'd soften and relax, he'd close his eyes and hum gently in their ears, 'There pet, there there pet, ssshhh.' Dixey used to say that with his coarse black hair and thick toenails, he was more horse than human.

The horses weren't just Dik's passion, they were our livelihood. To earn money, he did deals with the tinkers, buying and selling horses and hiring out the use of his stallion. We usually had one stallion at a time. Dik would breed or buy a strong stallion with nice markings to breed with his mares. Our prize stallion for many years was called Silver. We kept him close to the camp, tethered on a long chain on the various pieces of grass. He didn't run with the herd, as Dik controlled when he covered the mares, and which ones he covered.

In the spring the foals would be born. Sometimes Dik would limit the numbers to five or six, other years most of the mares would foal. We'd hope for black-and-white piebald fillies, as they made the best money. When the foals were due, he would be out at all times of the night helping the mares. If the foals got stuck he'd give the mare a helping hand, sometimes by gently pulling on their legs as they came out, other times by putting his hands right up inside the mare and easing the foal out. Usually they were born without any problems and he'd be there just to make sure it went okay, other times we'd turn up in the fields and there would be a surprise arrival. The little wobbly-kneed, long-legged foals soon found their feet and grew into stocky little workhorses. Breeding cobs is all about getting a short, but strong pony with a long mane, the hairier the better in the cob world.

It was from the tinkers – or Irish travellers as they are mostly called now – that Dik learned about horses, and with the tinkers that we did most of our business. We weren't tinkers, although the settled locals saw us as just as much of a plague and a nuisance. The tinkers were generally light-haired and cleanly dressed and lived in glitzy Buccaneer or Roma caravans – as spacious and open-plan inside as our little old wooden wagons were tight and dark, and were covered wall-to-wall with mirrors, carved glass and pink or blue Formica. The women had no end of gold jewellery: big hoop earrings and chunky rings; the men wore shiny leather dealer boots and had their hair greased down on their heads. The women and children would sit in the van while

Dik talked to the men about getting their mares covered or about buying a lurcher pup. In return they'd offer a range of things for sale, anything from a van of woollen rugs to a cob, sometimes 'chordi' (meaning stolen or hot) sometimes not – it depended on the day. They all spoke with the distinctive tinker slang that seems to be pretty universal. The favourite words from the tinker men were, 'How much for da dag? Will we have a deal, der boy, will we have a deal?'

Dixey would sometimes try and talk to the wives from the tinker families but she struggled to relate to them. They spent their days polishing the chrome on their shiny caravans and gossiping. Dixey was too busy battling through each day to worry about polishing anything. In contrast, tinkers considered even reading and writing to be a sign of weakness, a sign of participating in a society they didn't belong to. They had their own communication methods and reading and writing had no place in their lives.

One of the big tinker families in Tipperary was called the Rileys. The father, Lee Riley, had over a dozen children with his first cousin, Marie. It was a tradition to marry cousins in tinker families. Ironically, they considered it a way of keeping their genes pure. They didn't seem to register the fact that after generations of marrying cousins they might as well have married their own siblings, their blood was so similar.

Lee's kids had various disabilities and deformities. He had a wee lass called Anne-Marie, about my age, whom I'd see from time to time. She had one clear blue eye but the other eye was halfway down her cheek. It was swollen and sealed tightly shut. I was sure she'd never seen out of the closed eye and wondered if there was even an eye underneath the closed lid. She also had a cleft palate. Another child was completely deaf and mute and a few others had learning difficulties. Dik told me that if my cousin Jerry and I had babies together they may well turn out like little Anne-Marie.

Yet there was also something desirable about the tinker way of life – theirs might have been a rougher, more macho culture than ours, but they formed strong communities. A close clan moved as a group and always supported one another. You couldn't always trust them and there were times when we were ripped off or scammed by a tinker family (if they wanted a particular goat, or puppy or foal, and it wasn't for sale, they would come back in the night and take it) but they'd do anything for each other. Once a tinker, always a tinker, no matter what you lived in or where. And although we weren't really anything like the tinkers – we were darker and scruffier, and lived mostly out in the open rather than inside our wagons – and didn't really aspire to be, we had more in common with them than we did with settled people. They accepted us for who we were and we accepted them, no questions asked.

Apart from Uncle Bob and his family, there were a few other travelling families living on the Loony Line and in the surrounding area at that time, some of them proper gypsies, some of them not. Romani people were originally from India, although the word 'gypsy' originates from the Greek word for Egyptian and it is thought that many of the English Romani came over from Egypt in the 1320s. They're a more peaceful bunch than the tinkers, quieter and more in tune with nature. We suspect Dik's relatives are of Romani stock, but confirming his heritage is very difficult. Tinkers and Romani people generally choose not to be counted in the census and if they are they are recorded according to their trade rather than their origins. If we trace generations back some of our Smith family descendants are registered as horse breeders, others as blacksmiths and most of them are registered with no fixed abode or simply as nomadic.

Gypsy, traveller – as I child I never worried about who was who, or what I was. But as I've got older I've found that people like a label. Most of the people around us back then in the early 1980s were ordinary people that had gone on the road and chosen to raise their families in an alternative lifestyle. They became known as new age travellers. Then there were the convoys of travellers, or the Special Brew Crew as we called them. We saw these people from time to time, but their way of life was very different to ours. They were loud, anarchistic, alcohol-fuelled groups of people that were rebelling against society and had a point to make. They'd travel in massive groups, take over places and refuse to leave without a fight.

We had different relationships with different groups, but because Dik and Dixey had both found their own paths to this life, we didn't exactly fit in anywhere. We were as dark and scruffy as the gypsies, but we didn't have their folklore or wide, extended families. We were as free-spirited as the new age travellers, but we worked the fields or sold horses for money. We sometimes lived with other families like the convoy travellers, but we had no political agenda – we were just living our lives.

I have never known how to categorise myself and I dread the question, 'Where are you from?' I don't know if I am supposed to tell them where I was born, where I spent my younger years,

where my parents are from, or where I live now. We didn't seem
to come from anywhere: my siblings and I had no recognisable
accent, we still don't. I suppose it's a result of moving around a
lot. No accent ever had a chance to stick. Dixey has never
sounded American in my memory span, so we didn't either;
Dik has a bit of a Kentish twang but nothing strong. We were
surrounded by Irish people, but none of us went to school so we
didn't pick up that accent in the playground. We didn't seem to
belong anywhere other than together. In my memory, home was
where the fire burned and where our mama sat. That was where
we cooked our dinner, socialised and kept warm. Finding a log
without knots to sit on was one of life's priorities; if there
weren't enough logs we'd sit cross-legged on the ground. We'd
sit in a circle with our food on our laps; no knives, napkins or
place settings, just a bowl or a plate and a fork.

When I was very little, about three or four years old, we
camped with a sort of extended community that came and went.
At dinner time we'd normally all eat together. Men have a way
of smelling when dinner's cooked and appearing at that precise
moment. Rollin and Jerry used to gauge who was cooking, and
when it would be ready, then they'd do the rounds so they got
more than one meal as often as possible. Only the lads could get
away with it.

There was a sense that the kids belonged to everyone. Many
of the children didn't have both parents around and some of the
parents weren't particularly committed or child-orientated so
the kids could be neglected, cold, hungry and wild. Dik and
Dixey tried to keep their brood close and under control – or as
under control as you could in a travelling life – so I grew up with

a sense of security that many children around me lacked. I loved the fact that my parents were married, that we all had the same parents and same surname.

There was one woman called Roz who was good friends with Dixey and stayed on the Loony Line with her two sons for quite a while. Roz had fluffy blonde hair, blue eyes and a strong figure – she towered above Dixey. She was with a man for a bit, but mostly she was bringing up her kids on her own, and it had made her tough. Many of the children back then were scared of Dik and his gruff nature, the rest of us were scared of Roz and hers. Roz's eldest, Tristan, who was about eight years older than me, had a fiery relationship with his mother. He had her temper and their set-tos sent me running for cover on more than one occasion.

Tristan was always kind and loving towards me, though. In the mornings I'd often wake up and wander straight over to Roz's caravan. Never brave enough to knock on the door, I'd hover around outside until Tristan appeared.

'Mornin', what ya doin', Rox?' he'd say before picking me up and throwing me onto his shoulders and dashing around the camp with me bouncing around, my legs clenched around his neck and my hands clinging on to his curly black hair. I felt like I was on top of the world when I was on the shoulders of the oldest child in the camp.

Roz's other son, Zeal, was blond and soft-natured and had a calmer temperament than Roz and Tristan. The brothers were very close and spent most of their days together, usually making complex structures out of tat they'd gathered from around the camp or in the ditches. I enjoyed nothing more than the two

brothers taking me on the go-cart they'd made out of a couple
of broken bikes and some pieces of wood salvaged from the
dump.

But maybe our families were too close. I don't remember the
birth of Roz's youngest, Harmony – she was a few months
younger than Perly – but I grew up with the knowledge that
Dik had fathered Harmony and that she was our half-sister. Was
it her birth that meant that Roz and her family weren't around
much after that? I was so little that all I recall were some arguments and tears between Dik and Dixey and that shortly
afterwards we moved away from the Loony Line and travelled
alone for a while.

When I was very young, Dik went on a trip to India. He always
had an affinity with the country and said he felt more at home
there than anywhere else in the world. Perhaps the gypsy ances-
tors he spoke of were of Asian descent. He certainly looked the
part, and never more so than on his return. His shiny black hair
hung around his shoulders; his skin was dark with a weathered
look and his eyes deep brown and wide-set, those powerful eyes
that so rarely softened.

He had earned the money to get to India by doing some deals
with the tinkers and while he was there he bought things to sell
at the horse fairs when he got back. Long after he arrived home
we'd get shipments of clothes, silver jewellery, rugs and baskets
– things that would appeal to the gypsy families. He also brought
back a handful of chunky gold rings that were stashed away in a
box. He told us they were 24-carat gold and one day he would
pierce our ears and put them in. I snuck into the wagon and

opened that box many times over the coming months, rolling the rings around in my hands and looking forward to the day we could wear them.

One morning he came out of the wagon with the rings in his hands and announced that he was going to put them in our ears. He searched through his toolbox to find the sharpest leather awl before sticking it in the fire to sterilise it. I watched as he called Essie over, held her between his legs and pushed the awl through her earlobe. She squirmed and squealed as he forced it through the skin, pushing out a small triangular piece of flesh. He pressed a piece of rag onto her ear to stop the blood, before inserting a thick gold ring into the hole.

I waited anxiously for him to squeeze Essie's ring shut with his pliers before releasing her from his strong grasp. Her ear was swollen and red but the ring gleamed brightly. I was eager to go next. An almighty sting quickly replaced the sharp pain of the awl cutting through my skin as he poured cider vinegar into the piercing to sterilise it. I yelped with pain and felt his thighs tighten around my waist as I tried to wiggle away. He forced the thick chunk of 24-carat gold through my ear and let me go. I begged him to do the other one but he refused.

'I don't have more rings and, anyway, I don't want you looking like the chavvies from the tinker families,' he said. I knew that was the end of the conversation.

Dik used a lot of terms that I later learnt were of Romani origin, like 'chavvi' or 'chav', a general term used to refer to young children. He also often said 'cushti' meaning good, referred to money as 'vonga' and men as 'moosh'.

Then it was Perly's turn. The poor little girl can't have been more than two or three years old. She screamed briefly before scrambling to look in the mirror, beaming from ear to ear. We hurried out of the wagon hand-in-hand to play and show the shiny new possessions to our cousins.

It must have been about an hour or two later when Dixey asked us to go and gather some watercress and sorrel for the salad. We grabbed a bowl and ran off towards the dry land. The long narrow green sorrel leaves were tinged with red where the sun had singed them and I nibbled away on the leaves as we picked them. They had a green flavour about them: they smelt like damp grass but had a sharp citrusy tang that made them refreshing on the palate. I liked the way they made my mouth feel clean, but Perly didn't like sorrel, she said it tasted 'yukky and sour'.

Once we had a decent bowlful we headed towards the marshland to find the watercress. I pulled off my wellies and stomped into the swamp where it grew abundantly and was easier to gather. Pulling up the watercress in handfuls, we just had to be careful not to take the roots which eagerly came to the surface. I carefully separated the leaves from the roots, pushing them back down into the wet soil so the supply would continue.

The bowl was nearly full when I noticed the gold ring was no longer in my ear.

'My ring! It's gone!' I cried, clutching my ear, frantically searching the marshland. I was ankle-deep in black boggy water with cress and weeds tangling around my ankles. I hadn't noticed the ring fall out but I was sure it must have worked loose and fallen in the water. I heard Perly's voice come from the trees nearby. She had drifted off and was hanging upside down from a branch of an elm like a monkey, humming a tune in a soft careless manner. From the moment she could walk, Perly spent more of her life upside down than she did the right way up; she was always hanging from a tree or lying on her back with her legs in the air.

'Perly, you've got to help me! I can't find my ring!'

She was reluctant to come down and said, 'Come an' play, Rox, doesn't matter 'bout the ring.' But seeing me sobbing in despair, she came down and we trawled through the water together, carefully kicking at the roots hoping to unearth the ring with our bare toes.

'We've got to find it. Dik'll kill me if I've lost it.'

Perly looked at me with sadness as we trudged through the watercress patch, from one side to the other, over and over again. 'It's no use, Rox, I fink it's gone.'

The water was so stirred up and black that we couldn't see an inch beneath the surface. I thought that if we left it to settle maybe we would see the ring sparkling away, but we had to get back to the camp before the sun went down. It was the most precious thing I had ever owned, possibly the only gift I had ever been given by my father, and there was no chance that Dik's sharp eyes wouldn't see that it was gone. I felt helpless and anxious.

It was starting to get dark as we walked sombrely back to the camp. Perly scampered along next to me clinging on to my hand.

'Don't cry, Roxy, it will be okay,' she whispered and I knew if she had lost her ring it probably would have been. But at just five years old, I had already accepted that I was Dik's least favourite child.

I don't know when or why Dik started picking on me. Maybe because I was so close to Dixey; maybe he just didn't like me. I was a very accommodating little girl, always striving to please people and to say and do the right thing, but I also had a naughty side, which usually showed itself when Ome was around. She was far more ballsy than me, and was forever getting us into scrapes and trouble. Later Dixey would say he had such high hopes that he always expected more from me, and that was why he was so tough. I'm not so sure.

Essie was a lot closer to Dik than me. She'd often go and check the horses with him, while I stayed at the camp with Dixey and Perly. At almost four years older than me, Essie seemed very grown up and was quite serious, but as the eldest child was also protective and responsible. She had thick, dark, curly hair, red cheeks and striking green eyes. Essie was also more outspoken and confident around Dik than I ever was. I'd hide behind Dixey's skirt when he raised his voice and felt much more relaxed and at ease when he wasn't around.

Rollin, as the only boy, was Dik's pride and joy. He looked a lot like him, with his dark colouring and distinctive features but then again we all did. Dik's genes are strong. All his children have the same unusual hairline, broadly set eyes and dark skin, regardless of what their mothers look like. Then there was Perly, the baby, a dreamy and happy little girl.

I kept out of Dik's way as much as possible, trying to be quiet and go unnoticed so as to avoid his bark and fury. I would busy myself helping Dixey with the chores or playing outside. Dik called me Cinders because I was expected to do a lot of cooking and cleaning and was often covered in dust or flour. Cinders stuck as a nickname for many years and was only replaced by the nickname Roxarella when I was a teenager.

Dixey was aware of our difficult relationship and tried to make my life better by holding me close and always offering me her support. Essie would sometimes comment that I was Dixey's favourite, but I think we all got an equal share of love, just some of us got it more from Dixey than Dik. My mother looked out for me, doing her best to make sure that I wasn't being bullied. She seldom questioned Dik's bad temper, but occasionally, when he was mean to me, she would challenge him.

'Stop using Roxy as the family scapegoat, she's a good girl,' Dixey would say.

'A lying little brat more like. You just encourage her behaviour,' Dik would reply.

I remember the feelings of guilt that would wash through me as their argument rose. They were fighting because of me. Guilt is an uncomfortable feeling for a child but it soon became a common emotion in my life. I learnt at a young age that if something was wrong, it was probably my fault, regardless of who was really to blame. Sometimes I would stand my ground but I learnt there was little point as I was ultimately going to get punished for it. I wound up admitting to things I hadn't done just to prevent the extra scorn I would receive for not admitting to it.

When Perly and I got back to the camp, Dixey was cooking over an open fire. She was bent down on her knees kneading bread dough in a large stainless-steel bowl, the very bowl that I had placed over her pregnant tummy the day before. We had laughed about how well her bump filled the bowl and put it under my top to see how I would look at seven months pregnant, while Perly rolled around on the ground laughing. I wondered what my husband would be like and how many children I would have when I grew up.

Dixey stood up at the sight of my tear-stained face and brushed my hair out of my eyes.

'What's up, Rox?'

I told her about the lost ring.

'Oh no, Roxy, why you?' she muttered in disbelief. 'Sshh,' she said to Perly, holding her finger up to her mouth. 'He'll be home soon. He doesn't need to know.' Then she climbed into the wagon and retrieved her own ring, which she eased into the tender hole in my ear.

Moments later Dik strode into the camp with a rope over his shoulder and a bucket in his hand. My puffy eyes and doughy hands instantly annoyed him.

'Pull ya self together, child. What have you got to whinge about?' he said, his eyes blazing. Essie and Dixey busied themselves with the dinner preparations and Rollin kicked the ground as Dik whacked me around the back of the head. He didn't hit hard, just hard enough to move me out of his way. Dik wasn't a beater, he just gave us the odd clout around the ear or slap on the arse. He ruled the home with his stern nature not his hand.

CHAPTER 4

Births and Deaths

From the moment Dik met Dixey, he talked about the babies they were going to have together. He wanted a 'horde of daughters' with her and thought they should start right away. At just seventeen years old when they met, Dixey felt confused by the talk of having children so quickly and thought they should be free and enjoy their time together first. But she didn't doubt that they would have children together in the near future and, by 1973, when Dixey was twenty-one their first child was on the way. They'd married at Carmarthen Registry Office, as Dixey was going to be sent back to the US otherwise. She wore a red dress that she'd made the night before out of a bedspread.

Dixey loved being pregnant and their son, O Ryan, was born in Kenmare in southern Ireland in the autumn, a dark-eyed, handsome boy just like his dad. Dik and Dixey adored the little man and did their best to keep him happy and healthy, even though a little wagon by the side of the road was not the easiest place to bring up a baby and life could be gruelling.

Esther and Peter came to meet the new addition to the family, their first grandchild, booking themselves into a B&B in the village. Peter could hardly contain his agitation at the conditions his daughter and grandson were living in, but when he tried to talk to Dik about changing his ways Dik just told him that it was a good life they were living, even if it was hard on the women. They had no plans to settle down and he thought Dixey was made for such an existence. Perhaps she was – Dixey always said that she had never felt comfortable living her parents' lifestyle, and that she belonged with the birds and the trees – but her father struggled to see it and was very upset by the conversation. During their stay, he and Esther came across a small stone cottage going cheap in the area and decided to buy it for Dik and Dixey in the hope they might settle down and make it their home. Instead, Dik moved the horse into the downstairs room and made a storage area upstairs, and, much to Esther and Peter's dismay, he and Dixey continued to live in the wagon and cook on an open fire.

Esther was worried by how weak and wheezy O Ryan seemed and she hoped Dixey would take him to the doctor, but Dixey had faith that with her loving care, he would be fine. He wasn't. Shortly after Esther and Peter's departure, O Ryan died of pneumonia. He was just one month old. Dixey's existence crumbled as she plummeted into the depths of grief and mourned the loss of her baby boy. She felt like she could never recover from such a blow and berated herself for not taking him to the doctor as her mother had suggested. She'd done all that was in her power to keep him warm and dry but living outdoors in Ireland was cold and damp and he simply wasn't strong enough to survive. The death of the baby didn't make them question their choices, it just made them retreat deeper into the hedgerows, and further away from a society from which they were already detached.

Dixey got pregnant again the following year and Essie was born in June of 1975, a curly haired, dark-eyed beauty. Her smiles and laughter helped ease the pain of losing their first-born, but losing O Ryan has stayed with them for their whole lives. Rollin was born a year and a half later and I arrived next, in a birthing unit in County Galway, on 5 April 1979. Perly followed less than two years after me.

From the start Dixey was a natural mother. She often had a child on each hip and one in her tummy, and she was constantly overworked, but she was kind and loving. She offered us unconditional love as well as healthy food. She taught us how to be polite and considerate to each other, and she always looked for the best in people. Dixey is an optimist, like me; she'd sing as she trudged through the mud laden with buckets. But the tired eyes in her fresh young face told another story.

In the autumn of 1982 we were all looking forward to the arrival of a new sibling. We'd discuss whether it would be a boy or a girl. Of course Dik said he fancied more daughters, and that he wanted to populate the world with beautiful Freeman girls, but Dixey thought another son would even things out a bit.

Dixey went into labour a few days later while we were all sleeping. She had given birth to most of her babies at home without any problems – how much professional help she received depended on how far from a town we were camped, if there was a phone box within walking distance, and how quickly the baby arrived. Dik delivered some of us himself. But this baby decided to arrive at night when Dixey was all alone. We had a bus by this point and Dik and Dixey slept in their own space, so we all remained asleep, oblivious to the fact that our little sibling was trying to make its way into the world. And although there were various people scattered over the area living in caravans, tents or trucks, there was no one about that night.

When Dik got back from the horses or wherever he had been to find Dixey in labour, he realised something was wrong and set off on foot down the long track to the phone box to call the hospital for a midwife.

The baby boy was born while Dik was gone. He came out with the cord tangled around his neck. Dik never got to see his son breathing, and the midwife never arrived. We woke up the next morning to be told that our brother was born but that he didn't wish to stay with us and had gone to join all the other stars in the sky. I felt sad that I had never met him and noticed how tired and sad Dixey looked. All those months carrying the baby and we had just a corpse wrapped in a blanket.

Generally, when a foal or a kid goat died, we made a bonfire and burned the body, and after much discussion it was decided that we should do something to mark the baby's brief existence. So we burnt his body in a big bonfire before gathering up the ashes and burying them under an old oak tree. It seemed the most natural thing to do, to release his spirit to the sky. Dik told us that we shouldn't feel sad because the body was just an empty shell and the soul of the little boy had gone to a better place.

He pointed to the sky and said, 'The brightest star you can see is your little brother, he's up there with all the other people that were too good for this world.' Despite his positive outlook we couldn't help but feel a sense of loss and sadness. I held Essie's hand tightly and noticed tears rolling down her cheeks as Dik lit the fire. We stood by and watched the sparks disperse into the branches of the trees above, turning our baby brother to ash.

A few months later, a police car pulled up at the camp. Instinctively we hid, watching out the window of the bus as Dik and Dixey spoke to the officers. Police normally came to move us on, so we didn't think much of them turning up. But the look on Dixey's face let us know this was no normal eviction notice being served.

It turned out that Dik's call to the hospital for help when Dixey was in labour had been recorded and, although the midwife had failed to find our camp, they had noted the birth and were investigating why the baby had never been formally registered. They took Dik away for questioning and when they returned made him take them to where we had carefully buried the baby's ashes. They stood and watched as Dik dug them up. Of course there was no way they could determine the reason for his death as there was nothing left of him.

Dik and Dixey were investigated for murder and questioned extensively. There had been an unspoken sadness over the camp since the loss of the baby. In a time that should have been a joyous celebration of life, we were mourning our little sibling and Dik and Dixey were mourning a son for the second time in the space of a few years. The investigation made things more intense. Dik's mood deepened and Dixey became more subdued with each day.

Rollin has never been a boy of many words. He's smart but thoughtful and I'm sure he felt the loss as much as we all did. He coped by being extra helpful and keeping busy.

Essie's emotions boiled close to the surface. She shouted and cried, 'It's not fair, why did he have to die?'

I spent as much time as I could away from the camp. Desperate to escape from the sadness and tears, I disappeared into my own little dream world in the corners of the fields and under the trees. I found patches of moss growing in the woods and carefully detached their small roots from the soil so I could roll them up like a carpet. Over the course of a week I had a patch that measured approximately four feet square of soft, uprooted moss to lie on and play in. The green dewy smell of the moss made me feel comforted and safe. I captured ladybirds and butterflies and brought them onto my patch of moss to enjoy it with me. I lay on my back on the damp moss, looking at the sky with the bugs fluttering around above me, dreading the moment I would hear my name called.

'Roxy, come and milk the goats', 'Roxy, fetch some water', Roxy, can you help me cook?' I knew the calls would come before long, but for the hours my absence went unnoticed I lived in a world of my own imagining.

After a bit I ventured into the woods a bit deeper, and found a circle of trees with a clearing in the middle – a place I had visited once or twice with Perly. There was a big tree stump that had been neatly sawn off and served perfectly as a table for our imaginative picnics of blackberries and elderberries. I told Perly that we were in the fairies' home and that the tree stump was where the fairies dined and danced. When I talked to my family about the fairy woods, it was never questioned or contradicted and it seemed like the most real and perfect thing in the world. I brought my moss carpet into the clearing so the fairies could use it when I was asleep. I knew that they were nocturnal because I never saw them, but in the evenings as the sun went down I would feel their presence around me. I would get the odd glimpse of their silvery wings appearing from behind the trees but they were shy and rarely came out to play with me. I left them dishes of berries on the log and every morning I would scurry down there, hoping to get a glimpse of them before they made their way home. I would find little footprints and marks in the moss and empty jam-jar lids from the food gifts I had given them.

It had never occurred to me that anyone could not believe in fairies. To me they were a fact of life: shy, ethereal little people who lived in the woods and danced under the light of the moon. They were my friends. Every night for many years I lay tucked up on my little wooden bed in the wagon and dreamed of going away to their silvery sleeping place, walled with moss and sheltered with leaves and petals. It was a peaceful place where my colourful imagination was embraced.

After a while the police stopped coming. Dixey stopped crying and the charges against Dik and Dixey were dropped. They were cautioned for not registering the baby's birth and death but nothing more. We got on with our lives, moving about from place to place. Sometimes the police moved us on but often we left for pastures new of our own accord. Then, in the spring of 1985, Dixey got pregnant again and we looked forward to yet another addition to the family.

* * *

We travelled all over southern Ireland that summer and met up with Roz and her family at a camp where lots of other people where living. Roz and Dixey made peace and became friends again. They cooked together and chatted around the fire. We were all delighted to be reunited with Harmony and the boys. Rollin spent his time with Tristan and Zeal, and Perly and Harmony, who were just a few months apart and had similar spirited natures, played together from morning till night. I was a little left out. We had moved away from Uncle Bob and his family, so I was without my great friend, Ome. Essie was kind to me but, being four years older than me, she was preoccupied with friends who were older and cooler than me – so that left me fairly alone, though I still had my dream world for company.

There was an old man living at the end of the track, named Bill. His abode was a small caravan, no more than twelve feet long, which we referred to as a 'blim'. He lived alone and was quite grouchy. I really had no reason to go and see him, but the smell of his bacon frying each morning wafted down the track and tempted my nostrils. Bacon was another one of those things that rarely came into our home, and when it did it was served to Dik in a sandwich, not to us kids. I'd wander up the track and wait quietly outside the caravan until Bill finished frying his bacon, then I'd sit patiently outside the window where he sat and ate, oblivious to the fact that I was crouched down outside. After a few minutes he'd throw the rind over his shoulder, out the window and into my hand. I didn't think twice about eating the rind that he was rejecting – on the contrary I wondered why anyone would throw away such delicious morsels! I'd sit outside the caravan window until the bacon rind stopped coming, then I'd sneak off back down the track.

One morning I was so preoccupied chewing away on the rubbery rind that I didn't notice Bill emerge from his blim. He spotted me though, sitting on the ground gnawing on his leftovers.

'You little beggar, always eating my bacon, I know you do it,' he snapped. 'Doesn't your mutha feed you? Well, you can make yourself useful and do these dishes for me.' He gestured towards the counter in the kitchen inside, which was piled high with dirty plates and pans.

Now, I didn't actually like grumpy old Bill and I certainly didn't want to add any more dishes to my long list of chores, but I saw an opportunity and cheekily replied, 'What's it worth?'

'What's it worth? I ain't paying you if that's what you mean.'

'Well then, I ain't doin' 'em,' I said, turning to walk away.

Then Bill said, 'I'll give you a sweet, if you do them and do them well.' So we made a deal.

Every morning after I had done my chores I waited until I could smell the bacon cooking and I went up to that mouldy little caravan and washed Bill's dishes. When I finished, he checked over my work before getting down a long clear tube of shiny blue sugared almonds from the highest cupboard. He gave me one almond for a morning's dishwashing. It seemed like a perfectly good arrangement to me. I came to resent my parents on the mornings they kept me busy and I missed the opportunity to wash his dishes and get the sweet, but I knew I couldn't tell them as I wasn't supposed to be working for Bill or eating sweets.

Now, when I wasn't busy with my chores or dishwashing for Bill, I still spent a lot of time with Dixey and looked forward to the baby arriving. I'd pat her tummy and talk to the baby inside. While Dixey was heavily pregnant it became obvious that Roz was pregnant too. I didn't dare ask who the father was. She was travelling alone with the three children and spent a lot of her time with our family. We often ate together around the fire and she and Dixey sat up chatting after we were all tucked up in bed.

Not long before our new baby was due all that came to an end. I remember walking back to the camp and hearing Dixey wailing and Dik stomping around the camp as Roz threw her possessions into her truck, gathered up her kids and took off. The period of unrest and turmoil didn't finish there. My parents never explained what was happening, but shortly afterwards Dik went off to India and Dixey took Essie, Rollin, Perly and me to stay with a friend at a run-down old cottage in Leitrim. It had no water or electricity and was less comfortable than the wagon we were used to. Then Dik returned from India with rugs and embroidered clothes to sell at Ballinasloe horse fair in Galway. He brought us each a pair of little velvet shoes with mirrors on them – mine were green – and we were all together again.

I lost my dishwashing job shortly before we left that camp. Rollin rumbled me doing Bill's dishes and said I was being ripped off and should get two sweets rather than one. I agreed to negotiate a rise and to give Rollin one of the sweets if he didn't tell Dik and Dixey. Bill was furious at my request and I lost my job on the spot.

'You ungrateful little brat,' he said. 'Clear off, out of here.' So I did.

★   ★   ★

Wanda Ra was born in Leitrim in the winter of 1985 and shortly after Dik's return from India. Perly was four years old, so the new baby seemed very overdue: the rest of us had less than a two-year age gap. Daughter number four, five including Harmony, and Dad's dream of taking over the world with daughters was shaping up nicely.

Dixey came home from the hospital with Wanda one foggy afternoon in November. I peeked into the pile of clean, white blankets and saw a fragile little face sleeping away. She looked like a tiny china doll, with her pale skin and dark-blonde hair. 'This is your new little sister, my Roxy Riddle,' Dixey said, as she placed Wanda in my arms. 'She is more delicate than the cast-iron bread bastibles, so don't drop her.'

The bread bastibles were big black pans made of cast iron that we baked the bread in on the fire. I knew they were fragile and expensive to replace and had always handled them very carefully. I had seen one break after getting a knock from the kettle iron and noticed Dixey's distress. So something more delicate than them must be very delicate indeed.

A couple of days after Wanda's arrival, I awoke to find her gone. No Dixey, no Wanda and no Dik. The camp was unusually quiet. I found Essie making breakfast by the fire, a pile of fruit and some cornbread ready next to her, a serious look on her face. I sensed something bad had happened but was scared to ask; scared of being told Wanda had gone to join all the bright stars in the sky, like the last baby. Rollin was sitting by the fire kicking a smouldering log, his feet covered in ash, as sparks glittered into the sky.

Finally I couldn't contain myself. 'What's happened? Where've they gone?' I asked.

'Baby's sick, really sick, taken her to hospital,' Essie replied, without looking up.

The day went slowly. Nobody said much. When Dik came back in the evening, he told us that Wanda had pneumonia. The hospital was treating her with antibiotics but she was very ill. A couple of days passed but Dixey didn't come back. The mood around the camp didn't lift; we all feared the worst. Dik came and went between the hospital and the camp. He brought little news and rarely spoke. He held his head low and kept his brow furrowed.

On the third day, when he came back in the evening, Essie asked, 'How's she doing?'

'Not good. She's not responding to the antibiotics and they don't think she'll make it through the night.' They spoke in whispers. Essie was trying to be brave but I knew she was hurting as much as I was.

By this stage Essie had outgrown the cupboard under the bed, so I was finally tucked up in my own little space, the cosy den I'd coveted for so long. I'd made it my own with stickers on the walls of fairies and butterflies. Usually I could hear the bed above me creak as Dik and Dixey moved or turned over. When Wanda had come home for the brief few days after her birth, I could hear her whimper and gurgle above me. Now there was no sound; it was all so still and silent, a deathly silence I think they call it. I went to sleep thinking about Wanda's little face, the first and only time I'd held her. She was more delicate than the basti- ble after all; she hadn't been dropped or hurt but she was teetering on the edge between life and death. At times like this many people prayed, but I had no understanding of God, so I closed my eyes and hoped she'd pull through but I felt helpless in my hoping.

Dik didn't come home that night, and he wasn't there when we got up. I missed Dixey and knew she must be having a terrible time at the hospital. The camp seemed to have lost its heart and centre with her gone. There were no family meals, and no laughter; we all just muddled through as best we could. We milked the goats and ate lots of muesli, rarely bothering to cook or clean. Dik was gone all day. Then, just as the sun was going down, a car approached. I didn't recognise the driver but Dik got out of the passenger seat. He held his head a little higher than he had in recent days, and he smiled as he got out. Then Dixey emerged from the back seat of the car. She looked happy too. As I walked towards them, I saw Dixey lift something out of the back passenger side. Had they brought Wanda's body home to bury? Was it her blankets and clothes? The bundle started to wiggle and let out a scream. I nearly jumped out of my skin with shock. Wanda had not only got through the night, she had completely recovered.

Dixey took her inside and wrapped her up double warm. Now Essie and I had even more work on our shoulders; Wanda's arrival meant fetching water and cooking and cleaning took up a lot of our time. I had less time to play but I cherished little Wanda and quickly learnt to look after her, how to change and wash her nappies and which fruit I should puree through a sieve to make her face light up. I rocked her to sleep at every opportunity and believed that at six years old I knew most things about babies and was nearly old enough to start a family of my own.

*   *   *

Wanda wasn't the only baby of Dik's born that year. It wasn't long before Dixey told us that we had another half-sister: Roz had given birth to a little girl named Emily. Dixey didn't seem particularly upset by the news and said that she knew Roz was carrying Dik's baby for the second time. I was puzzled and it made me feel less secure about our strong family unit but it didn't seem to be particularly out of the ordinary. Lots of the families we knew had different mothers and fathers.

I remember having a chat with Dixey around that time when she told me that she and Dik loved each other very much but that he needed a lot more sex than she did, so sometimes he went elsewhere to get it. It seemed very matter of fact and logical and she expressed little emotion. It wasn't like the idea of sex was a shock to me: living in such a small space it was part of our lives from an early age as Dik and Dixey had to make all those kids one way or another. But I wondered where else Dik went, apart from into Roz's caravan, my busy little mind skipping through the various names and faces of women we had camped with over the years. I thought perhaps he went to see them for sex as well. But no one else had his babies as far as I knew.

I recalled a Swiss woman, Frida, who came to stay from time to time. She was the very opposite of Dixey, tall and angular with blonde hair. She didn't fit in around the place like most people did. She had a kind of stiffness and was always looking for chairs to sit on or getting Dik to sort out somewhere comfortable for her. I knew she was a friend of Dik's rather than Dixey's as she and Dixey rarely spoke to one another, but

Dik spent a lot of time with her – they went for walks and talked in whispers. I concluded that she must be one of the friends that Dik went to for sex as Dixey's revelation had clarified things in my mind.

CHAPTER 5

England

In 1986 we left the sleepy marshes of southern Ireland and moved to the UK. I don't know what motivated my parents to move then or why they decided to go to England. Dixey said she wanted us to have more opportunities, that Ireland had nothing to offer us other than bogs and freedom, and that if we didn't go now we'd be stuck there forever. So we took the wagon and put everything in the bus, including some horses and a couple of goats, and boarded the ferry to Wales late one night. I had never left Ireland before, apart from a trip to see Esther and Peter in America when I was very young which I had no recollection of. Dik was seasick and grumpy on the journey. We didn't have a cabin, so we slept under the stairs in the corridor above the car deck, wrapped in our coats. The weather was stormy and the sea was rough, but it was an adventure.

I heard Dik and Dixey discussing how expensive the ferry was and that we didn't have much money to survive in England.

We'd spent a few weeks camped by a farm doing mushroom picking before we left Ireland. They said the money we'd earned paid for the crossing, but that we'd have to find work quickly when we got to England.

Our first stop was on top of a grassy hill near the town of Wellington in Shropshire. I was struck by how different the scenery was: big old trees dominated the landscape and the ground was dry. There were none of the leaves and herbs I was used to finding in the marshy bogs of Ireland. Perly was happy and content climbing high in the deep-rooted oaks and elms though, and Rollin quickly settled in and started dismantling and remaking bicycles and electrical things he came across in the dumps and ditches of the area. Dixey was heavily pregnant again and she and Dik decided to stay put so she could give birth to the baby in the local hospital in Shrewsbury. I think she was still haunted by the memories of her little boys and the fright of nearly losing Wanda. Whatever the reason, she didn't wish to endure another home birth.

Our home was much the same as in Ireland – the wooden wagon and the bus camped next to each other but we now had the addition of a frame tent to cook in when the weather was bad. It had a simple gas hob and a trestle table inside as well as a large metal cupboard for food storage. Dixey had painted the cupboard bright green with red scrolls. She had been doing more painting recently on various wheels and pieces of furniture. She practised lining and scrolling whenever she had the time.

It made things a bit easier not having to always light the fire in the rain and cook outside but we still spent most of our time outdoors. We didn't have any water, but we had large metal churns and buckets. In Ireland there were often public water pumps on the outskirts of towns and villages so we could easily fill the churns but in England water was always a problem. Sometimes Dik would ask if he could fill the churns at a garage or shop, but we were always very aware of not wasting it, as it wasn't easy getting them filled up.

The memory of one day when I was about seven has stayed with me. It was wintertime, snow had fallen and then the ice had set in, freezing the snow in hard, sharp mounds. We hadn't been in England very long and were out of water again. Dik and Dixey had been arguing and Dik had stomped off in a bad mood. Dixey asked Essie to mind the little ones so she and I could go and get the water churn filled up. We walked down the hill holding on to a handle each. The metal was cold, so I pulled my jumper down over my hands to stop them sticking to the handles. We could see lights in the windows of the houses. I was tired and relieved as we approached the door of the first house. We just needed to fill the churn and we could get back to the camp and warm up. Dixey knocked on the door.

A stern-faced man greeted us. 'What do you want?'

'We're out of water, just hoping you'd be so kind to fill up the churn for us,' Dixey said in her soft, calm voice. I looked behind the man and saw a TV flickering away and a fire burning in the background. The house looked warm and cosy; I imagined him inviting us in and giving us a cup of cocoa while he filled our churn. Then his reply came shattering my daydream, 'No, and don't come begging around here again.' He slammed the door in our faces.

I was shocked at the negative response and wondered how someone could be so mean. We went on to the next house only to get a similar reaction, and the next and the next. People told us we should be ashamed of ourselves scrounging at their doors or to get a job and pay our taxes then we'd have water for ourselves. We were losing hope and getting cold. I dragged my feet as we walked, and tried to keep my balance on the cold slippery ground. I looked up at Dixey and saw tears tumbling down her cheeks. Eventually we got to the house of a lady who took pity on our situation and gave us half a churn of water. We then had the horrible task of getting back up the hill, lugging the churn between us. It was pitch-black and freezing cold. I thought I would collapse with the cold and exhaustion, but I tried to stay strong and get the water home so we could cook some dinner and warm our tummies. I became a little less naive that night and realised that to other people we were the scrounging, begging no-gooders that lived on the hill.

On the up-side, England meant that we were closer for some visitors. Shortly after arriving in England, we met Tanya for the first time. She was Dik's eldest daughter, the result of a brief relationship Dik had had with a woman called Ruth before he met Dixey. We were all very excited to meet her and scurried around trying to make ourselves respectable before she arrived. We knew she existed but we'd never met her – she lived in Kent and even Dik had only seen her once or twice, when she was a small baby. I was curious to see what she looked like but imagined she would look like all the rest of his children: dark with eyes set far apart and thick hair.

She did. In fact, she looked even more like Dik than any of us, with very similar features and she shared his love of horses. I coyly eyed her from head to toe noticing that her eyes were darker than mine but a similar shape and her hair was dark but not as curly. Tanya was far cleaner than we were, despite our efforts to tidy ourselves up. My shabby dress looked scruffy next to her immaculate skirt and ironed shirt while my hair was hidden under a spotty headscarf. Tanya lived in a house and went to school. I was fascinated and plied this new grown-up sister of mine with questions about her life. I wished she'd take me home so I could see what it was like to live a nice life in a proper house. Tanya didn't stay long but I thought about her for many months afterwards and looked forward to meeting her again.

Then, not long after Tanya left, we had a visit from Dixey's parents. Esther – who was too youthful ever to let us call her grandma – and Peter were still trying to accept the life that Dixey had chosen, and tried to maintain contact. They would visit every year or so, and between times Esther would send parcels of books and clothes for us, and old clothes of hers for Dixey, to the nearest post office. This time they had come to help Dixey prepare for the birth of their eighth grandchild. They checked into a hotel in Wellington before coming to pick up Perly and me.

In comparison to us, my affluent grandparents were like creatures from another universe. Peter was a tall gentle soul, perfectly turned out in suit trousers and a shirt. His silk ties and smart hats mesmerised me. Esther was, and possibly still is, the most well-presented person I have ever seen in my life. Her hair was always set and tidy, she had perfect make-up and immaculate clothes with a wide belt cinching in her small waist – a look that took her hours to prepare each morning. Esther still had her dancer's bearing, straight as a die, her head always held high. And though we were raised not to answer back to any adult, there was something about Esther's light American accent, dignity and sharp diction that was particularly authoritative. She demanded respect.

When we got to their hotel, Esther sat us on the bed and went into the bathroom. We had never been to a hotel before. We eagerly eyed the bowl of tea bags and mini milk portions that sat on the table next to the bed, picking up each thing and looking over it until we were sure we knew what everything was.

'That's mint tea, smell it,' I said passing the tea bag to Perly.

She held a shortbread tightly in her hands. 'I've got a biscuit,' she replied, her eyes huge.

Esther came back into the room and looked anxiously over to see what we were doing. She took a bottle of pink liquid from her shopping bag and went back into the bathroom. We could hear water running, and smell the scent of soap in the air. Before long she summoned us into the bathroom.

'Put your dirty clothes in there,' she pointed to the empty shopping bag, 'and let me know if you need help washing your hair.' She left us to it, leaving the door ajar. We quickly undressed and climbed into the steaming bath of bubbly water. The bath seemed enormous and very full of water, much hotter than we were used to. Perly and I sat one at each end grinning from ear to ear. We washed and rinsed our hair with more ease and delight than we had ever experienced.

All my life Dixey had talked about how she longed for a hot bath and in that moment I finally understood why. We were used to having strip-washes with a bucket of water and a rag or giving ourselves a soap-down in the rain when it poured on a warm day. If the weather was cold we'd heat some water in the wagon and just wash the essentials – hands, faces and bums – with a damp cloth.

Esther and Peter had arrived, as always, laden with gifts and after our bath Esther presented Perly and me with starched tartan dresses with white collars and cuffs and matching tights. We put our dresses and tights on and brushed our hair before being dropped off at the camp with the strict instruction to stay clean while they took Rollin and Essie to have their bath at the hotel.

Dixey told us that our grandparents would be taking us out for dinner.

'Promise me you will be really good in the restaurant, very polite and quiet. Promise,' she pleaded.

I sat at the table, clean and smart for once, quietly basking in the pleasure of not receiving the usual scornful stares from the locals. But I wasn't totally at ease – there was still my deep dread at being presented with a menu. I was eight years old and could not read or write. None of us could. I longed to learn though, and spent many afternoons staring at the books Esther and Peter gave us, hoping that if I looked long enough the words would make sense to me – but I didn't know what the letters were called let alone how to pronounce them. To my relief Peter leant over and read the menu to us before asking what we'd like. It contained many things that I had never tried but hearing Peter mention sausage and mash, I quickly announced that was what I'd be having. Rollin opted for sausage too, but with chips. (Rollin had always hated mashed potato and refused to have it on his plate, making Dixey take his potatoes from the pan before she mashed them. We never questioned why Rollin had the luxury of stipulating how his food was prepared when the rest of us ate what we given, but there was always a degree of double standards in our home: the men had certain privileges.) But when I turned to Perly who was sitting next to me to see what she wanted, I found her in tears.

'I don't wan' to choose dinner!' she cried. 'I jus' wan' something given to me like normal!'

We had a very healthy but basic diet – brown rice, vegetable stews, curries or dhal, mostly cooked by Dixey with the help of Essie and me. Occasionally Dik would come back with a rabbit or a chicken and make a curry, something he did very well, probably having learned his skills in India. He'd start by dry-roasting spices in a heavy-bottomed, cast-iron pan. The heady aroma would drift far and wide, tickling our noses and tantalizing our taste buds. Then he'd roughly chop onions and garlic, before tossing the meat around in the pan with some fresh tomatoes and herbs. He cooked with ease and confidence. I wondered why he didn't do it more often, but I didn't ask. But apart from that, we didn't eat much meat and had no sugar or processed food in our diet. There was never a question of not liking something or not eating at mealtime. We had two choices, take it or leave it. We ate exactly what was put in front of us without question and without grumbling. In between meals we would eat fruit, or nibble on the things the hedgerows and fields provided.

'Perly'll have sausage and mash like me,' I said.

I was surprised to see my plate of food appear without a vegetable in sight. On the odd occasion that we were given things like sausages they were always accompanied by a pile of steamed or raw vegetables. We struggled to eat with a knife and fork and wriggled around on our chairs; used to eating with just a spoon, a fork or our fingers and having our food on our laps, our table manners left much to be desired. Nonetheless I devoured the plate of food, delighted by the smoothness of the potato that was entirely devoid of the skins and lumps that I was used to. I savoured each mouthful and decided that, even if the goodness of the potato was in the skin, as Dixey had told me on many occasions, when I grew up I was going to make smooth mash for my children. I filed this in my memory along with baths, and the fact that I would never make my children eat lentils on Christmas Day.

Christmas, like Easter, was never celebrated in the Freeman home. I think Dik was rebelling against his Catholic upbringing – he refused to acknowledge or partake in any religious or commercial celebrations. Christmas was just like any other day of the year apart from the fact that we seemed to eat even more lentils and brown rice than usual. We weren't totally deprived of celebrations though, our parents always made sure that birthdays were very special days and sometimes we celebrated other events, like the winter and summer equinox. Then we'd make a big bonfire and bake potatoes in the embers. Many an evening was spent sitting or standing around the fire laughing and joking.

One Christmas Eve when we were camping in Telford, a well-meaning local man took pity on our lack of festive arrangements around the camp and presented us with a turkey. Dixey gratefully accepted the gift and stored it away in the outdoor food cupboard.

Essie was beside herself with joy. 'We've got a turkey and we're gonna have a Christmas dinner this year!' she announced to us all.

'Can we have roast potatoes?' Rollin enquired.

'And gravy?' I piped up.

'Yes, I don't see why not. I don't know what Dik will think about us celebrating Christmas, but we can't not eat it, now we've been given it.'

'Yippee!' we sang in unison.

I woke up early on Christmas morning, filled for the first time with some excitement, looking forward to a day that was going to bring something out of the usual, a proper roast dinner and our first Christmas turkey. Essie and I started to scrub the vegetables as Dixey attempted to get enough heat to cook the bird.

She went to get the turkey from the cupboard. Seconds later we heard her say, 'Oh!'

She emerged with a sad look on her face. 'It's gone, girls, the turkey is gone.'

'What do you mean, how can it be gone?' Essie asked, disbelieving.

'The cupboard door was open and it's not in there.'

I thought it was a practical joke at first, and went to the cupboard to look. The usual staple packets of rice and lentils, chickpeas and tins of tomatoes lined the back, but no turkey. Rollin and I started to search the camp for the missing bird but lost hope of recovering it with every minute that passed. Eventually Rollin returned with a chewed-up piece of plastic wrapping with a picture of a turkey still visible on one corner.

'Dogs had a nice lunch anyway,' he said, flinging the plastic in the bin and walking off.

We all argued about who'd left the cupboard open. But whoever's fault it was, the fact remained, Christmas was cancelled again.

Dixey tried to raise our deflated spirits by saying, 'Oh well, we can still use all those lovely veg to make a nice big soup,' but her cheery voice and enthusiasm just made us feel worse.

Essie cursed and said, 'When I have kids, I'll give them the best Christmas, every year.' She found the lack of Christmas even harder than most of us. For me it was just a fact of life – but for Essie it was a disappointment time and time again, and she didn't mind saying so.

Dik and Dixey's sixth child was born in October that year. They went to hospital for the labour, leaving us in the capable hands of our dear grandfather, Peter. We were delighted to be left in his care but he looked woefully out of place in the camp. He leant his 6 foot 4 inch statuesque frame awkwardly on the side of the wagon, and balanced on the water churn when eating while we all sat cross-legged on the ground, giggling at how he struggled to relax in the chaotic surroundings.

A marvellous part of the weekend was when Peter returned from shopping with a box of chicken and mushroom pies. We'd never eaten anything so processed in our lives and thought it unbelievably exciting. The rain was beating down outside and we hadn't lit the fire, so we decided to warm the pies by putting them on top of the woodburner in the wagon and putting the milking bowl upside down on top of them. They scorched on the bottom and were congealed and lukewarm inside – nothing like as nice as the wholesome pies that Dixey made out of wholemeal flour and vegetables. Still, gloopy and over-salted though they were, we were thrilled. In fact we were so abuzz with the excitement of the pies that when we found we had a new baby sister the news scarcely registered as the highlight of the day.

I wasn't surprised that we had another girl in the family, although there had been constant talk of how this one would be a boy. A few weeks before, an old friend of the family, Ray, had come and doused Dixey's tummy with a ring on a piece of thread; when it spun around in circles, instead of swinging from side to side, he announced that there was definitely a boy in there. Dixey said he had a very good track record and he was bound to be right. We had compiled a long list of possible names for him which we now threw into the fire and started racking our brains for yet another girl's name.

Going to meet the baby was a surreal experience. I had never been inside a hospital before. It was so bright and I was surprised by the clinical whiteness of everything. I remember the first time I set eyes on the baby lying in Dixey's arms. She seemed so tiny and perfect. Dixey looked exhausted and I thought they were going to keep them there forever, but they were home the next day and our family was complete.

Well-versed in the care of babies, I quickly settled into the role of the caring big sister. The baby was the cutest little thing; podgy and smiley from the outset, she quickly developed a strange habit of munching things around inside her round apple-red cheeks like a little hamster. There was just one problem: this little baby had no name beyond 'the baby', and the debate about what to call her went on and on. Dixey was adamant that she was to be her last child and liked the idea of a name starting with 'Z' to represent this fact, but we couldn't come up with anything appropriate. I requested that we call her Sofia or Natasha but Dik said they were too common, as was Dixey's suggestions of Zena. As the weeks of debate ran into months, we finally decided on Zeta. It was the last letter of the Greek alphabet, Dik told us, and it signified that she would be the final child of the family. But after calling her 'the baby' for so long we all struggled to start calling her anything else. Zeta continued to be known as 'the baby' until well into her toddling years.

Some of the families we knew from Ireland came to see us in Shropshire and of course Uncle Tony still appeared from time to time. We'd spot his familiar old grey van trundling up the track and would all gather around outside to greet him with hugs and kisses. Dixey would put the kettle on and Dik would come in to have a chat around the stove. I've never known how he kept track of where we were living but he always seemed to find us one way or another.

But one family remained absent: Roz and her children. I guessed that Dixey wouldn't still be mad with her, she always thought the best of people and wasn't really one to hold a grudge, but for whatever reason they were no longer part of our life. I often thought of them, wondering where they had gone and if we would ever see them again. Perhaps Harmony and Emily might like to know that they had another sister but I wasn't sure how to let them know and didn't want to bother

Dixey with my ideas. Dixey had told us before Esther and Peter
arrived that we shouldn't mention that we had two other sisters.
She said it would hurt them and they didn't need to know.
Shortly after our grandparents left, a couple of old friends, John
and Esta, who were musicians from Ireland, turned up in a van.
They knew Roz, so I asked about them.

'They've gone to Spain to start a new life, Rox.'

Spain sounded like a very long way away. I felt sure that we
wouldn't see Harmony, Emily, Tristan and Zeal ever again. We
were very close as a family, our sibling bond so strong despite our
different mothers, that it was strange to think of them living a
different life in a different country.

My memories of Shropshire in the mid-1980s are mostly of cold
bleak weather, hostile neighbours and poverty. The Battle of the
Beanfield, the largest mass civil arrest in British history, when the
police attacked hundreds of travellers converging on Stonehenge,
was only a few years past, and although we were just one family,
and not a convoy of travellers and vehicles like the ones in
Wiltshire, we still felt the suspicion that settled people, and the
police, held towards us. Travellers, gypsies – we were all the same
to them – meant trouble.

The only thing I knew of politics when I was growing up
was the little snippets I overheard when Dik turned on the
radio or talked about something in the newspaper. I knew
that Britain had its first female prime minister, a horsey-
faced woman called Margaret Thatcher. She seemed to be
responsible for a lot of unease across the country, but she
didn't seem to have much effect on our lives. The only

economic fluctuation that impacted on us was the price of brown rice and the availability of cheap land to graze the horses. But life did become very difficult for travellers in the 1980s when the homeowner was king. Common land was more or less a thing of the past and any camping on it was illegal. Other traditional stopping places, green areas on the outskirts of a village, little lanes that led to a dead end, were barricaded off. A lot of gypsies were so scared of losing their places in the few authorised caravan sites that they didn't move at all. Later, a 1994 Act of Parliament removed the obligation of councils to provide such sites at all, supposedly encouraging gypsies to look after themselves, but increased the power of police and authorities to evict gypsies and travellers from unlawful stopping places. The result was to criminalise a whole way of life.

I recall just one friendly face among the many sour stares. An elderly man called George. He befriended Dik and liked to come and sit around the fire, chatting with a cup of tea. Dik and George did a bit of business together but nothing much. It was during a lean patch – I can pinpoint times of poverty in my upbringing by the meals of endless rice and dhal, or rice and vegetables – so we thought all the missed Christmases of our past had come at once when Dik came home one day carrying a box full of chicken wings.

'Look at this, kids, five kilos of chicken. Only cost three quid.'

George had taken Dik to the local chicken farm and introduced him to the farm manager. They had more chicken wings than they knew what to do with and would sell them off cheap. Dixey quickly got to work, tossing the wings in marinades and cooking them up. We had those wings in curries, stews, soups, roasts and numerous other dishes.

'Back home in the USA,' Dixey told us, 'people marinate chicken wings in chilli sauce and call them buffalo wings.'

'Buffaloes don't have wings,' was Rollin's smart reply.

When the box was empty Dik got some more and then some more and then some more. The bony, fatty little morsels soon lost their appeal; and it wasn't long before we were all craving the old healthy meals of dhal and veg. But the wings kept coming. That winter will always remain in my memory as chicken-wing winter. It wasn't the first and it wouldn't be the last time we lived on one particular food group simply because it was cheap and available. I couldn't look at mushrooms for most of my childhood after we spent a season picking and eating them every day for months on end.

We stayed in Shropshire for less than a year. Before long the police clamped down on us and made us leave the area. They turned up with an eviction order within days of our arriving at each and every camp. We'd find a quiet lane, park the wagons and vehicles and before we'd even had a chance to light a fire, a police car would pull up, so finally we figured it was time to move out of the area.

Dik secured some work doing rubbish clearing with the horse and cart at a festival in Norfolk, so we packed up camp and made the long journey across the country. We travelled for a few days and it was slow going with the big old truck and the horses and wagons. We stopped in lay-bys at the side of the road when it got dark and Dik was too tired to drive any further. I remember trying to sleep in the back of the truck with vehicles flying by, the noise of the engines booming through the walls and every passing truck making our vehicle rock. I missed the peace of the bog and sound of the wind whistling in the trees. But at least the chicken-wing supplier was far behind us.

CHAPTER 6

Dereham

Dik's bad moods had become more frequent since we had moved to England. I guess he was under pressure. It was harder to make a living and find somewhere to stay in England, which was so much more densely populated than Ireland. I could tell by his eyes in the morning whether I should speak to him: if they looked raging and angry I kept well out of his way. Dixey did all she could to try and keep him happy but the disorder and mess of the camp enraged him, as did her cooking much of the time. He wanted to eat full-flavoured food such as a hot lamb curry, not Dixey's 'bland slop'. Sometimes when a mood took hold of him it could last for days. When that happened I would hide away and daydream of a different life: I wished I were an only child, living with just Dixey in a pretty house with dormer windows on a cobbled street.

I have often wondered what it was that took hold of my father. What was burning away inside him to make him express such a lack of satisfaction with the world and the life he had? Was he beaten and abused as a child? Did he feel cheated or betrayed by something or someone? He rarely spoke of his upbringing so I knew little about what he'd experienced as youngster, but from what he did say it never sounded particularly traumatic or difficult. I was frightened of his temper, but saddened by his moods. They seemed to dominate our lives.

When I was around eight years old, my interest in books and stories was increasing with each day and I was gradually learning to read. Dixey helped me whenever she had a chance, explaining to me what sounds the letters made and how to pronounce the words. I took up the stack of books that Esther and Peter had bought us; they had heavy blue covers and pictures of children around the world. The stories were about families and children living unusual lives, goat herders in Switzerland, a travelling circus in Italy. Some of them I could identify with – the children in the circus rode horses bareback like we did and lived in wagons, the Swiss children milked goats and lived off the land – but my favourite one was about a little girl who lived with her mother in France, working from home, side-by-side with their sewing machines. That's the life I wanted: just me and Dixey in a little house with a bath, a toilet and a washing machine. I knew I'd miss my siblings but I just couldn't see how we could have the life I longed for if they came with us, so they were left out of the dream.

While Dik's clean-up job at the festival was in full swing – he'd sit on the cart steering the horse around the fields while we children ran behind throwing boxes and bags of rubbish on board – we explored the area looking for a quiet place to set up camp. As in Shropshire, we quickly got moved on from every-where we stopped. Finally we arrived outside the town of Dereham in North Norfolk, where we found a long green track with a field running down one side, which backed onto a housing estate. It was the closest we had ever lived to a residential area and the sound of the children's voices coming from the playground intrigued me.

'Don't even fink about 'em, Rox,' said Rollin, 'and definitely don't try an' talk to 'em.'

Unlike many gypsy children, we weren't brought up to fear settled people, but we knew we were different and unaccepted by most of them, so we kept out of their way. But I was an inquisitive little girl who longed to make friends with children who lived in houses. The mere sound of children playing made me dream of sleepovers in tidy rooms with bunk beds and hot-water bottles.

One day Rollin and I wandered up the lane and into the woods. We were collecting firewood when I heard the voices of some of the children from the estate. They sounded much closer than I had ever heard them before. I walked slowly to the edge of the woods and could see a group of five or six children, about the same age as us – maybe eight or nine – walking towards me. They spotted me in the trees and coaxed me out with friendly voices. Filled with excitement – they wanted to be friends! – I slowly walked away from the shelter of the trees.

From behind me I heard Rollin say, 'Stay here, Rox, stay here,' but I ignored him and headed towards them, straightening my headscarf and spitting on the sleeve of my dress in an attempt to wipe my face clean.

But I was hardly out in the open when the children started to chant in unison: 'Gypsy, gypsy, dirty, dirty didicoy'. They hurled pebbles and clumps of hard soil at me as I ducked and shielded my face with my arm. Rollin yanked me back into the trees as the children ran back to the housing estate.

'I told you not to go,' he snapped.

'I jus' wanted to talk to them,' I whimpered.

'Well they didn't wanna talk to you, did they?' he replied.

'Why'd they do that?' I asked. I couldn't understand it.

'Dunno, they're probably scared or stupid or sumfink. Don't worry about it,' he said and patted me on the back lovingly.

I saw the children a few more times, but I never trusted their kind prompts again. It was a lesson well learnt: I stayed out of their way and put the ideas of having a friend in a house out of my mind.

Shortly after arriving at the Dereham camp, Dik came home one day with two fluffy black rabbits. We'd had a lot of animals in my life, but never any pets as such, so I immediately presumed they were for the pot and started preparing the veg for a stew. But much to my surprise he then presented a run for the rabbits and announced that we could keep them.

'There's a girl and boy there,' Dik said. 'I got given them. Do what you want with them. They're domestic rabbits, whatever that means.'

I could hardly believe my ears, but was delighted with the new arrivals. Essie and I busied ourselves making the rabbits comfortable and decided to call them Bill and Penny. We combed their fluffy coats and hoped they'd soon have babies – as if we didn't have enough babies to look after already.

But it soon turned out that the rabbits were not a harmonious pair. Instead of snuggling up and making babies, Bill and Penny did nothing but rip holes out of each other's fur. After some close examination, we discovered that Bill and Penny were in fact both male and didn't like occupying the same run. Our dreams of baby bunnies evaporated and we renamed them Bill and Ben. Their appeal faded and we told Dik we didn't want them any more. He responded by breaking their necks. Essie and I skinned one each and ate our first ever pets without a second thought or a single regret. We weren't cold or heartless children, we were just brought up to know what an animal was for: if they were no longer entertaining us they may as well be fulfilling their primary role and satisfying our bellies.

Bill and Penny/Ben were not the only couple scrapping around that time. Dik and Dixey weren't getting on very well and it felt like we were always ducking away from a row. Dixey worked hard to keep the family happy, she rarely complained and received very little gratitude but she struggled to accept Dik's casual attitude to 'other women'. Sometimes our calm mother would break down and yell that she'd had enough of him sneaking off to see the Swiss woman Frida and that she was leaving him or she would cry and plead with him to get rid of her. Sometimes I hoped Dixey would leave, and take me with her, but I knew she wouldn't. We kids would huddle together when our parents were fighting. We'd judge how bad it was by how long it went on and we'd discuss what we hoped the outcome would be.

'She shouldn't put up with it. It's time she stood up for herself or left him,' Essie would announce.

'Don't be stupid, of course she shouldn't leave, relationships are just like that,' Rollin would reply.

'Well I'm going with her if she does leave,' I'd mumble.

'No one is going anywhere,' Perly would say. 'We're a family, we all stay together.'

Eventually the dust would settle and they'd make up. And there were times when they were completely in love. Dik would start to sing and joke again and Dixey's face would lose its tired appearance. Sometimes the good times lasted for days or even weeks. During those times it felt like we had the strongest, warmest family in the world.

At other times Dik would roar away in the cheap car he'd got from one of the local dealer men, sometimes disappearing for days on end. One day shortly after my eighth birthday he took me with him – a surprise because I felt like the last person in the world he'd want as a companion. Maybe Dixey had been pestering him about showing me more attention. We seemed to be travelling for ever. Dik said we were heading to Bath to see some friends that he had business with. But once that was done, we met up with Frida. I hadn't seen her since we'd left Ireland but I knew Dik had from the arguments I'd overheard between him and Dixey.

Frida was dressed in a short black skirt, tights and a buttoned-up blouse. She had the same fake blonde hair I remembered and she wore make-up, something Dixey never did. She hugged Dik and nodded at me. Dik and Frida talked for a few minutes before Dik got back in the car, leaving me with Frida in the middle of Bath.

'Meet you back at yours in a bit. Take her shopping, 'twas her birthday last week,' he said, putting a note in her hand and driving off.

'So,' said Frida, looking as uncomfortable as I felt, 'let's go. Come on, follow me.' She marched ahead, with me lolloping behind, leading the way to a toy shop. I had never seen anything like it. It was wall-to-wall dolls. 'Go on,' she said sternly. 'Choose one. It can be for your birthday.'

I was awestruck by the events of the day. I didn't know why Dik had decided to bring me with him, that in itself was extremely out of the ordinary and now I was in a toy shop being told I could have anything I wanted by a lady who never before even acknowledged my existence. My toy collection consisted of a few books, a pack of cards, some sewing stuff and a stuffed llama with mirrors on it that Dik had brought back from India a few years before. We didn't have toys or games, we played cards and made things and we certainly didn't have dolls. Dixey encouraged us to draw and paint although I never enjoyed painting as much as Perly and Dixey.

I looked around at the dolls in their grand attire; some with sets of clothes, other with ponies or ball gowns. I'd longed for a Barbie ever since a girl had visited with one the year before but I couldn't choose a Barbie. I didn't believe that I could have whatever I wanted. It must be some kind of trick, I thought, scared of getting caught out. Also I didn't want to choose anything that looked too special in case Dixey noticed it and asked me where I'd got it. I knew that the honest answer would upset her.

I hung my head. 'I don't wan' anyfink,' I said through my hair. 'I jus' wan' to go home.'

'Don't be silly,' said Frida briskly if a little more kindly. 'Choose something you like. Anything.'

I looked around me for the smallest, ugliest doll in the shop. After a bit I spotted a little wooden character on the counter, no more than two inches high. She was poorly carved and unpainted, and was glued onto a bike with stabilisers.

'I'll have her,' I announced.

'You can have something bigger, you know,' said Frida.

'No, I want this one,' I mumbled, not letting myself look at the gleaming plastic Barbies.

'Well, all right then,' said Frida. 'If you are sure.'

I stuffed it into my pocket satisfied that I'd made the right choice and pleased that there wouldn't be any big deal about it when I got home.

Next she took me to a sweet shop and told me to choose some chocolates. I shook my head shyly so she shrugged and picked a box of chocolate-covered almonds for me, before taking me back to her flat.

We hadn't been there long when Dik returned and the two of them disappeared into the bedroom, leaving me with the chocolate almonds and the small wooden doll. I can still taste those bittersweet almonds in my mouth: the sweet chocolate that was such a rare treat but the sensation that trickled down my throat with each nut was bitterness over my mother's unhappiness about Dik's relationship with Frida. It seemed to be a long time before they re-emerged. Frida was dressed in a silk gown and had her bleached blonde hair flowing down her back.

'Com'on, Rox, time to get off home,' said Dik, pulling on his boots and reaching for his jacket. He turned back and gave Frida a kiss. I watched them out of the corner of my eye, glowering at the floor. I'd never seen Dik kiss anyone but Dixey before. Then Dik shovelled me into the car and we set off. Exhausted from the confusion of the day, I fell asleep almost at once and only woke up when we pulled into the camp.

We had been in Dereham a couple of months when a familiar van drew up. I immediately recognised it as Uncle Tony's and ran to greet him. As I drew nearer, I saw a little girl climbing out of the van behind him.

'Roxy, this is Emma, the daughter of a friend of mine. Thought she'd like to meet you lot for a few days,' Tony said. She was slightly older than me with blonde hair and blue eyes. I knew Tony would want tea, so I set off to fill the cast-iron kettle, hooking it over the fire to heat and Dixey busied herself making the bed Perly and I shared big enough for Emma to share with us. There was plenty of room in there, as it was actually a large horse lorry. Rollin often slept in the Luton – the sleeping cab over the driver's seat – while Perly and I shared a double mattress that took up just a tiny corner of the otherwise empty space. Usually we slept in little sleeping bags that Dixey had made out of blankets but now Dixey got a big duvet and told us that we could all share it while Emma was staying.

'Don't worry about fixing her a bed, Dixey,' said Tony as I brought him his tea in the biggest mug I could find without a chipped rim. 'Emma can sleep in my van with me.'

'It's all right,' said Dixey. 'It's better for the girls to be together.'

I was excited to have a new friend and pleased that we would all be sleeping together. When bedtime came, Emma was shocked that Perly and I slept in our clothes, or if it was warm, completely naked. She had pretty matching pyjamas that Perly and I eyed enviously.

We hadn't been asleep long when I was woken by someone opening the door of the truck. Half asleep, I thought perhaps it was Rollin going to bed in the cab of the truck like he often did, but the footsteps walked the length of the lorry, clanking against the metal floor. Gradually I became aware that the person had stopped walking and was close to the bed. I couldn't see who it was – it was too dark as we'd blown out the candles and the truck had no windows – so it wasn't until the overwhelming smell of smoky breath came close to me that I knew who it was: Uncle Tony. He moved the covers and climbed in, pressing himself close to me, his scratchy jumper against my bare body. He didn't speak just made a soft 'ssshhh' sound before kissing my face and neck. The sensation of his stubbly face on my soft young skin was horrible while the smell of tobacco made me hold my breath. I lay completely still, somehow unable to move or make a sound, and before long he turned his attention away from me and over to Perly and Emma. I wondered what I should do. After a few minutes he left, pacing back down the length of the van and closing the door behind him.

Yet, although this is my first memory of such a thing happening, in another part of my mind I wasn't surprised that he came in that night. Somehow it all seemed very familiar and I knew it wasn't the first time. He didn't stay very long, just long enough to kiss me, caress my body and nestle his head into my skin.

I wasn't particularly upset, but slightly confused by what had happened. The next day when I brought the morning cup of tea to his van, he was up and dressed, sitting on the edge of the bed with a cigarette. He told me I was the most beautiful girl in the world and that he was going to teach me lots of things – as long as I didn't tell anyone about it.

'They'll be upset with you if they know, Rox. Let's keep it between us.' I basked in his compliments, but worried about keeping secrets. So I nodded and didn't say a word to anyone. I carried on as if everything was normal, making his tea, cooking and cleaning but I played less with the other children and spent more of my spare time in his van or going for walks. Unlike the adults, who were always too busy to talk, Tony was always available. He didn't always touch me in the early days, often he would just take me for a walk, we'd chat and he'd sing sailor songs or tell me humorous stories. But he always wanted a kiss.

He taught me how to French kiss and made me feel proud with praise about what a quick learner I was. He often tried to fondle me, but I would try to resist his grasp. He never forced me to do anything, but he held me so tightly to keep me from squirming that he left bruises on my arms. Though he also spent time alone with Perly and Emma, he always told me I was his favourite girl, which made me happy. I'd never been anyone's favourite girl before and considered it to be a very good thing to be. Now I realise that he was saying that to all of us. That was how he kept us quiet.

Emma and I became quite close: we played together and I enjoyed hearing about her home and school, but she didn't play games I was used to. Emma was more mature than us; she had little interest in climbing trees or making daisy chains with me and Perly. Even though she was only nine, she wanted to play with boys and pretend we had lovers. Then, after about a week, Tony took her home. Half term was over, he said, and she had to get back to school, so they'd better be off.

Not all that long after Emma's visit I was woken by the sound of Dik rampaging through the camp. Except this time it wasn't about him and Dixey or Frida. He wanted to talk to me.

'Roxy! Get out here! I want to talk to you!' he hollered.

I made my way out of the truck. Dik looked furious, his eyes blazing.

Immediately my thoughts turned to Uncle Tony. Although he always said we weren't doing anything wrong, I couldn't help wondering if it was true. Had Dik found out? Dixey was close behind him, crying and telling him to calm down.

Dik had found out, but not about us. Dixey told me that Emma had accused Uncle Tony of some terrible things and had been arrested.

'I just had no idea that grown men could have an interest in little girls,' Dixey sobbed, shocked and bewildered. In the sheltered Brooks household she and her siblings had been protected from such behaviour. 'You made friends with her, Rox, you played with her. Do you think it's true?' Dixey asked me gently.

'Don't be daft,' Dik roared before I could say a word. 'Of course none of it is true! She's a fucked-up little girl, love, that's all this is. She wants attention.' He asked me about Emma, what she was like, what games she liked to play and if she'd said anything strange.

I told them that sometimes she wanted to play grown-up games but that usually we just played together outdoors with the other kids. It was true but I knew that the accusations she had made were also true. But Dik was so outraged that I immediately got caught up in the drama and found myself standing up for Uncle Tony along with the rest of my family. I wasn't the only one that knew Emma was speaking the truth, Perly knew too but we never spoke about it and we certainly never dreamt of coming clean.

'How could anyone say stuff like that about the Bird Man? Him of all people. He's one of the kindest men I know. He adores the kids, always has. He wouldn't do a thing to hurt them. And definitely nothing like that. It's disgusting!' Dik shouted. And it was true. Tony was a kind, loving old man. I felt bewildered about how everyone could be telling the truth and yet there seemed to be such a massive drama erupting.

'I trust that man,' raged Dik. 'I trust him with my children, I'd trust him with my life. We'll fight to get his name cleared.' And I knew as soon as Dik uttered those words that he would do all he could to get him out of prison. Tony was 'family', after all.

Rollin loved finding things and fixing them and he was always on the lookout for things he could transform. One day he had found an old bike abandoned at the dump, dragged it back to the camp was trying to get it working.

'Needs a new chain and the back tyre's punctured,' he said, spinning the wheel on the upturned bicycle. 'Get us some water, Rox. Gonna find the hole in this inner tube.'

I walked towards the water churns, bucket in hand, secretly hoping that if I helped him enough, he might give me the bike.

As I turned the corner with the water I heard Rollin yell, 'The pigs are 'ere!'

The police served us with an eviction notice and said we had seven days to move on. Normally we just packed up and got on with it, but this time Dik said, 'Fuck 'em. They can move us if they want, but we don't have any fuel for the truck so they'll have to push it onto the road and we won't be going far.'

We'd never heard Dik defy the law before, but we could see that this time he'd had enough and he wasn't going to make it easy for them. It was scary for us kids – not just seeing our dad so defiant but because we'd always simply moved when the police told us to. We worried about what would happen when they came back and found us still there. We spent the following week collecting rubbish from the hedge-rows and lanes so the place would be tidy when we left it. Each camp had to be left immaculate, so it seemed that we'd never been there.

When they did come back it was with five or six cars full of men in waterproof glowing jackets covered in badges. They talked to Dik for a while before starting to push the carts and wagon along the track and on to the road themselves. We looked on with astonishment as our homes were pushed the mile or so down the lane and dumped on the busy road at the end. When the last wagon was gone and only the truck remained, I overheard Dik ask if they had any idea where we could go, somewhere quiet and out of the way.

The chief policeman replied, 'Get over the border to Suffolk and don't come back. I don't care where you go. You won't be my problem any more.'

So we headed for the border of Suffolk, but stopped in a lay-by just past Norwich for the night as the lights weren't working on the lorry and we had hardly any fuel. Dik was driving the horse lorry, laden with animals, possessions and children, Dixey was close behind driving the car and towing a trailer, Rollin was tucked in at the back with a horse and wagon, Essie sitting by his side. Dixey got out of the car, carrying the baby and climbed into the Luton of the truck where Perly, Wanda and I were all huddled together under a duvet.

'All right, kids?' she asked, tucking the baby into the bed beside me.

'Yep, all good,' I replied, cuddling the little one close for warmth, while peeping out of the tiny window onto the busy road.

'What's 'appening, Dixey?' Perly asked.

'Nothing much. Don't worry,' she replied.

But before too long, a shiny black Mercedes car pulled up behind us. Dik swore and Dixey sighed as a stout man approached our vehicles.

'Jesus Christ, what now?' Reluctantly Dik got out of the truck and headed over to speak to him. We waited in the dark.

'Well, I didn't expect that,' Dik said, approaching the lorry a few minutes later with Rollin beside him.

'What did he say, love?' Dixey asked.

'Said we can head over to his land and camp up, first light tomorrow.'

It turned out the man in the Mercedes, Bob, was a landowner. He was having problems with the neighbouring gamekeepers and landlords and was quite happy to allow gypsies on his land. So we could haul our wagon, truck and rusty old car, not to mention the goats and horses, into his field.

Another night was spent on the side of the road, another

night being rocked by the passing trucks and kept awake by the tooting horns. I lay in my bed with Perly on one side and Wanda on the other. The words of Christy Moore's song 'Go, Move, Shift' ringing in my ears: 'The big twelve-wheeler shook my bed, you can't stay here the policeman said.'

CHAPTER 7

Hempnall

When I woke we were on the move again. But later that morning the back of the truck was opened to reveal our new home, the runway of an old US airbase near the village of Hempnall. I was struck by how peaceful and also how flat it was; the only sounds were birdsong and the wind in the trees. The bright blue sky stretched as far as the eye could see, while the crops of barley swayed gently in the breeze. We were parked on concrete, a welcome protective layer to keep us off the mud, and a rare treat.

Setting off to find a suitable place to light the fire before tethering the horses and goats and setting up camp, we were glad to be left alone to get on with our lives, without visits from the council or the police. Before long, Rollin went to the local auction with Dik and returned with a pile of yet more rusty old broken bikes that he proceeded to take apart and put back together so that we could explore the local area. The runway was the perfect ground to learn to ride on, but a hard landing when it went wrong. No soft forgiving peat here. We soon got the hang of it though and were nipping down to the local shop and off into the woods in no time.

Feeling more secure than we had in months, our camp soon began to grow. We got a caravan, a shiny but tired old Vickers with chrome panelling on the outside and an abundance of pink Formica and cut mirrors inside. We used the caravan as a kitchen and dayroom. It made things much easier – it didn't have a sink or running water but it had a gas cooker and counters to prepare dinner on, whatever the weather.

I loved the shiny surfaces of the Vickers, but Dixey much preferred the atmospheric wooden gypsy wagons we'd brought from Ireland. She and Dik slept in one, a beautifully decorated bow-top with woodcarvings that had been painted with gold leaf. Dixey had long been perfecting the art of gypsy scrolling and lining, painting delicate straight lines in red, and beautiful scrolls in gold as well as other more intricate shapes, and was currently working on a set of wooden wheels that Dik had picked up. He hoped to sell them on when she'd finished decorating them.

Dik kept cages of songbirds, goldfinches and red house-finches hanging inside his and Dixey's wagon. Their pretty little cages were no bigger than 14 inches high and their restricted life made me feel sad, but they sang from morning to night, which gave Dik great joy. Dixey didn't like the birds being caged but let him get on with it. I'd often sneak into their wagon after they got up to sit with the birds, thinking that my company made their existence more bearable. I'd chatter away to them like they were little people and they'd reply with a twitter and a tweet.

Now that our troublesome rabbits were gone, those songbirds were the only animals we had that were without a use or purpose. We had a gang of lurcher dogs that we'd brought over from Ireland. We bred them – each puppy would fetch a hundred quid or so, more for the pick of the litter – and use them for hunting. We'd take them out coursing and 'lamping'. Rollin and Perly, who really loved the dogs, were more into hunting than I ever was; my job was skinning and cooking their catch. But every now and again I enjoyed going out with them.

We'd wait until the dead of night before setting off across the fields with a large, powerful light attached to a small car battery that we strapped around Rollin's shoulders. Perly would keep the dogs on their leads until we were out in the middle of the stubble fields and we could hear the scurry of rabbit feet. Then Rollin would turn on the light so the rabbits would freeze and Perly would release the dogs. The sleek, long-legged dogs were so fast the rabbits scarcely had a chance. The hares put up a bit more of a race, but even they tired before the lurchers and were often caught, unless they reached the cover of the trees and undergrowth and managed to escape. Once the dogs had hold of the catch we'd run over to take it from them, gut it on the spot and tie it to a rope before throwing it over our shoulders. We'd often come home with enough rabbits and hares to feed the whole family for a couple of meals, giving us all a well-desired meat fix.

I still hated the goats but they were essential to our lives. Dixey bred them for their milk, and had strong bonds with the old nannies, but the billy-goat kids were kept for a year or so before being slaughtered and eaten. The goats' meat was the best meat we ate: they grazed on the grass and hedgerows so their meat was lean, tender and full of flavour. There was nothing more satisfying than a good goat curry. The rich flavours and aromatic aromas still linger in my mouth and nostrils to this day.

With the goats' milk we could make yoghurt and cheese as well as drink and cook with their yield. Dixey developed lots of recipes to use up the glut of goats' milk, and she taught me to make yoghurt early on. We'd warm the milk in a large pan, add the starter and then pour it into large glass sweet jars that we'd been given by the local shopkeeper. We'd then wrap the jars inside a duvet and put them in a warm place overnight. The yoghurt was silky and surprisingly mild for a goat product. We'd always keep a bit aside as a starter for the next batch so we didn't need to buy any live cultures.

We also made cream cheese by getting yoghurt to the 'warm stage' in a pan and then leaving it for twenty-four hours before pouring it into a piece of muslin and hanging it over a dish so the liquid would drip out and we were left with the soft cheese, to which we'd add fresh chives or lemon juice. I enjoyed making little cheese tarts, by adding honey and cinnamon and baking them in small shortcrust pastry cases.

Dixey didn't really bake much, apart from bread, cornbread and birthday cakes but I developed a passion for pastry work and dessert-making at a young age. I loved nothing better than to be left alone with the oven and a cupboard full of ingredients to experiment with. My attempts weren't always successful, and my progress was hindered by the fact that I wasn't allowed to use sugar or refined grains but I got pretty good and could confidently make cakes and tarts at eight or nine years old.

The more time we spent at a camp the more visitors we received, as old friends worked out where to find us. During our time at Hempnall, lots of people came and went; we even had the odd party. Musicians such as John and Esta would turn up with their band members – back then they were in a band called the Seven Kevins. One of the band members was a young woman called Maxine, who sang and played the fiddle. She was probably in her mid-twenties then, with the most amazing voice – sweet and powerful enough to make the birds in the trees envious. I'd sit beside her and beg her to put down her fiddle and sing to me.

'"Spancil Hill", just one more time, *pleeeaase*, Maxine,' I'd beg her.

'Fine I'll sing it again, but I know other songs too, you know?' she'd say, her bright green eyes sparkling. But I wasn't interested in other songs; I knew the words of 'Spancil Hill' off by heart and would dance around in delight while she gave me my own personal concert.

From time to time, Bob, the landowner, turned up. He was a loud, jovial man with a big belly and a pretty foreign wife. Sometimes he'd come into the kitchen caravan for a cup of tea and eat his way through my latest batch of baking. I was filled with pride when he commented that my cheese tarts where the best he'd ever tasted.

'You ought to sell them,' he said. 'You'll make good money with this girl,' he told Dik as he munched on the tart, reaching for another. 'And she's a pretty one an' all.'

And for once I saw Dik give me an appraising glance, like I might not always be a pain in the arse.

✶ ✶ ✶

Uncle Tony at this time was in prison, awaiting his court hearing. Dik asked me to appear in court for his defence.

'Jus' tell the judge what a kind and loving uncle he's always been to you and what a mucked-up kid Emma is,' he said. I was confused by the request. I did care about Uncle Tony, I even missed his company and attention but also I knew that Emma wasn't lying. Nevertheless I wasn't confident enough to say so – and I was scared that all the anger Dik was expressing towards Emma would be directed at me if I told them the truth – so I agreed to stand up in court as did Essie and Rollin.

The court case hung over us for months, until finally the lawyers decided that no minors would stand up in his defence. I felt hugely relieved to be let off the hook. Uncle Tony got sentenced to seven years' imprisonment due to Emma's accusations. The outcome made Dik so furious that he quickly started preparing material for an appeal. I mostly felt sad that we wouldn't be seeing him for a while; I still felt so muddled when I thought about him. When Dik and Dixey went to visit him I pleaded with them to take me too.

Eventually a visiting order arrived at the local post office granting Dik, Dixey, Rollin and I permission to visit Tony in prison. Essie stayed at home to mind the little ones. As we approached the prison I noticed the barbed wire around the top of the walls and was surprised that I got searched before I was allowed through the gates. The Polaroid pictures of Wanda and Zeta, which I had worked so hard to get, asking a friend who visited to take them so I could show Tony how much they had grown and he could have them to brighten his cell, were confiscated. I was puzzled when the guards took the photos from me.

In my mind Tony wasn't a bad or dangerous person, he was just good old Uncle Tony. I didn't know how wrong his advances towards me were. Now, as an adult looking back, I'm shocked by my innocence, the innocence he stole from me.

'Don't worry, Rox,' said Dik. 'I'll have him out of here soon enough and he can see for himself how they've grown.'

Tony was glad to see us. He picked me up, put me on his knee and patted Rollin on the head. It was cold in the dim, concrete visiting room. Tony wrapped his jacket around me and slipped his hand under my skirt. I wasn't wearing knickers as usual and squirmed around trying to avoid his probing fingers. No one noticed. Dik and Dixey were busy chatting away about our new camp and how nice it was to be left alone, and telling him about all they were doing to get him out. It seemed like the easiest thing to let him do as he wanted but as soon as I could I wriggled away from his clutches to try and explore the visiting room.

'Roxy, come back here and sit down!' Dik snapped, so I sat on the floor a short distance away from them. We hadn't been there long when a loud bell rang; time up. We all kissed Uncle Tony and set off on our way home. I sat in the back of the car, utterly bewildered by the day. I had started to wonder if I had imagined the things Uncle Tony asked me to do in his campervan, but now I knew that they weren't a figment of my imagination, and that being caught for it wasn't going to make him stop.

One morning I woke up to find Dik making a bed up in the other wagon, which sat next to his and Dixey's pretty wagon. He put a colourful cover over the bed and told me to light the stove.

'Who's it for?' I asked. We were used to having people come

and go, but people didn't very often stay in one of our wagons and I'd certainly never seen Dik making a bed before.

But Dik didn't reply. Instead he got in the car and drove off. He returned a couple of hours later with Frida, who he led out of the car like a princess, presenting her with the wagon like a prize, which I suppose it was, their own private love nest. Later that day I stood in the kitchen chopping carrots and watched the wagon rock from side to side. Dixey sat on the floor scrubbing potatoes with tears running down her cheeks.

'She'll be gone soon, won't she, Dixey?' I asked, wishing Frida would leave that instant.

'No, Rox, she's here to stay for a while,' Dixey replied in a small voice. 'It's a good arrangement, you'll see. Maybe Dik'll be happier, less grumpy.' Dixey seemed to accept it as a fact of life, but I feared Frida becoming too involved with our family. Unlike a lot of the families I'd grown up around, our family had a sense of completeness that I loved and I didn't want her coming in and changing things.

I needn't have worried. Frida looked miserable from the moment she arrived, picking her way through the mud in her white jeans. She did not get involved in camp life. She spent most of the day in the wagon, only emerging to go somewhere with Dik. On the rare occasion when she did come out of the wagon to eat with us, she hung back, so stiff and inflexible she struggled to sit cross-legged on the ground or to mould to the tree stumps like we did. Her body just didn't seem to suit the lifestyle.

Frida must have been with us for over a month when, one day while I was cooking with Dixey, she came rushing to the caravan door.

'Give me a knife!' she screamed. 'I need a knife!'

'What do you want it for?' asked Dixey reasonably. It wasn't as though Frida ever helped with the cooking.

'Just give me the sharpest knife you have,' she demanded.

There was something about the way she asked that made me do what she wanted. I handed over the knife I was chopping with. Frida took it from me and stormed off, heading, we presumed, to her wagon.

'Make sure you bring it back!' yelled Dixey after her. 'That's a new Sabatier that is! Cost a lot of money!' We always had one decent knife about the place, mainly for killing the goats.

'She won't be staying much longer,' Dixey said softly as she turned back to the sink. 'It's not working the way Dik thought it would. He says he's taking her to the station later.'

It wasn't long before we heard the rumble of Dik's car drawing in.

'Where's Frida?' he barked, the car door slamming behind him. 'She's going to miss that train.'

'Dunno,' said Dixey, her face unreadable. Dik marched towards the wagon.

A little later he returned. 'Come on,' he said to Essie and me, 'help me look for her. I can't find her anywhere and she's going to miss her bloody train.'

Frida was nowhere to be seen. All we found was her suitcase, sat outside the wagon, all packed and ready to go.

'She must be already on the way to the station,' said Dik getting back into the car. 'Stupid cow must be walking.'

An hour later, Dik returned with a tear-stained Frida in the passenger seat. 'Where was she?' Dixey asked.

'In the woods on the way out. She had a knife, said she was gonna kill herself if I made her leave, daft woman,' he said. 'Where'd she get the knife from anyways?'

'I gave it to her,' I mumbled. 'Thought she wanted to cut a bit of rope or sumfink.'

'There's a "th" in the word something, and no "f", Roxy,' Dixey said with a light sigh.

Dik tutted, picked up Frida's case and drove away. Dixey said nothing.

'Wouldn't have been a bad thing if she had slit her wrists,' muttered Essie, watching them go.

Esther was due to visit. Dixey planned to meet her first in London. She said she would be away for a few days, she'd be taking just baby Zeta with her and told me to help Essie hold the fort while she was gone. Dixey being away only showed me how hard she worked. Between us, Essie and I juggled taking care of the little ones with the cooking and cleaning and it felt like we were toiling non-stop. I longed to get outdoors, to ride my bike and play in the fields or read a book.

I was hoping Esther would bring more books with her as my reading was coming on leaps and bounds. I'd spend afternoons tracing the words with my fingers to get used to the shapes and sounds of the letters and was delighted when I first realised I could read signposts. I started off with simple books like *The Little Red Hen* but quickly moved on to more advanced novels, and by the time I was nine, I was on my way to becoming a bookworm. The first proper book I ever read was *Little Women* by Louisa M. Alcott, quickly followed by *Jo's Boys*. I loved to read about people living in houses and going to school, it all seemed so mysterious and magical to me.

Essie could read but the rest of the family weren't interested in books; they enjoyed the odd story being read to them but the burning desire to read and to learn from books made me something of an oddity.

'Poxy Roxy's got her head in a book,' Rollin would chant at any opportunity.

There was no chance of hiding in a quiet corner and ploughing my way through a novel that week. While Rollin worked with Dik most of the time, wooding, sorting out the horses or scrapping, Essie and I were up at dawn to lay the fires, and scratching through the veg baskets to find a meal. As usual, washing the dishes was a constant chore. They'd pile up, stacked like the Leaning Tower of Pisa. We had a system with trestle tables set up around the caravan and dirty dishes would get piled on one table, with the other one for clean dishes. But washing up at the camp wasn't a case of filling a sink with hot water and wading in. First we had to fetch the water from the local garage or a friendly shopkeeper, then heat it in a bucket, before filling up the washing-up bowl and washing the dishes.

There were different bowls for everything, one for washing up and one for rinsing. We also had a couple of milking bowls, a face-washing bowl, a body bowl, a salad bowl, a food prep bowl and so on, not to mention the animal feed bowls. Most of the bowls were round, shiny and stainless steel. The sizes varied, but they were all kept immaculately clean and no cross contamination was allowed – if Dik or Dixey spotted us milking into the washing-up bowl or vice versa all hell would break loose. (It still shocks me to see people washing their salad in the sink where they wash the dishes, or putting a putting a food prep bowl on the floor for a dog or a cat to eat out of. My home is full of bowls, each with their own purpose; it's a habit I can't break.)

On the second day Dixey was away, Dik went out and left a man called Matt at the camp to keep an eye on us. He was a tall, skinny man with a big nose and playful nature who loved the horses and often came out to help Dik renovate the harnesses. Late that afternoon I was cooking with Essie when we heard a distant but loud scream.

Then I heard Matt at the door shouting, 'Help! Get out here quick! Perly's hurt!' We ran out of the caravan into the dark. I could hear Rollin shouting in the distance.

'What's happened?' Essie asked.

'Perly was helping me an' Rollin move the horses when one of them bolted,' Matt said breathlessly. 'His chain wrapped round Perly's legs, tossed her eight foot in the air. We've got to get her back to the camp quick.' Rollin was still in the field with Perly who was lying on her back, unable to move.

Matt took Dik's overcoat to carry her in and went back out to the field with Essie. I stayed with Wanda and waited for them to return. Was there blood? Was she going to be okay? Eventually Matt and Rollin walked slowly into the camp with Perly cradled between them in the coat.

She was awake but curled up in a ball with pain. Matt told us that she could have broken her back, but he didn't think she had. Eventually Dik got home and sent us off to bed. When I woke, Perly was propped up on the sofa with a cast on her leg. She'd broken the femur in her thigh in two places. She said that everything in her body hurt, that her bones ached and she didn't think they'd ever stop. The poor girl was covered in cuts and bruises down one side of her body from the impact of hitting the ground.

A day or so later, Dik told me to light the fire in his wagon ready for Dixey's return home with Esther. I was relieved that she was coming home and hoped she'd know some remedies for Perly. I found an armful of twigs and went into their wagon to light the little Queenie. Relieved to find a box of firelighters stashed away, I soon had the fire raging. I chatted to the songbirds and was filled with sadness as they chattered their beaks on the wire cage. They seemed so desperate to get out, I almost went to open the door to release them. How far and quick could they fly? Would Dik know it was me that let them out? I thought better of it and left the door closed, leaving them safely in their cages. I went away from the wagon confident that it would be warm and dry when Dixey got home.

The evening dragged on and there was no sign of Dixey and Esther. Dik was chatting to a friend called Ray, the same Ray who had doused Dixey's tummy and predicted that Zeta would be a boy. Perly was stuck on the sofa with her cast and the rest of us children were sitting cross-legged on the floor of the caravan eating dinner when Dik suddenly yelled, 'Jesus Christ!' and flew out the door. I got up and looked out to see huge flames licking from Dik and Dixey's wagon. My heart missed a beat. I pictured the blazing fire as I left the wagon: where had I left the firelighters? Had I moved any books or paper away from the stove? Had I closed it up properly? The songbirds!

It must be my fault. Filled with fear and guilt, I fled the

caravan and headed for the woods. I ran and ran as far into the woods as I could before falling over in a convulsion of tears and distress. I looked back to the camp and could see the flames and smoke billowing into the sky. I could hear Dik and Ray shouting as they tried to get the raging fire under control. I knew they had no chance; it was too far gone and they only had a few churns of water. I found a soft batch of moss and curled up in a ball covering my ears and closing my eyes. I hoped it was a bad dream and that soon I'd wake up. I thought about the songbirds perishing in the flames and wished I'd released them when I had the chance. I thought about Dixey coming back with her mother to find her home burned to the ground. I thought about how much trouble I was going to be in for letting the wagon catch fire. I dared not go back to the camp and instead fell asleep in the woods, my eyes sore from a mixture of tears and smoke from the fire.

At dawn I woke to the sound of someone calling my name. I could see smoke gently wafting from the wagon. I was cold and damp, lying on my blanket of moss. I stayed still and quiet, trying to work out who was looking for me and how much trouble I was in. A few minutes passed before I could make out the figure of a man silhouetted against the grey sky.

'Roxy! What ya doing out here?' Ray exclaimed when he saw me. 'We've been looking for you for hours! You must be freezing, you daft little urchin.' He reached out for my hand while offering me his jacket.

I wrapped his big jacket around me. 'I'm not coming back to the camp,' I sniffed. 'I can't. Dik'll be mad. I burnt the wagon down!' I burst into sobs all over again.

'What are you on about? Why would Dik be angry with you?' he asked, bemused.

'I lit the fire. I must've not closed it down properly or somefink.'

'Don't be daft, Roxy, the stove was knackered. The fire bricks had fallen out and everything.'

I looked at him, trying to work out if he was tricking me or telling the truth. Ray was an old friend of the family; he met up with us from time to time and often travelled with us before disappearing on his own for a few months. He was a kind man but I didn't trust his personality as he had an unpredictable grouchy side that appeared when I least expected it.

I looked at him again. This time his bright blue eyes seemed to be genuine, and so I timidly let him lead me back to the camp.

We found Dik picking the few surviving items from the mound of glowing dust. I watched him drag the birdcages out and strained my neck to see what remained of the finches. He shook the cages and threw them to one side, ashes fluttering into the sky. Tears streamed down my cheeks. To my relief he looked calm and unflustered: 'Don't worry, love, it's just stuff and stuff don't mean much in this life,' he commented softly. Ray walked me to the truck; I climbed up inside and snuggled in next to Perly, glad of the warmth her body was generating.

I woke up a couple of hours later to the sound of a car pulling into the camp. I'd almost forgotten that Dixey and Esther were due home. Dixey stepped out of the car carrying the baby with a look of disbelief on her face. Everything she owned was now a pile of dust.

CHAPTER 8

Thorpe Abbotts

We quickly got over the fire. Esther checked in to a hotel in the village before taking Dixey out to get essentials for herself and the baby. Dik and Dixey moved into the wagon Frida had been living in. Our life, which wasn't based on material possessions, soon moved on from the loss. But the guilt over burning the birds stayed with me for many months.

Life at Hempnall was, by our standards, peaceful. Perly wasn't allowed to move for a while but eventually the pain eased and she became eager to get outdoors, so Rollin, ever resourceful, got an old armchair from the dump and ratchet-strapped it onto four wheels so we could push her around the camp and play. And Dik and Dixey seemed to be getting on better since Frida had packed her bags, even if Dik still had the odd mood and temper tantrum.

One grey spring morning I helped Dixey make the corn-bread for breakfast and washed the dishes before sloping off with

my book under my arm. Minutes later I heard my father shouting and the sound of breaking crockery. I gingerly approached
the kitchen caravan, just as the pile of plates I had washed minutes
before came flying out the door, breaking into a thousand pieces
on the concrete runway. Over the next hour every item in that
caravan came out the door and landed on the ground.

I could hear Dixey inside saying, 'Get a grip of yourself for
Christ's sake, Dik! Stop it! Why are you doing this?'

'If the place wasn't such a tip, I wouldn't have to, would I?'

After the pots and pans came a hailstorm of potatoes and
onions. Then, once everything was outside, Dik came steaming
out, rounded us up and told us to bring it all back in. 'And put
it where it belongs this time.' So we set about gathering up the
items that hadn't broken and putting them in neat piles inside
the caravan. Of course many things were smashed and went
straight in the bin. However the caravan was certainly tidy, if not
a little bare and until we had the money to get new crockery, we
ate off pan lids and chopping boards.

Then, one morning, about a month or so after the fire, we
woke to find we were sharing the runway. Another family had
camped next door. We were used to convoys of travellers turning
up hoping to share our patch and, because we wanted to keep
relations with Bob cordial, Dik always went over and told them
they couldn't stay. He'd explain that we had an arrangement with
the landowner. But this time the father of the family replied that
they did too. Dik wasn't happy but there was nothing he could do.

The family were rough travellers. They had four angry
Alsatians chained to the corners of their caravan – you couldn't
get near the door without risking life and limb – who barked

from morning till night. The only thing that drowned out the sound of the dogs was the bellowing of the father, Colin. He was a bad-tempered and violent man who made our dad look like a pussycat. The sight of him holding his wife's hair and banging her head against the caravan as she whimpered has stayed with me throughout my life.

They had two children, a daughter called Sophie and a son, Davey. Rollin, Essie and I spent afternoons with them, hiding away from Colin and gambling pennies on card games. Dik reckoned we'd learn more about maths from cards than any school could teach us and showed us how to play cribbage with a wooden board. Rollin banged holes in it with a hammer and nail and we used matchsticks as markers. Rollin and Dik were the champions but I liked to have a game, usually with Essie or Rollin. The sing-song style of the counting fell softly on my ears like poetry, '27, 4s in heaven' we'd chant, or '29, 2s a chime' as we eagerly approached the desired score of 31 for an extra 2 points.

Sophie, a quiet and troubled girl who took solace in music, was about Essie's age, and the two of them hung out together listening to her cassette player and doing teenagery things. Sometimes they'd deign to let me join them; it was Sophie who introduced Essie and me to Elvis Presley, and sparked my lifelong romance with his music. I got a personal cassette player shortly afterwards and listened to Elvis's *Greatest Hits* over and over again until I knew every word of every song.

But no matter how hard we tried to get along, there was no ignoring the fact that Colin was becoming more aggressive and confrontational with each day that passed. His wife was getting more and more beatings and his children were becoming more introverted. Apart from a fight in Ireland that, in my very young memory, seemed to last all day and pulled in every male member of my extended family, I can't remember my dad ever fighting, no matter how nasty the traveller that pitched up. Dik had a way of looking at you with his wild black eyes that meant people simply did as he said. But Colin was a very determined man; if he wanted a fight he'd have one.

Then one night the set of wagon wheels that Dixey had been painting during most of our time at Hempnall disappeared. She had just finished them and they were beautiful. Dik was planning to take them round the gypsy families in the area the next week and hoped to get a good price for them. But in the morning they were gone, and we knew who had taken them.

We all knew that Colin had stashed them somewhere but his vicious dogs and horrible temper put us in a difficult position. Most families would have just called the police, I guess, but the police weren't people we turned to for help and if we did I doubt they would have assisted. So there was no way we could prove that Colin had the wheels and no way for us to get them back. Dik was furious; he stormed around the camp shouting and swearing that he would get revenge. He was so incandescent that we all ran for cover.

But after a few days, Dik had had enough of being pushed around. Late one evening he went round to Colin's caravan and demanded them back. Colin responded by getting out a gun and putting it to Dik's head. Thank God Dik didn't carry a gun himself. He quickly retreated and we packed up the camp and left that same night.

★   ★   ★

As morning broke I woke up brimming with excitement. New camps always filled me with enthusiasm and joy. Unknown territories beckoned, sparking my explorer side into life. I opened the door of the truck to find we were on another disused runway, but this one was much bigger and had lots more concrete. The runway was longer than at Hempnall, with an aeroplane hangar and some collapsing red-tiled barns. But there was something that felt different about this place; already I had the feeling that something new had started, not like all the previous camps. This place felt more real, more permanent. The empty barns resembled the house I had dreamt of for so many years. In my mind I had already moved in and didn't want to leave. I quietly snuck over to where Perly and Rollin were sleeping.

'Hey, wake up. We've moved, let's go and explore.'

Rollin stretched his arms and yawned. 'What's the time?'

'Dunno, but it's light,' I replied. Perly hobbled out of bed, and into her wellies; she was dressed already. Shouting with glee, we turned each corner to find a different landscape.

Since Ireland we had missed the freedom of the bogs. Now we ran around the ruins of barns and the aeroplane hangar, skipping through the fields and paddling in the pond. The horizon was dominated with acre after acre of agricultural land: there was sugarbeet and ploughed fields as far as the eye could see – ideal for lamping – and the area had an amazing open feeling about it. At the top of the runway was a cluster of ancient oak trees but these were the only trees within half a mile of the camp. The stark planes made for bigger skies than anywhere else I'd ever been.

We jumped a ditch and started to walk across the fields to

some woods we could see in the distance, but the clay soil was heavy; soon we could hardly lift our feet with the weight of it.

'We better head back to the camp, girls. There'll be loads to do,' Rollin commented, tugging me by the shoulder of my coat, and gesturing towards the camp.

'Yeah, but let's just check out what's down there,' I said, pointing to the end of the runway we hadn't yet seen. Across from the runway was a field containing an old quarry with some machinery, and beyond that lay the quaint village of Thorpe Abbotts: a small cluster of houses with perfectly manicured gardens and shaped topiary as well as a phone box and post box.

But within hours of waking up at Thorpe Abbotts, the shiny black Mercedes of Bob Reynolds rolled into the camp. He emerged from his car frothing at mouth and waving his fists in the air.

'You blasted gyppos, you're all the same, give an inch an' you take a mile. You ain't staying here, that's for sure. Pack up and get out!'

Dik approached him and explained about the trouble with Colin and said we really needed somewhere to stay until we could get something else sorted. Bob started to calm down. But we couldn't stay long; he said he and his wife had plans for the barns.

A few days after we arrived Rollin and I came up with a plan to build a bender tent to store things out of the rain. We ran across the ploughed fields heading for the woods to find some sticks. The wooded area was quite small compared to the forests we were used to but it had some big oak trees and a lovely familiar smell of moss and bark. We were looking for ash or hazel or something that was flexible and strong to make the frame for the tent which we'd then cover with a tarpaulin. Rollin had a bow saw over his shoulder; I had a piece of rope to tie the branches together, so we could pull them back to the camp.

It was dark inside the wood; the tall trees towered high above us. We searched for young saplings to make our tent, but couldn't find anything suitable; there was a scattering of elm but they were too big for the job. Oh well, we thought, if we couldn't find branches for a bender we may as well get some firewood, so I started to gather dried wood from the forest floor.

I was down on my knees tying the wood into a bundle when I heard an angry voice behind me. 'Oi, what the bloody hell are you doing in here?'

I looked up to see a portly red-faced man in a waxed coat, with a beard. He had an air rifle in his right hand.

'Just getting some wood,' Rollin replied nervously from close by.

'Not in here you ain't, you little scamp. You'll disturb my pheasants. Now clear off! Meddling kids!' he shouted waving his gun in the air.

'Come on, Rox, run!' said Rollin bolting for the edge of the wood. I grabbed my bundle of wood and scrambled after him.

'And keep them dogs of yours on a chain or I'll shoot the lot of 'em!'

We knew he meant it.

It was a shaky start but it turned out my first hunch had been right: we could lie low at Thorpe Abbotts. We were outside the village, and out of sight of the road, so apart from the odd nosey dog walker, we were ignored by the locals. The police left us alone. Even Bob got over his fury, and decided it was useful having us there; we could make sure no one came onto the runway to dump stuff or interfere with his machinery. So our position was fairly stable. For us, permission from the landowner was a godsend, even if we were still illegally camped in the eyes of the law. I found it strange living so close to a village but having no involvement whatsoever with anyone; it made me even more aware of how unaccepted our way of life was. People would stare at our camp as they walked past, but look the other way if we acknowledged them.

For Dixey, being closer to civilisation had its benefits. She'd been talking about finding a dance teacher for a while – she wanted something to do other than being a mother and wife, and she thought that we girls might enjoy it too. So not long after we arrived, she went to the phone box in the village to find out about adult education centres and returned with the news that she was going to start taking flamenco classes, and Essie and I could go with her if we wanted. They were every Tuesday at 1 p.m. in the centre of Norwich.

Norwich was about 22 miles away, the closest we had ever lived to a city. We had visited on occasion but not often, as there were so many of us we couldn't all fit in the car and we rarely took the horses into a city centre. But when Tuesday came, Dixey, Essie and I dug out our fullest skirts and smartest shoes and climbed into the tatty old Peugeot estate. Dixey still hadn't taken her UK driving licence and was driving on her American one which was invalid after living abroad for fifteen years (she often talked about taking her test but the expense was always too much for it to become a reality), and the Ole Rust Bucket, as Rollin called it, was more rust than paintwork, but we made it. The classes were held in the Duke Street Centre, a large ugly concrete block that overlooked the gentle Wensum river.

The class had already begun, a whirl of women in their thirties and forties wearing high-heeled shoes and elegant skirts. The teacher, a tiny, muscular woman with dyed black hair called Liz Lee, told us just to come on in and do our best to follow the steps.

'It'll take a while to sink in,' she said gently.

Boy, was she right! Most of the class had been attending for some time, so they stamped their feet and swirled their skirts confidently, spinning around me until I was giddy. Apart from Essie, I was a good twenty years younger than anyone else in the room, so I felt quite out of my depth.

But instinctively I loved the music Steve Homes played on his guitar, and I loved the dancing. We'd always been surrounded by music. I had grown up with musicians and singers round the campfire, so the complicated rhythms of flamenco came easily to me, as it did to Dixey.

'You'll make a lovely little dancer one day, Roxy, it's obviously in your genes,' Liz Lee told me, and after a few weeks she took Dixey aside and told her that she needn't pay for lessons: she wanted to teach us and didn't want money to be a reason to stop coming. Soon we were attending on Thursdays too. Dik got us a piece of plyboard to practice on, which we placed under the trees. A few months after arriving in Thorpe Abbotts, we moved the board inside one of the empty, ramshackle barns, so we could practice in all weathers.

Flamenco wasn't the only class Dixey introduced us to that year. Rollin went to guitar lessons and Essie was thinking about going to school. Even Wanda and Zeta, at just six and four years old, had started taking violin lessons. Knowing how I loved to read, Dik and Dixey said I could go to school too if I wanted, but I knew school every day would mean not being able to go to the dance classes and having to try and fit in with all the ordinary children.

When Liz Lee said I 'had the flamenco fire burning inside me', I hoped she was right. I could feel something burning inside me when I heard the music but I was quite self-conscious and I knew how much I had to learn before I'd be any good. Essie started school that year. She was thirteen, she could read and had Dik's very bright, analytical mind and confidence but she had a lot of catching up to do.

Shortly after we settled at Thorpe Abbotts, Uncle Tony turned up. After eleven months in prison, his case had been quashed on appeal. Dik had gone to court to support him, but in the end the case was dismissed due to lack of corroboration; in other words, it was Emma's word against his. So Tony was free, and he took up where he had left off: arriving like an elderly uncle in his campervan, expecting a constant supply of cups of tea, and inviting you in to 'chat'. He looked the same – or perhaps he always seemed old to me – his face permanently grey and jowly, his eyes small behind his thick glasses – but he was less jovial than before, a little more gruff. He spent more time at the camp now – maybe he was less welcome in Kent – but did less. All I knew was that he had a new campervan and now he locked the door whenever I brought him his morning cup of tea.

The grooming started up again. He said he loved me, bribed me with crisps and sweets and attention. His was a slowly, slowly, approach, a gradual build-up of feeling and kissing, taking my clothes off, and getting me to touch him – teaching me things no child needs to know. He always tried to get me to touch his penis; as he kissed me he'd drive my hand onto it and tell me to stroke it, but I mostly refused. He'd get annoyed when I didn't obey and hold my hand in his as he stroked it. Or he'd try to get me to lie down, pushing his tongue so far into my mouth that I'd end up squashed beneath him. At times like this, I focused on the tartan blanket that was neatly folded on the shelf above the bed. There were twenty-one squares visible from where we sat. I'd count them every time. It had three colours: brown, yellow and green. I used to wish he'd move that blanket so the squares would reposition, or replace it with something brighter, to give me something new to focus on.

He did it to Perly too, sometimes when I was there. In a way that was worse. It was horrible seeing him force his tongue into my eight-year-old sister's mouth, to watch her squirm and wiggle in distress. But in some strange way it was easier knowing I wasn't the only one going through it. Although we never spoke of it, it gave us a strong bond. Yet I could also see Perly was changing from the open, bubbly personality she'd been: she was growing more shy and withdrawn by the day. I didn't know what to do.

I knew it wasn't right, what went on in that van, but I didn't know how wrong it was, or how to make it stop. I thought about discussing it with Rollin or Essie but the warnings Uncle Tony gave me rang in my ears.

'If your family find out what you've been up to, Roxy, they'll throw you out on the street, so keep quiet.'

I couldn't bear to think of Dik turning on me with the same anger he expressed towards Emma when she told people what had been going on. And while I still thought Tony was kind, I had also seen him riled. Once, when I was about five or six, I'd asked him about his life before he was part of our family.

'Did you have a wife, Uncle Tony?'

'Yes, I did. Once upon a time.'

'And kids, didn't you have any kids?' It seemed a fair question to me – our lives were full of kids.

'I had a daughter once,' he said gruffly.

'What d'you mean once? What happened to her?' I was confused about where she could have gone.

'She was a lying little brat,' came the reply.

How could someone lose a daughter because they lied? 'What did she lie about?' I probed, hoping to understand. I was only little.

Tony stood up abruptly, quite agitated, and headed for the door. Then he slammed the door leaving me sitting alone.

Now when Tony told me that what went on in that camper-van was our secret, that my family would throw me out for being dirty if I told them what we had been doing, I believed him. And besides I knew no one would believe me.

Each time we moved camp, Dik had to find ways of making money. He and Rollin made a bit collecting scrap on the cart. Rollin especially was good at cleaning down old cars to the carcass and selling them for a good price. But mostly Dik would drive around until he spotted another camp, then he'd go and have a bit of a chat, find out who they were, see if there was a chance for a bit of wheelin' and dealin'. Everything was done face-to-face, never by phone. It was harder in England to find pasture for the horses and for the first time Dik had started paying for the use of the land, which meant we couldn't keep quite as many horses as we previously had.

But we still had our big old Irish stallion Silver, and once word got round, tinkers from all over would turn up at our camp with their mares. Dik would joke that it was 'time for the ole guy to do some shaggin''. Silver, a chunky fella with a long mane and dark silver colouring, would give them a good sniff and if they were in season his top lip would curl and he'd mount them. He made quite a name for himself.

Our lurcher Ross was going strong on the breeding front too, though life for a lurcher wasn't as free as it had been in Ireland. After our encounter with the gamekeeper, we never let any of our dogs loose to explore the woods across the field again but tried to keep them chained up. It was a miserable existence for a dog, especially a lurcher that's bred to roam. Sooner or later they'd wriggle themselves free, or someone would let them off for a runaround and they'd never be seen again. If they weren't shot they were poisoned. Every time it would break Perly's heart – she'd go out looking for them at dawn and search for hours. Finding a corpse was a blessing because at least we could stop searching and stop hoping. So we were limited to lamping at the dead of night. On those wide open fields the rabbits were doomed with nowhere to hide.

の

In the meantime, Dixey, Rollin and I started working for a local farmer picking daffodils. I was about twelve or thirteen. We got up at daybreak every morning, filled our flasks with hot drinks to fight off the morning frost and set to work. We were allocated rows that we had to work, walking up and down methodically picking the flowers, being careful not to damage the stems and only picking the plants that had tight buds.

The money wasn't good but it was piecework so the quicker we picked the more we earned. It soon added up and between us we made a decent amount, but it was hard, cold, back-breaking work. There were other people picking too, but not many people stayed for the whole season. I got on well with the man who ran the farm, Mark, a jolly pink-faced man with grey hair and a thick Norfolk accent. He was impressed with the speed that Rollin and I worked.

'There's not many adults could earn what you kids do in a day,' he'd tell us.

At the end of the day, Mark came around and noted how many we'd picked before giving us a small brown envelope of cash. We always counted our money before giving it to Dixey to use for shopping; sometimes we'd keep a fiver for ourselves but we weren't supposed to.

One day we counted our earnings and discovered that we had each been paid £10 too much. We took the overpayments out of the envelopes and put them in our pockets without mentioning a word to Dixey or Mark. When we got home we discussed what we should do about it. There was nothing we wanted more than to keep the money and buy ourselves something next time the opportunity arose, but we were suspicious that he had overpaid us both and we smelt a rat. The next day we gave the money back to him.

'Ha, 'onest lettle ones, aren't ya?' he said. 'Thought you gyppos were meant 'a be devious little baastards. Well, whaa' d' ya know?'

We were sorry to say goodbye to the cash but knew that if we kept it we'd have been sacked the next day and our family's reputation would have been ruined in the process.

Daffodil season turned into roses, roses turned into asparagus, asparagus turned into apples and then winter came and the potatoes were ready. Essie came to do the farm work with us from time to time but she was usually busy with school. Perly came too but she was still quite young and struggled with the cold and intensity of it. Usually it was just Rollin and me and sometimes Dixey but she came less and less.

Settling had its perks and its downfalls. Essie was working hard at school but often came home upset or angry. She was struggling to make even one friend and couldn't fit in; she didn't have the latest designer clothes or Nike sports kit, her uniform came from the charity shop, and as we didn't even own an iron she always looked crumpled. Even though she was a strong and feisty character, she felt the whole school was against her. She hated the ways we were different, even that we all called Dik and Dixey by their names, and started to insist that we called them Mum and Dad. I could never get my head round that, though a few years later I took to calling them Mama and Papa.

Once the school realised there were school-age children living here they sent the education authorities sniffing round the camp. The council seemed most worried about Wanda and Zeta as they were still young and could start in primary school, so in the end Dixey decided she would home-school them. The council were quite strict and said they would be assessing the level of education they were receiving at the end of each year.

'Teacher Tim' came to the camp once a week for quite a few months, sent by the council to get us older children interested in school. He had his work cut out with us: at thirteen and doing a lot of the man's work with Dik, Rollin was already quite grown up and wasn't interested in sitting in a classroom, especially as Essie was having such a hard time. I was too absorbed in my dancing to pay much attention and Perly just refused to even discuss the subject and just wanted to play the guitar instead. But Tim was a do-gooder who was willing to try anything. Long after he'd had no luck he still came to the camp, even turning up one Christmas dressed as Father Christmas with a sack of gifts over his shoulder, much to Dik's horror and our amusement.

Knowing that dancing was my real passion, one day Tim turned up at the camp and announced he wanted to take me on a tour of Suffolk schools. He thought it would be 'interesting' for the children to see me dance and hear about my lifestyle – and maybe if I saw how friendly some of the children were, I would change my mind about school. Before I knew it I was being packed into his old black Volvo with a bag of costumes. He took me to one school after another; I'd get changed, put on a cassette and dance. Then, when I finished dancing, all the children would sit in a circle around me and ask questions about my life. I tried my best to answer them, as Tim was someone official, and I knew Dixey was getting a lot of hassle due to our lack of conforming but I found it all quite embarrassing and strange.

The children asked questions like 'Where do you sleep?' and

'Do you have toys?' After question time we'd have some lunch or a drink and move on to the next school. The tour went on for many days; we must have visited over a dozen schools, all within the Suffolk district. I felt a bit like a circus monkey traipsing around from one school to the next dancing and talking but I was surprised how friendly most of the children were – there was very little teasing or laughing, as least amongst the younger children. Some of the children my age or a bit older giggled under their breath and whispered. The young children were inquisitive and friendly but the older ones had already learned about being cool, and I wasn't it.

When we were done with our tour, Tim asked me which school I liked best. I told him they were all okay, but that I wouldn't be going to any of them. He sighed and rubbed his head, perplexed. I realised that the children's good behaviour would soon go out the window if I wasn't under the watchful eye of Teacher Tim. The following week Tim turned up at the camp with a sack full of letters from all the little children at the schools we had visited. They'd drawn pictures of me dancing, or of horses and wagons. They thanked me for coming and asked me to come back soon. But that was the first and last time I would go into a school classroom.

As the weeks turned into months and the months turned into years, our camp grew and spread. The centre of the camp was the kitchen caravan, outside that was the campfire. Nestled around the hangar, on the concrete and out of the wind, were the sleeping caravans and wagons – we started off with two but ended up with four or five. We tethered Silver and the goats on the grassy areas either side of the concrete. Dik and Rollin loved going to the weekly auction in Diss and picking up a bargain. Rollin went from fixing up old bikes to fixing cars and all manner of machinery would lie about the place in various stages of dismantlement.

We also acquired things that normal families had, like a television. It was a small black-and-white one that we had to plug in to a car battery, but it was a television nonetheless. It was only allowed on after dark, when the generator was running and the jobs were done but occasionally we would all huddle round and watch a programme. It soon became the norm for us to be allowed to watch *Worzel Gummidge* on a Sunday and one or two other programmes a week. Rollin and I would sometimes sneak off and try to watch something without anyone noticing but we'd always get discovered by Dik or Dixey who would go ballistic. Dik liked having the TV, but he didn't like us watching it; he said we'd get square eyes and go brain-dead if we watched too much. Kids belonged outside as far as he was concerned.

But most exciting of all, for the first time in my life we had an address and a letterbox. It was beyond the barns, on the side of the road that led into the village. Dik went to the post office and registered the camp as Red Barn, Rollin fashioned a letterbox out of a traffic cone with a sheet of metal strapped on the front as a flap door, Dixey painted the name on the front and we hung it on a hedgerow by the side of the road. And soon enough things started to arrive, mostly junk mail, but occasionally the odd letter or parcel from Esther and Peter, or a letter from the school. We no longer had to use a care of address or get important documents sent to the post office. I was thrilled, and jumped out of bed every morning to check it before anyone else woke up.

After a while packages started arriving with my dad's name scrawled on them. They always looked the same – squashy brown paper packages tied up with string – and the contents were always the same too: home-knitted wine-red socks. Dik would open them, fling them to one side, never bothering to look at them but never bothering to hide them either. To me they were a tell-tale sign that Frida, even though we hadn't seen her since she left Hempnall that day, was still on the scene. I hated the sight of those wretched socks. Dixey and I would find them when we were tidying up; they seemed to multiply with every day that passed, scattered around the floor like a constant reminder that Dik had a mistress. I guess that's partly why she sent them.

Uncle Tony worked away part of the year, taking driving jobs here and there but he was at our camp more than he wasn't during those years. Sometimes he'd stay for a week, sometimes he'd be there for a few months, taking chauffeuring jobs in the area. Mostly though, he sat in the kitchen caravan or by the fire smoking cigarettes, expecting to be waited on by Dixey or one of us girls. The more comfortable at the camp he became, the less he did around the place: he no longer helped Dik with the horses or went wooding, and he no longer took us for walks.

I recall Dixey getting wound up by him around this point.

'He's a burden, I don't need another mouth to feed. He's lazy and demanding. Surely he's got some family he can go to?' she'd say.

Dik would reply, 'What's one more mouth when there's already so many of us? He's getting on now and we're the closest thing to a family he has.'

Gradually I noticed him getting less careful. He didn't always lock the door when I was in his camper and he'd started touching and kissing me in the kitchen caravan while Dixey was outside getting a bucket of water or emptying the slops bucket into the hedgerow.

One day I delivered his cup of tea in the morning and tried to leave the van quickly. He grabbed my arm and held my wrist tightly.

'Where are you rushing off to?' he asked. 'Come in here and give me cuddle.' He held open the covers, flashing his saggy grey boxers.

'I don't want to,' I told him, 'I don't like it.'

'What don't you like?' he quizzed me. 'You don't like being my favourite? I'm sure one of your little sisters will happily come in here and give me cuddles if you don't want to.'

Instantly I locked the door and climbed into his bed. His hands were clammy and hot on my body; his breath was stale and smoky. I tried to hold my breath as he put his hands in my trousers and his tongue down my throat but he got angry. He scolded me for not responding how he'd taught me and said, 'You won't be getting any treats or crisps off me today,' but the crisps and treats had lost their appeal in recent months. I just wanted it to stop. But I knew that if I didn't oblige he'd get Perly in, or worse, start on little Wanda and Zeta – if he hadn't already.

CHAPTER 9

Dancer

After I had been attending her classes a year or so, Liz Lee gave me this advice: 'A good flamenco dancer feels the rhythm in their bones, but shows the emotion in their eyes. You have very expressive eyes, Roxy, don't be scared to use them.' In a short time flamenco had become everything to me: my self-expression, my identity, my outlet. As Liz took me under her wing, it was wonderful to find there was something I was good at. When I was dancing, I didn't hear the guitar playing in my ears, I felt it strumming in my stomach and penetrating to the depths of my soul, each chord releasing some of the pent-up anguish or unexpressed joy from within me.

Liz, as an ex-ballet dancer herself, urged me to join the ballet classes she ran in Bungay, Suffolk, for girls my own age – she believed ballet was good discipline for any dancer and would benefit my flamenco – but I was reluctant. I had grown to trust and be comfortable with the class of thirty- and forty-year-olds I danced with; I couldn't be sure that girls my own age would be so accepting. I knew I'd look dirty and untidy next to them, and worried that they would tease me.

Finally, however, I agreed to enrol on the Saturday and evening lessons with the children of my own age. It was hard leaving our messy, muddy, doggy camp to join those neat pink girls with their spotless pale tights and scraped-back hair. I made a great effort to be as clean as possible but my curly hair wasn't tightly pulled back in a bun with a hair net, my tights were black and woolly and I didn't have the leg warmers, jazz trousers or umpteen other things that they all seemed to have. But I enjoyed it and was proud to be able to pick things up as quickly as everyone else, even if I found ballet more challenging than flamenco. It was far more structured and rigid; the music didn't stir my emotions like the flamenco guitars and I didn't feel the emotional release I felt when dancing flamenco.

In those years the camp was a constant hive of activity, with Dik and Dixey driving us to different classes and schools, the little ones practising their violins, Rollin working on people's cars or collecting scrap from around the place, Dixey and me dancing. People were coming and going all the time, tinkers and gypsies for Dik, visitors from Spain and Ireland popping in to see us, but local people never came. In all the time we'd lived in Thorpe Abbotts, just a couple of hundred yards out of the village centre, not once had I exchanged a single word with anybody local. Until one day a car pulled up and a stout man with a long beard got out. He wore a blue shirt and overalls and his round belly and beard gave him a friendly look. He came towards the caravan, holding the hand of a girl not much older than me. When she saw me looking from the window of the caravan, she buried her face in her hands.

Dik spoke to the man for a while before inviting them in for a cup of tea. The man's name was Jerra Hart.

'We live just down the road,' he said. 'Dulcie and I want to buy a horse.'

Dulcie was unusual looking, but I couldn't figure out why. She had pale white skin and big pink lips and wore a little round hat with embroidery on it, similar to some hats that Dik had brought back from India a few years before. But it wasn't the hat that was strange. She had no hair underneath it, not a single strand. Then I realised that not only did she have no hair on her head, she had none anywhere, not an eyelash or eyebrow in sight. Her pale face was completely bare and her eyes squinted almost closed as if she couldn't bear the light.

'D' ya think it's a girl or a boy?' Perly whispered in my ear.

'Girl I reckon; not sure though,' I replied. She was so quiet and shy she didn't say a word.

They didn't stay long. They agreed to buy a black-and-white filly foal and said goodbye.

'They seemed nice,' Dixey said, as their car headed off.

'Yeah, poor family,' said Dik. 'They've had a rough time. Hopefully the horse will help with the girl's recovery.'

A couple of days later Jerra came back, this time on his own. He came to ask Dixey if I could go and play with his girls. He said Dulcie's sister Cleo needed a friend in the area and that all the focus trying to get Dulcie better had left Cleo rather lonely. He hoped Perly might come along too. To my surprise Dik agreed to let us go.

It was the first time Perly and I had played with children our own age in a house. The Harts' house was warm – to us it seemed overpoweringly warm – and homely and both Dulcie and Cleo were shy but welcoming. Soon we looked forward to getting our work done so we could go and spend the afternoons with them. Knowing just one family in the area made me feel like we were a little part of society, and maybe not complete outcasts.

Dulcie was three years older than me, but she seemed the same age. She spent a lot of her time with their lambs or kittens and didn't seem to like people that much, but we got on well and became very close. I suppose we were both unusual children, but our peculiarities clicked. We discovered that we both loved to cook. The Harts had a lovely big kitchen, weighing scales, mixing bowls and no end of ingredients so the two of us spent many an afternoon experimenting. Dulcie often told me to bring the cakes back to the camp with me but I knew Dik wouldn't approve of the sugar and white flour we used, so I always said no.

I still wondered what was wrong with Dulcie but no one mentioned it. Cleo, her sister, had long thick hair and thick eyebrows, so the lack of hair obviously didn't run in the family. One day we were painting our toenails when I looked down at Dulcie's feet and saw her painting the polish straight onto her toes. She had no nails at all.

'What's happened to your toes?' I asked.

'The nails fell off when I lost my hair, they haven't come back yet. It's from the chemo,' she answered without looking up. She was six months into the treatment.

The Harts invited me for a sleepover many times but Dik didn't like the idea of me staying in a house with people he didn't know very well and always said no. But one weekend Dulcie and Cleo asked if I wanted to spend the night when Dik was away. I skipped home and asked Dixey what she thought. Much to my amazement she just agreed.

I walked back to their house just before dark and had dinner with them.

'Where are your things?' Dulcie asked me.

'What things?' I replied. She meant pyjamas and stuff, but I didn't have any.

It was arranged that I would sleep in the bunk beds in Cleo's room.

'Top or bottom?' she asked me.

I opted for the bottom, as the top one made me anxious about tumbling out onto the floor. Cleo gave me a T-shirt to wear. It smelt very fresh and clean, in a way that none of my clothes ever did, but it wasn't cotton like most of my clothes, it had a prickly feeling to it. Cleo and Dulcie's mother, Erika, came up and gave me a hot water bottle, before putting a thick blanket over me. I watched her carry a lead to the socket and plug it in before leaving the room.

I snuggled under the covers and contemplated the evening: the luxury of the hot bubble bath and fluffy white bread and sugary cakes. I was filled with a warm contentment – my own friends, my first sleepover and cosy bunk beds.

As I lay there thinking, my bed got hotter than anything I'd ever experienced and I started to sweat.

'I'm boiling,' I told Cleo.

'That's the electric blanket. Great, isn't it?' she said before rolling over and going to sleep.

I'd never heard of an electric blanket and lay there terrified by the fact that I was holding a bottle full of hot water and was wrapped up in a blanket that was plugged into the electricity. I threw the hot water bottle out of the bed and crept over to the socket to turn off the power. Then I took off the T-shirt and wrapped myself up in just the cotton sheet. I wondered if they'd notice if I snuck out and slept in the garden. I didn't want to seem rude or ungrateful but I couldn't sleep a wink. I opened the window and crouched down where the fresh air flowed in. I breathed deeply, relieved that the feelings of suffocation and panic were quickly easing.

Eventually I crept quietly back to bed and lay down leaving the window open. I dozed off but was awoken intermittently by lights flickering outside. I couldn't hear the subtle sounds that I heard lying in my wagon back at the camp. There were no birds walking on the roof and no branches gently swaying in the wind. Instead the sound of the odd car passing by disturbed me. Did I really want to live in a house?

Late one afternoon, Perly and I came back from the Harts' house to find the camp unusually quiet. We looked for Dixey, but couldn't find her anywhere. There was no sign of anyone around the barns or in the caravans. We never left the camp empty because nothing was secure, so I was sure someone was home. Perhaps Tony was minding the place. I didn't want to go into his van voluntarily – nowadays I only went in to deliver the endless cups of tea – but I needed to know what was going on. I opened the door, and held my breath as the smoke wafted out. Tony was there, sitting on the bed with Wanda and Zeta.

I was filled with panic and anxiety. Why had I gone out and let him get his hands on them? I quickly took in what was going on. It seemed to be early days. The girls were fully dressed and smiling; four-year-old Zeta sitting opposite him with a multi-pack of crisps and some Jaffa Cakes. Six-year-old Wanda, lying on her back on the bed, was closer to him but his hand was just touching her on the outside of her clothes.

'Come out here, kids,' I said. They ignored me and carried on munching through the goodies. 'Come out here now,' I said more sharply. I entered the van and whisked them off the bed and down the steps. 'Don't go in there again,' I snapped in a mixture of fear and anger. 'Never again, do you hear me? Promise you won't.'

Perly came over as I brought the girls into the kitchen cara van. She'd been looking for Dixey in the goat pen. 'Who was minding them?' she asked.

'Tony,' I said. A look of sadness came over her face.

The abuse had been going on for at least three years at this point. Tony seemed to switch between Perly and me quite frequently. He'd still tell me I was his favourite girl, praise that made me feel good and made the unpleasant bits bearable, but he told Perly that too. He played us off against each other, claiming that Perly was a more passionate kisser than me, or more willing. Sometimes he'd leave me alone for a few days but that was no relief because I knew at these times Perly would be the focus of his attention. I felt sad she was going through the guilt and self-loathing that I was experiencing but I felt helpless. Sometimes I'd offer myself to him to protect her, other times it was easier to pretend it wasn't happening. I could do my best to keep the little ones away from him – wherever we slept, Zeta would sneak in and sleep by my side, and I was happy for her and Wanda to be around me as much as they wanted if it kept Tony from getting his overly friendly hands on them – but his claws were in too deep with Perly, who was only a year and a half younger than me.

I often thought about telling someone – I hoped someone could make it stop – but who could I turn to? Maybe Essie? She was always brave enough to speak up. But she was a teenager, and was quite distracted with school and boys. She probably didn't want to know.

Rollin had his own caravan now and was often busy fixing cars and working but we were still quite close. I went to his caravan late one night, when all the adults were asleep and I was supposed to be asleep too. I opened the door of the little blim trailer to find him and Essie inside smoking a pipe. Rollin had got a little piece of hash off someone. They were stoned and giggling.

'Hiya, Rox, what's up?' Rollin said. He and Essie were pushing each other around playfully.

'Need to talk to you,' I said. 'It's about Tony.'

Essie's face became serious and stern. 'What's up, Rox?' she asked.

'All that stuff Emma said about him,' I began. 'It's all true! I know it is.'

I looked at them, waiting for a response. The caravan was smoky, and my head was spinning with a mixture of marijuana smoke and fear of what I'd started.

Rollin, Essie and me on horseback in Ireland, with Dik holding the rope. Taken the summer after I was born, this is the earliest picture I've ever seen of myself, 1980.

Dik, selling harness, surrounded by gypsy and traveller boys, at Ballinasloe Horse Fair, County Galway, 1981.

Rollin, me and Perly, inside the wagon, all looking uncharacteristically clean after being washed and dressed during a visit by Esther and Peter, Ireland, 1982.

Feeding time at the
zoo – me, Rollin,
Essie and Perly,
Ireland, 1984.

Me, aged 5, at a fair in Ireland,
1985. My hair was still growing
back after the ringworm drama.

Perly, Essie, Rollin
and me, with our
faithful lurcher Ross,
collecting scrap on
an old pushchair. This
was taken shortly
before we left Ireland
and moved to the
UK, in 1985.

A double rainbow over our amenities building, and the mollycroft wagon that I lived in as a teenager. Thorpe Abbotts – our first and last stable family home. © Ramona Carraro, 2009.

A rare family portrait: Mum, Dad and their six children, with our champion stallion, Silver, and sandy lurcher, Katie, at Thorpe Abbotts. © Fred Mustill, 1989.

Zeta and Wanda take a bath, traveller style, at our first camp in Thorpe Abbotts, 1980.

Dixey practising flamenco in the barns, Thorpe Abbotts. © Fred Mustill, 1989.

Dik and a young gypsy cob, Norfolk. © Stefanie Borkum, 2003.

Dixey sign-writing, while I cook in the kitchen caravan. Taken during a short period when Dik didn't have his signature long hair and top knot. Thorpe Abbotts, 1990.

Taken on my 12th birthday by Tom Carrigan, shortly before he got carted off to prison. I remember wondering why people didn't wear balloons in their hair more often.

Me joyfully dancing at the camp, with Rollin playing the guitar. Thorpe Abbotts, 1990. © Tom Carrigan.

Me, Perly and Zeta. This photo was taken for postcards by Caroline Arber in Norfolk, 1992. © Caroline Arber.

Riding one of the yearlings bareback. I'd never ridden this horse before. Dik got me to hop up and show some traveller boys that it was a calm cob. Norfolk, 1994.

Standing outside the caravan, Thorpe Abbotts, in the summer of 1996. Back row right to left: Perly, Rollin, Essie, me, Dik and Dixey. Front row, right to left: Zeta and Wanda.

Rollin and Cousin Jerry rounding up the horses on the bog during a visit to Ireland in 1999.

A photo taken for
performance publicity
and my professional
portfolio by
Monica Curtin,
Norfolk, 1996.

Dancing with a
flamenco group on the
island of Terschelling
during our tour of
Amsterdam in 1997.

Mum and Dad in India: their first and last trip together as a couple before they separated, 2001.

Graduating at Brighton Dome, with Mama and Papa by my side, seven years after I first walked through a classroom door, 2008.

With Arnaud, all dressed up on our way out to celebrate the New Year, Brighton, 2010.

They both looked at me in disbelief. No one said anything. Then the door of the caravan opened. It was Perly.

'It's true, isn't it, Perly?' I said, turning to include her. 'Uncle Tony does things to us, things he shouldn't. Tell them.'

'Stop it, Roxy, just stop it. What are you saying? You're going to ruin everything,' she replied.

I looked at Essie for help, but she didn't speak. She had tears welling in her eyes, but she didn't say a word. I started to cry too, but I carried on talking.

'I know it's true because he does it to me too, all those things Emma said and much more. He does it to Perly too.' I looked again at Perly, the only person who knew I was speaking the truth, hoping for some back-up or support.

'Think about what you're saying, Roxy, think about what will happen. Nothing will be the same again if you keep talking; our lives will all be ruined if this gets out,' Perly pleaded with me, her eyes full of anguish.

Finally Essie spoke. 'What do you want us to do?' she asked.

'I don't know, but I want it to stop.'

Perly was still standing in the doorway of the smoky caravan. 'You don't know what you're doing,' she nearly yelled. 'If Dad finds out about this, he will hit the roof. He'll kill Tony, then what? No dad, no family, everything will be ruined, Rox. We can't say anything, nobody can.' Then she turned and ran, slamming the caravan door as she went.

'Do you want us to do anything, Roxarella?' Rollin asked me, breaking the silence that followed. I could see the fear in his face, the same fear that I felt inside.

'Of course we're doing something,' Essie interrupted. 'We're doing something right now. Let's go and tell Dik and Dixey exactly what that creep's been up to.'

'No, stop, I don't want you to do anything,' I replied. My head was racing. Somehow just voicing the truth for the first time gave me the relief I was looking for. I knew Perly was right: we didn't have to do anything. Life would just carry on as normal. Of course I didn't want to ruin things. It was all so easy and settled, why would I ruin it?

Every year Esther and Peter visited us in Norfolk. Every year they brought their usual gifts of clothes and books and every year they checked in to a hotel in a nearby village. They still found the camp a challenging place to be. The noise and chaos made Esther wince and sigh dramatically, while the rough surroundings made Peter look and feel completely out of place. Esther would be dressed in a long black skirt, a polo-neck sweater, and a blue pashmina and smelling like exotic flowers. Peter was always in a suit, or suit trousers and a cord jacket. He appeared a little more stooped in the shoulders with each passing year. I looked forward to seeing my grandparents but found them intimidating. They were strict about little things that had never been of much importance in our family. Although we were always on our best behaviour when they were around, Esther often said things like, 'Roxy deary, must you sit like that? It's not very becoming for a young lady,' and Peter would ask questions about what I planned to do when I got older and how I was going to make a career. They talked about politics and the economic climate, things that seemed to be from a different universe to the enclosed world of the camp.

Esther and Dik would have heated debates about politics but even if their attitudes were in fact similar, they'd rarely agree as they were from such different walks of life. Two huge personalities, neither of them were scared to voice their opinions. Theirs was a strange relationship. Sometimes they seemed really close and genuinely fond of each other but a lot of the time Esther struggled to see past the hardship her daughter was enduring and ultimately blamed Dik. She was always wanting to give Dixey a break from the camp, even if for Dixey moving back into her old life and adjusting to her mother's ways offered its own difficulties.

That year I'd overheard Dixey and Esther talking.

'Dixey deary,' said Esther, 'I do hope you can bring the children to Spain. We're there from December to May, so maybe Easter would be a good time. Essie could come and the girls won't miss any of their music lessons. Of course we'll cover the flight costs, you won't have to worry about a thing.'

Esther and Peter still spent a lot of time in Europe and were thinking of buying a property in Spain. They had organised the rental of a place while they looked for somewhere of their own.

As spring eventually sprung, talk turned to Spain. I was pleased when Dixey said she was booking flights. We'd never been on a holiday before.

'Maybe we'll do some dancing over there too,' she said. But for me it mainly meant a chance to escape Tony's attentions.

We flew to Andalucia in April, just after my twelfth birthday. Esther and Peter's house was in Nerja and it was beautiful. It was on a busy residential street, was spacious and bright, and had two bedrooms. To reach the extra bedrooms you walked out of the house and up some stairs to a landing that overlooked the garden. But the appeal for me wasn't the house, it was the garden. The property was surrounded by mature citrus and avocado trees which provided welcome shade, as well as a glut of delicious fruit. The realisation that we could wander outside and pick whatever we fancied, whenever we fancied, took a while to sink in. Perly could usually be found in the avocado tree; we'd gather down below and get her to throw us the ripe fruits from the top of the branches. We'd catch them, squeeze lemon juice on them and eat them like apples.

At the back of the garden was a long winding staircase that led down to a quiet little cove and an idyllic beach where we spent afternoons playing in the sand and learning to swim. Dixey sunbathed and read books and Esther made the most extravagant picnics I had ever seen. I set the table each day and helped to wash the dishes. But despite the luxury and comfort, I wasn't relaxed. It was strange staying in a house. I didn't understand it at the time but the feeling of being trapped was quite over-whelming. I enjoyed being with my siblings away from the work and cold of the camp, but I couldn't sleep.

The house had thick stone walls and heavy curtains. As soon as the sun rose each morning, I ran straight to open the windows. I needed to get some air and light. During the day we were outside most of the time, so the strange feeling of being suffo-cated was held at bay. But in the evening, when Peter closed the door and turned the key, I felt like someone was locking me in a cage. I knew for a moment how the little songbirds must have felt, and for the first time I felt relieved that the fire had freed them from their prisons.

I thought constantly about Tony and what he was doing to me. Being away from the situation seemed to make it worse; perhaps it was all the time I had to reflect on what was happening. I cried myself to sleep each night and woke up having dreams about living on the street and never seeing my sisters and brother again.

During our second week in Spain, my nightmares grew worse. I'd toss and turn but as soon as I managed to fall asleep, the nightmares would begin. I rarely remembered the details but the sense of anxiety and stress would wake me up, my pillow would be drenched with tears and my sheets soaked with sweat. Then I'd try to stay awake, but would drop in and out of fitful, restless dreams. I began to dread going home.

There was a story on the news about a man's body being found on the rocks further out of town and I started to think about what it would be like to die that way. I stood on the five-foot wall at the back of the garden looking down on the ocean. The craggy rocks lined the steep bank that fell at least a couple of hundred feet, before it met the beach far below. How quickly would I die if I threw myself off? I wondered. I walked up and down the wall with tears rolling down my cheeks, weighing up the options until I heard Dixey's voice shouting, 'Roxy, get off the wall! You'll fall and kill yourself!' When she asked why I was crying, I told her there was bird with its wing trapped down below.

I gained some insight into suicide that afternoon, an understanding of how easy it is to focus on only the negative parts of life, not think about the good or the people that care about you. Of course I didn't want to die, but for a split second it did feel like I'd found an easy escape from the mixed-up emotions I felt.

My otherwise happy life had turned into a nightmare. I'd always been a joyful soul, I still was in most ways; those feelings of hopelessness were based purely on the fear of what would happen when it all came out in the open. For it was no longer a case of if, just when.

Despite my internal struggles, I loved Spain. I loved the country, the people, the warmth, the food and the beach. I felt more at home there than I ever had in England – there were many gypsies in Spain, they seemed to be accepted as an important part of the culture. Their faces did not look odd on the street, like ours did in England but part of the natural order. Yet for the first time I was on the other side – a 'normal' person, living in a house, on a cobbled street, showering every day, wearing new clothes and taking pictures with my disposable camera of the 'gitanos' as they called them over there, just like any tourist.

There were posters around town advertising flamenco shows by real Spanish gypsies, and during our stay Dixey and I took classes in castanets and Sevillanas with a Spanish woman in the town. She was certainly a tougher taskmaster than our gentle friend Liz Lee. A tiny lady with dyed black hair and a shrill voice, she barked out the castanet rhythms at the top of her voice. 'Tar, re ar, re, ap pi, tar, re ar, re api,' she said rolling the 'r's off her tongue.

At the heart of Nerja was the Balcón, a large, tiled viewpoint that stretches out over the sea, where travellers and gypsies congregate to play music and dance. One night, as we came out of our last class, Dixey and I found Rollin waiting for us there, looking down at the sea. Dixey headed back to the house leaving

Rollin and me to look around the shops. As we made our way back to the house for dinner, we noticed some people juggling and doing circus tricks in the square. They had juggling clubs, unicycles and wore top hats and were surrounded by an enthusiastic crowd clapping and cheering them on. We pushed through the crowds to get a better look before we realised it was Tristan and Zeal!

We hadn't seen them for six or seven years. I wouldn't have even recognised them if Rollin hadn't been with me. They were tall and grown-up, wearing black drainpipe jeans and T-shirts. They took off their hats and passed them around the crowd to collect money. A look of pure disbelief came over their faces when they spotted us.

'Wow! What you two doin' here?' Tristan asked us, grabbing me and hugging me tightly.

'We're visiting our grandparents but it's nearly our last night – we could have missed you.'

We chatted for a while, before giving them the phone number of Esther and Peter's house. 'Promise you'll come back?' I asked Zeal.

'Yeah, course we will, we only live half an hour away.'

They came back the next day bringing Harmony, who was now ten, and Emily, who was six, with them. We met up at the beach and played and chatted all afternoon. It felt like we had never been apart; Perly and Harmony were joined at the hip. Wanda, Emily and Zeta barely knew each other, but instantly clicked. When we took them back to the house, Dixey was as surprised as we had been. She seemed genuinely pleased that we had all been reunited and told them that they must come and see us in England. But she was a little anxious about having them in Esther and Peter's house: our grandparents still didn't know that Harmony and Emily were related to us.

Harmony and Emily came to stay with us in England that summer. They flew over in their holidays and stayed for a few weeks. Dik was happy to have us all together but soon found the extra additions to the family quite challenging. Harmony and Emily hadn't been brought up with the strict rules that we had; they were wilder and less respectful, disappearing when chores needed doing, and refusing to go to bed. Harmony wasn't quelled by a single look from Dik like I was. She would shout and scream at him if he tried to discipline her in any way, which led to a fair few fights between them.

One afternoon in July, Dik and Dixey went out and left me at home with Perly, Harmony, Emily, Wanda and Zeta. We were in the kitchen caravan tidying up from breakfast when Tony came in with a multipack of crisps under his arm.

'Morning, kids,' he greeted us cheerfully. 'Why don't you all take some of these crisps and go off and play. Roxy and me, will finish up in here.' They all gratefully grabbed a pack of crisps each and ran off, glad to get out of the cleaning up. 'Come and sit down with me, Roxy,' he said, patting the couch.

Since returning from Spain, Tony had started making lots of remarks about my emerging breasts and my body. He constantly told me that I was ugly or fat and not the little girl he had adored. I was quite slight at that time, but I was developing quickly and no longer looked like a little girl. The comments had a big impact and made me even more self-conscious than I already was.

'Not here, Tony,' I mumbled, conscious that the caravan had no curtains and no lock on the door; it was in the middle of the camp and the busiest place. He'd touched me in there before, even kissed me once or twice, but nothing more.

'Don't be difficult,' he said. 'Come over here.' He smiled to make the request seem more appealing.

I will never understand why he did what he did next. After so many years of gentle progression and soft grooming, it was very out of character. I went and sat down next to him and he kissed me on the lips but pressed harder than he ever had before. I sensed a kind of urgency and force in him and squirmed away. But before I knew what was happening he'd whipped off his trousers and was pinning me down on the sofa. I started to struggle and tried to wiggle out from underneath him but he was twice my size and held me tightly in place. He forced his tongue into my mouth, ferociously biting my skin. For the first time in my life I was truly scared of him. He didn't care that I was distressed and ignored the tears running down my face. I begged him to stop but he pressed himself against me, his penis pushing hard between my legs, until finally I stopped struggling and resigned myself to the inevitable.

Then I heard a car pull up beside the caravan. It was Dik and Dixey returning home.

'How could you forget to put the washing in?' Dik's voice calling from the car was clearly audible in the caravan. Tony quickly put his trousers on and tried to make the situation look normal, straightening the covers on the seat and wiping my tears away.

'All right, my Roxy Riddle? Why the sad face?' Dixey asked

as she walked in the door. My head was racing, I was desperate to tell her what she'd nearly walked in on, but Tony replied for me.

'She's okay now, just had a tumble, was playing in the trees.'

'Are you hurt?' Dixey asked.

'No. I'll be okay.' I stood up and scurried towards the pile of dishes, worried what Dik would say if he came in and they hadn't been washed. He didn't come in but waited in the car for Dixey. She grabbed the bags of laundry from outside the door and got back in beside him. Tony didn't return for the rest of the day.

I avoided Tony as much as possible over the following days, and he avoided me. I felt a sense of relief that he didn't seek me out to carry on where he'd left off. But in a strange way I also missed him. I missed the attention and the close relationship that he and I had built up over the years. But he had broken the trust between us. Perhaps that's why he stopped – he knew he'd gone too far – or maybe my womanly figure was unappealing to him. He went away that autumn and didn't return for many months.

CHAPTER 10

Trust

We had been at Thorpe Abbotts for five years and were in the weird position of being almost settled. The police left us alone. No eviction notices were served. The locals didn't complain about our presence. We even had friends – the Harts and Chris and Jenny, a couple who lived across the way. Dik had built up his network of tinkers and gypsies and we were all growing up and maybe not turning out as badly as he'd feared. We couldn't help noticing that Dik wasn't as grumpy as we were used to. He even fooled around and got involved in games with us.

One warm summer's day Liz Lee dropped me off after a class. As I got out of the car I was suddenly drenched from head to foot with water. I looked around stunned as my dad darted around the corner, chuckling maniacally, his pink silk shirt hanging off him from an earlier dousing. He headed for the pond to refill his bucket. Before I knew what was going on, I was involved in a massive water fight that lasted the entire afternoon and into the evening. Perly and Rollin hid behind the wagon, thick as thieves, chuckling with their water pistols and squirting anyone that walked past. Wanda and Zeta had taken charge of the hose-pipe and were spraying it high into the sky. There was no safe territory. At one point Perly and Dulcie ended up marooned on the pond floating inside an inflated tractor tyre, while trying to escape the buckets of water that were coming at them from every angle. By the end of the day the entire family, as well as the Harts, were soaked and exhausted but deliriously happy.

I was dancing constantly, practising and taking classes and exams, and when I wasn't dancing, I was cooking and cleaning. We seemed to have an ever-increasing flow of residents and guests, all of whom miraculously appeared at mealtimes. People would drift in and out of our lives, sit down for food round the campfire, joke with Dik and absorb the atmosphere. Some of them stayed for a bit and then drifted off, others lingered and became lasting friends.

Gypsies and tinkers would pull up in their vans and beep the horn.

'Is anyone home?' they'd ask. If you weren't male you didn't count as a person: 'anyone' meant Dik or Rollin. I'd noticed a few of the fathers eyeing me up and asking questions about my age and skills. They liked to marry their kids off early and talked about their boys like they were selling a car or a dog: 'He's a good worker, my boy, handsome too, he knows how to do a deal and's good with the harses.'

Dik would take a wicked pleasure in going along with it. Like a cat teasing a bird he'd reel off our talents, even calling us out of the caravan so they could see what pretty, hard-working girls we were; that was how you could tell he was proud of us, even me, although he could never tell us directly.

'She's a good-looking girl, to be sure,' they'd start before Dik nipped it in the bud with a swift 'I'm not looking to marry her off though.' If Dad had his way he'd have his tribe of Freeman girls around him forever.

When I think about the camp now, I realise how naive we all were. Everything about our way of life was based on trust, on accepting that people were who they said they were. There was one guy from London who called himself Yamir. He wore his thick curly fair hair in a ponytail, became friends with Dik and took to visiting regularly. He said he loved our way of life, how we all sat around the fire and ate dinner on our laps, the way that we sat cross-legged and danced a lot – he said it reminded him of India. His ex-wife and two kids lived nearby, so he would bring the kids up to play with Perly and sit chatting with Dik and Uncle Tony far into the night. He and Dik were of a similar age and had interests in common.

Dixey too was drawn to him.

'He's such a gentle, soulful man,' she'd sigh. Dixey always loved anyone with a spiritual side to them and Yamir practised reiki and claimed to be a healer. He was a follower of the guru Bhagwan Sri Rajneesh and had visited the ashram in India where Dixey's sister Melanie lived. Rajneesh was the guru who famously kept a fleet of Rolls Royces, who held all-embracing beliefs about sex, and who rechristened his legions of devoted, orange-clad followers, transforming Melanie into Gopa, and Yamir from his original ordinary British name. I watched Yamir talking to my mum, smiling and flashing his bright white teeth and telling her that 'No one should suppress their desires, man' and wasn't sure that it was all about spirituality. Yamir was flirtatious with most women – he was very physically affectionate and liked to touch you as he spoke to you, playing with your fingers or stroking your forearm – but especially so with Dixey. Lucky for him that Dik was busy with the horses.

Soon it was normal for Yamir and his kids to appear every Friday and stay until Sunday night. Sometimes he'd turn up with a girlfriend – London girls who found the camp 'charming' and thought they were getting back to nature by experiencing our way of life. I looked forward to Yamir arriving as he was funny and kind. He talked to me like an adult, not one of the kids, plying me with compliments and offering to help me with my chores. He was more of a hindrance than a help, though – I've never much liked being touched by anyone other than my family and found the hugs and massages while I washed up off-putting. He'd often appear while I was on my own practising flamenco in the barns. I always knew when he was nearby because the smell of his Indian petiole oil would drift ahead of him, tickling my nostrils before I heard his distinctive super-calm, 'Awlright, Rox? What ya up to?'

Yamir's children slept in a spare bed in the caravan that Perly and I shared. Yamir came every night to tuck them in and read chapters of different novels to us. Sometimes he'd lie next to his kids on the bottom bunk to read, other times he'd lie on mine and Perly's bed. It was about the third or fourth time he came in to read that I felt his hand slip off the page of the book and under the bedcovers. I thought he must be feeling the cold so I gave his hand a squeeze. He was such a tactile person I didn't think much of it when his hand rested on my thigh.

He finished the second chapter and said, 'Want another one then, kids?' We thought our luck was in, three chapters in one night.

'Come and read down here, Dad,' his children said from the bed below.

'Next time,' he replied.

I snuggled down and listened to the story. Then his hand left my thigh and crept up between my legs. It was a familiar feeling as Tony had done it so often before but it still caught me by surprise. He read through the story, holding the book with one hand and exploring my body with the other. I lay very still and closed my eyes, hoping it was a bad dream and that I would wake up soon. But instead the same thing happened the following night and the following weekend. I didn't whisper a word about to anybody, not even Yamir. He never said anything and we continued our friendship as normal during daylight hours. The guilt that I had been free from for just a few months had returned.

Tony was in Thailand. Dik and Dixey had received the odd postcard from him but I didn't pay much attention. I didn't want to think about him. Then one day a thick letter arrived with Tony's handwriting on the front. Dixey opened it and read it aloud.

'Dear all, I have married a local lady. I'm learning the language little by little, but my progress is slow. Here are some pictures of my new family for you to show the children.'

I stopped listening at that point and started looking through the images. The first one was of an attractive young Thai lady. She was younger than Dixey, probably in her thirties, definitely at least twenty years younger than Tony. She was petite, with dark hair and dark skin and wore a loose blue and green dress. The next picture was of Tony with three children sitting on a log near a river, two girls who looked no more than seven or eight and a boy slightly older. The children had the same colouring as the lady but were dressed in more normal European-style clothes. He'd written names on the back. Looking at the picture with Tony in it, all the familiar conflicting emotions of fondness and mistrust came flooding back. I was glad that he was away, far away, and would be staying away, but I feared for the little girls in the pictures.

By this stage we were so established at Thorpe Abbotts it was hard not to think we would be staying forever. I started growing vegetables and flowers with the help of a lady called Jeni-Wren who had come to stay. She taught me how to block out celery and get rid of greenfly. We planted daffodils all around the pond and put lilies in the water. Then we fenced off a little area behind the pond, leading up to the hedge that separated Bob's land from the adjoining landlord's plot, to make a garden. Dulcie and I both had a love of traditional English country garden flowers, like sweet peas, nasturtiums and pansies. We'd plant packets of seeds and swap seedlings, each striving to find an unusual colour or scent.

Jeni-Wren was motherly towards me and was happy to share her wealth of knowledge about gardening and plant care with me, but for the all the hours of love we put into that garden, it seemed to cause more tears and heartache than anything else. English country gardens don't mix well with goats and horses. It didn't matter how much chicken wire we put up, or what kind of barbed fences we constructed, they always got in just as things were taking shape.

Animals came and went but the herd of goats seemed to increase with every year. Dixey loved them as deeply as I disliked them. I still milked them and helped Dixey make the cheese and yoghurt but I resented them more and more every day. Dixey said I hated the goats because they were headstrong and intelligent like me, so we clashed. I just disliked the devilish look in their eyes, and their pig-headed natures. If they weren't eating my plants, they were making me get out of bed to milk them and nurse their kids. If they weren't getting me out of bed, they were chewing the cables that connected the wagons to the generator and plunging us into darkness. One day when I was battling with my emotions while milking a goat, Yamir wandered by and commented, 'It's so lovely to see you squatting down, milking the goats, Rox, you're obviously so at ease with them,' to which the goat responded by sticking its foot in the milk and standing on my toe. I stood up, whacked the goat around the head and fled in fury.

The goats had many kids; Dixey kept the nannies and we ate the billies. We often bottle-reared them and helped bring them up but it didn't upset me that Dik killed them. It was just the way life was. In fact much of the time I wished he'd slaughter the nannies as well and be done with the whole herd. We gave the billies names like Yumyums and Dindins so we knew where they were headed. Dik usually waited until they were about a year old before he slaughtered them.

One day I was standing in the field when he came out and took Yumyums by the scruff of his neck.

'Time for the pot for you,' he said.

He led the goat across the field and into the hangar. Normally I kept well away when he was slaughtering – I'd helped him skin and joint them in the past but I never wanted to see him actually kill them – but on this day I followed him and hovered around outside. He tied the billy up inside and came back out, took a knife and a sharpening stone from the kitchen and went back to into the hangar, sliding the doors closed behind him. I walked over to the doors and peeked through the hole.

I watched him methodically sharpen the knife before walking over to the billy goat. He straddled the goat as if he was going to ride him, and held his head in his hands as he gently caressed the hair under Yumyum's neck. The goat seemed to go into a trance; his head went all floppy and relaxed as Dik stroked him, making a gentle 'Sshhhh boy' under his breath. When Yumyums was completely relaxed, head laying back and eyes closed, Dik took the knife and slit his throat. One sharp movement and he was done. Yumyums fell to the floor and did a series of convulsions before going soft and still. Dik knelt down beside him and removed the skin, putting it aside to be salted and cured for use as rugs later, and took out the organs and cut off the ball sack. He then tied a piece of rope around his back legs and strung him up from the ceiling. He came out of the shed with the bowl of organs – we always ate the organs and testicles on the day of the slaughter – and left the carcass hanging.

I don't know if he knew I was watching; if he did, he didn't say anything. I was surprised at how humanely he had killed the billy, but felt a strange sense of sordidness at having observed a life being taken.

★   ★   ★

Early in the summer of 1990, a photographer turned up at the camp with an old family friend. He had a Scottish accent and ginger hair.

'Helloo, hen, I'm Tom,' he said as I came out of the caravan to see whose the car was. 'I'm hoping to take some snaps aroond and about. Is that okay, lassie?'

'Yeah, I guess so,' I said. 'Better check with Dik first though.'

He stayed for most of the day, laughing and joking as he wandered around taking pictures of everyone and everything. I noticed him sneaking around the door of the barn where I was practising my dancing and taking some shots. I tried to ignore him and carry on but had rarely seen a camera and felt quite self-conscious. He was a confident and charming person and had a way of making you relax in his presence – before I knew what was happening I seemed to be telling him all kinds of things. There was just something about him that put me completely at ease.

Tom was renting a large house just a few villages away and he liked to come by to photograph the camp and spend time with us all. He was the most generous person I'd ever met. He bought me new clothes, magazines, books and numerous other gifts every time I saw him. I think a part of me expected him to start having a fiddle and grope in exchange for all the presents he bought me, but he never did. It was a warm, brotherly friendship – nothing more. Tom didn't spend that much time with the adults, despite the fact that he was in his twenties; he was childish in his behaviour and would play hours of hide and seek or sardines in a can with us all. He also sang us songs. 'Skinny milinki long legs, big banana feet, went to the pictures and couldn't find a seat, when the picture started skinny milinki farted,' he sang in his thick Glaswegian accent, as he drove us to see *Dances with Wolves* at the cinema. It was a birthday treat. I took my passport to prove that I was old enough to get into a twelve certificate.

Tom had lots of girlfriends that came and went. None of them lasted very long, until he met Estee. Then, a little while after introducing me to Estee, he came around and said, 'You okay, lassie? Guess what? I'm gonna be a daddy. Estee's pregnant.' He was over the moon and scooped me up to go shopping in town for things for the baby. He dropped me off a few hours later and tucked £20 into my pocket. I wondered where he got all his money from. He seemed to be getting richer every day.

Tom's baby girl was born that year but within weeks of her arrival Tom was arrested and carted off to prison. He was accused of a string of armed bank robberies. I was shocked – both that my kind friend Tom could have done such things, and that he would be taken from my life. I remembered the barbed wire around the walls when I had visited Tony in prison and the sterile grey room where we had sat. It seemed unfair that someone so loving and generous should be incarcerated. Tom was the first man I had ever known that seemed to love me unconditionally and want nothing in return. It was an unusual friendship: I was a twelve-year-old girl and he a thirty-year-old man. He was a friend to all the family but he gave me the one-on-one time and attention that I needed without the sexual advances.

Estee and Tom got married while he was on remand. They had a prison wedding and lived in hope that the sentence wouldn't be too harsh. I saw Estee a few times and met the baby but we soon lost touch with her. I wrote to Tom a few times every week while he was on remand. It made me glad that I had learned to write. Tom always replied promptly. He told me he'd made some terrible choices and had got addicted to the money, but that he'd do his time and be back before we knew it.

Around this time Essie brought home a friend who we unofficially adopted. Amelia was a quiet girl, with straight dark hair and a well-spoken voice who wanted to be a schoolteacher when she left school. She was miserable at home, so for her the welcome of the camp was a refuge. Dixey adored her and asked if she would help with educating Wanda and Zeta. They made a plan that she would come and stay with us and help Dixey out in return for food and somewhere to sleep.

It was musical beds again. Amelia moved into the caravan that Perly and I shared, Perly moved into a section of an old unused bus and I moved into a little wooden wagon. It was my first place of my own. It wasn't a canvas bow-top one like the one we'd lived in before, or the one Dik and Dixey slept in, but a showman's wagon, entirely made of wood, with a tiny row of little mollycroft windows around the top. Dik had bought it to do up and sell, but said I could move in for a while they worked on the outside of it. It had no insulation and thin wooden walls. Inside the door was a small Queenie stove, a bench on each side and bed at the back. I put posters on the wall and bought trinkets in the charity shop to decorate it. Rollin, who liked nothing more than to wind me up and make me cry, took great delight in giving my wagon a good shake every time he walked by. All my trinkets would fall on the floor and break, I'd burst into tears and he'd walk off laughing. He wasn't cruel or malicious, but he'd learnt how to tease from Dik and I was an easy target.

Moving into the wagon had one huge benefit: I missed out on the evening stories read by Yamir each weekend. He soon found other times to get to me, however. He'd seek me out when I was sitting still, but oddly never when I was on my own. I think the thrill for him must have been doing it while other people were present. He'd come and sit next to me while Amelia and I were planning homework for Wanda and Zeta, or when I was snuggled up on the sofa with one of my sisters. He'd pretend to be caring and wrap a blanket around me or put his jacket on me. Then he'd sneak his hand underneath and have a fiddle. The abuse was less frequent or extreme than the things that Tony did, but it still left me feeling dirty and ashamed. When Yamir first turned up at the camp Tony was still around. They got on well, drinking tea and chatting late into the night. Maybe Tony had told him I wouldn't speak out. Many years later Essie said she wouldn't have been surprised if Tony had given him a tip-off. Yamir had tried it on with her and she'd sent him packing. I wished I'd had the confidence to do the same thing.

I wrote to Tom regularly and waited anxiously for his trial to come to a close. I imagined he might get sent away for a year or two and wondered how I was going to cope without my new friend. I had no idea of the extent of his crimes and somehow refused to see him as the criminal that he really was; I think I hoped it wasn't true. The newspapers reported on the case continually but I mostly kept track of what was happening through my letters from Tom. Then, in May of 1993, shortly after my fourteenth birthday, I went into Diss to do the laundry. I ambled carelessly into the newsagent to get some change and was confronted with the headline: 'Gang Jailed for "Ruthless" Raids'. The *Independent* as well as numerous other papers had reported the outcome of the case. I scanned the article looking for the sentence Tom had been given but was bombarded with information on the scare tactics that 'Glasgow's most vicious criminals' had used in their bank raids. The person I was reading about wasn't the kind, supportive Tom I knew and loved. This was a monster. Then in the final paragraph I found the informa-tion I was looking for: 'Thomas Carrigan, 31, sentenced to 17 years in prison'. I ran from the shop in tears colliding with a customer entering the store. I was upset at the things the paper said, but also deeply disillusioned. Who was Tom that could have done those things, and yet be so sweet to me? I didn't think I knew him after all.

But even then, once I knew the extent of Tom's crimes, I still kept writing to him. I missed our bizarre friendship and his letters gave me strength and a feeling of companionship. My replies were a kind of diary; he was going to be inside for so long that I knew I didn't have to worry about him talking to my family or anyone else so I expressed my experiences and emotions in my letters. I never told him about Tony or Yamir but somehow just writing to him eased the burden of carrying those secrets. And perhaps on some level he understood. He told me that he was ashamed of his behaviour and that he'd got in with the wrong crowd and now he was paying for it. He'd do his time and had learned his lesson. He said the papers were mostly fairly accurate, that they did terrorise people and stick guns in their faces, but that the person I knew wasn't a lie or false. He said, 'People have many different layers, hen, you know this already.'

One day Dik intercepted one of the letters I'd written to Tom before I got it to the postbox. He asked me why I had drawn hearts on the envelope.

'I miss Tom,' I told him, 'I really miss him and I love him.'

'I knew you'd been acting strangely,' he replied. 'What's been going on between you? What's he done to you?'

'I love him like a brother,' I said, 'not like that. He hasn't done anything apart from love me back.' Dik thought it was all very odd and told Dixey that he didn't trust my friendship with Tom and he didn't think I should be writing to him. And maybe I had been acting strangely but it wasn't Tom that was causing my erratic emotions. I thought how ironic it was that Dik was now getting suspicious over Tom when two different people had been abusing me. Child abusers weren't open and adoring like Tom was and they worked harder at keeping Dik and Dixey on side than he did. I guess because they had something to hide.

I was still living in the wooden showman's wagon as the winter of 1994 set in. That wagon was the coldest place I have ever slept in my life. I may as well have been sleeping outside with no protection at all. I loved having my own space, but hard as I tried, it wouldn't warm up. The icicles hung down from the windows, inside the wagon. If I lit the Queenie it would warm up just enough that icy cold water would drip onto the bed and the floor. I'd place cups and bowls under the icicles to catch the drips but there was rarely enough wood to keep the stove alight for very long anyway despite all the time I spent collecting twigs and sticks to fill it.

Every morning I was woken by an icy drip landing on my face. I'd hop out of bed, glad to be awake while the rest of the camp still slept, light my stove and skip across the field to the letter box. Collecting the mail had become a bit of a ritual for me. Apart from Tom's letters from prison, I didn't receive much post but I loved the fact that we had a letter box, and I liked to see what was in there before anyone else had a chance.

Frida's brown-paper packages still arrived on a regular basis. When the socks first started coming I'd deliver them to the kitchen caravan and leave them on the table for Dik to find when he got up. Then one day I noticed a tear trickling down Dixey's cheek as he put on the socks and fiddled with the pink silk scarf she'd sent with them. She didn't say a word. Dik was probably completely oblivious to the pain she felt but I was a sensitive person and was always aware of other people's emotions, particularly my mother's, so I picked up on it quite early on.

It soon became a matter of priority for me to get to the letter box before anyone else was awake. I'd collect the mail and as usual deliver it to the kitchen, but if there was a brown paper package, I'd tuck it under my clothes, before walking back through the long dewy grass to my wagon.

I'd climb up the steps into my wagon and kneel down in front of the stove. I always tried to get the fire raging before I left to collect the post. I'd open the package and take a quick look at what was inside. The socks were the first things to succumb to the blaze. I'd toss them in without a second thought. They'd burn brightly for a few seconds before fizzling out. The card said

'Dik' across the top and always had a hand-drawn heart with the letter F. There were no other words, but sometimes a scarf or a silk ribbon was included. It all went straight in the fire.

It never occurred to me that disposing of the gifts was a bad thing to do. I've always been the family peacekeeper and as far I was concerned I was preventing my mother's tears and keeping the home harmonious. And Dik never commented on the lack of gifts from Frida. I don't know if he even noticed. Of course there were still many of the socks kicking around the place. She'd been sending them for as long as I could remember – Valentine's Day, Easter, Christmas, his birthday and any other excuse she could find – so there was a bit of a build-up. But I gradually disposed of them; as I cleaned the caravans, I would fling them into the nearest bin or into the fire, and slowly they started to disappear. In some strange way I think I hoped she would disappear with them.

After six years at Thorpe Abbotts the council had finally noticed us. For once they didn't seem to want to move us on – a law had come in that meant they would have to provide us with a council home or somewhere else to go if they did – but equally they weren't happy about us residing illegally on the runway. So a notice went up near our letter box stating that we were seeking to make our position in the village legal and that if anyone had a problem with it, or thought it a good idea, they should let their feelings be known within twenty-eight days. We waited for the period to pass and all hoped that our many peaceful years in the area would stand for something with the local residents.

But when the month was up we were told that the response

had been overwhelmingly negative. It seemed that most of the villagers did object to our being there. They gave reasons such as our living there lowered the value of their properties, and the tone of the area, or they found our camp to be an eyesore when walking their dogs on the runway. The only people that had expressed a positive response to us being there were Chris and Jenny from across the road.

Dixey was particularly hurt by the number of letters of objection. She'd baked cakes – or got me and Dulcie to bake things for her to deliver – for the village fete. She'd even organised some benefit shows at the village hall to raise funds to rebuild the roof and had made a big effort to put something back into the community. Now she could see names she knew in the pile of objections.

'What harm are we doing them?' she asked, wounded. 'Why would they object to us staying? I really thought I was making progress around here. They're more worried about the value of their property than a family being pushed off onto the roads.'

Dik negotiated with Bob over buying the land, as it would have been easier to get permission to stay if we owned it, but they couldn't come to an agreement.

We sought help from the Gypsy Council of Great Britain, which specialised in helping gypsy families. They said we had a case hingeing on the fact that we had lived in Thorpe Abbotts for six peaceful years without a single complaint or problem being lodged against us. But our lack of hell-raising and fighting didn't seem to have made a wit of difference. When the local paper covered the story the headline still read: 'Keep Them Out'.

CHAPTER II

Teenage Kicks

I was fifteen and it was hard to be a teenager under Dik's eagle
eye. It didn't help that Essie had run him ragged staying out late
and dating boys from the earliest opportunity. Dik might not
have behaved like a tinker father, never letting his girls near a
man until she had a ring on her finger, but he liked to think he
kept us on as short a lead as any of his lurchers.

Mostly I was wrapped up with dancing – not just classes and
exams, but performing. Dixey and I became part of Zambra
Flamenca, a company put together by Liz Lee and some of the
people we had originally started taking classes with, and we
performed together a couple of times a month, doing a 'filigree
show', which means a fusion performance, in this instance com-
bining flamenco, Indian and Egyptian dance music. With Steve
Homes playing the guitar and various other musicians, we got
gigs in theatres, at festivals and even did a tour of the county's
libraries.

Liz was very supportive of me in those years and I learned everything from her. We performed with many different people: some of them were technically brilliant, but didn't show any emotion in their movements; others were fiery but lacked experience or skill. Liz Lee had both. Dik used to say 'she's got fire crackers in her knickers' when he saw her dance. He praised Dixey and me on occasions but back then he believed that criticism got better results than encouragement.

I also joined a can-can troupe that summer, Les Fi-Fi-Farfelous. The group was based in Bungay and practised in Liz's studio a couple of times each week. I had a dress made to the same pattern as all the other dancers but in my favourite colour, deep purple. We got a decent amount of gigs, birthday parties, work dos, festivals and even some foreign tours. One year, we did a tour of hotels in Malta and were flown over by a French wine importer to dance at every establishment that ordered over a certain number of crates of Beaujolais Nouveau.

Amelia was still living with us and had been working hard to get Wanda and Zeta up to the right level of education for their age, so they could start school the following year. They were regularly assessed by the education board and had made great progress in the time she had been working with them. She was pleased to get away from her family and had become a good friend to me. Dik and Dixey were happy to have her around, as she was helpful, intelligent and hard-working. We went to parties together whenever Dik would give us permission to leave the camp. As she was a few years older, Dik trusted her to take care of me. We dressed up and went out until the early hours. We flirted with boys and made some friends but neither of us was really interested in a steady boyfriend.

I stopped doing farm work and got a job taking care of an old man named Mr Brown. At first I did regular housekeeping, cooking and gardening but he wasn't very well and before long I was doing full-on personal care in his home. He was a big man who suffered from Parkinson's disease and was often inappropriate and rude but after all the abuse I'd experienced it was like water off a duck's back. I learnt that I was incredibly resilient, and despite his comments, gropes and advances I became quite fond of the old git.

I spent most of my spare time with Dulcie baking cakes and puddings. We'd perfected the art of caramel tuiles and took pride in garnishing and dusting our creations so they looked like something from a posh patisserie. I'd never eaten much sugar and still didn't have a taste for it but I enjoyed the process of baking complex puddings. Seeing people's faces light up as they tried my creations filled me with a feeling of delight. I've always had a desire to please. I think because I felt like a nuisance and an inconvenience as a child, I have subconsciously fallen into a role where I seek to satisfy people. Performing was the same: it was the applause I loved. The feeling of being appreciated made me feel singled out after a childhood in the middle of a big family.

Then, a couple of years after we started trying to make our position in Thorpe Abbotts legal, we finally made some progress. Various organisations assisted us with the application and, despite the negative response from the locals, the council eventually granted us rights to stay on the land indefinitely. They stipulated

the permission was for Freeman family members and their partners only, and a maximum of seven caravans or temporary
structures. We could stay on the land as long as the landowner
was happy for us to do so – Bob was pleased and quickly wrote
out a contract so we could pay him rent. The council would be
making regular checks to ensure that the camp did not increase
and we were not allowed to build but we could put up a non-
permanent amenities block. The travelling Freemans were free
to stay put.

I was happy with my life and felt strangely untouchable.

Dik said to me one day, 'You'll always be okay, Cinders. You
were born under a lucky star.'

I contemplated that statement for a few days. I wondered if
that was his way of justifying his behaviour towards me, by telling me that he knew I could get through it all. I didn't feel
particularly lucky, I just cherished my life, my family and my
friends and I knew that no amount of abuse, or trauma would
ever change that. The nightmares still came, mostly about Tony
but even if he haunted me in my sleep, during daylight hours no
one could alter my positive outlook and persona.

With my sixteenth birthday on the horizon, and more and
more time spent away from home touring with Liz Lee and one
or other of the troupes, I began to fight for my independence.
Not that Dik was having any of it. It was nice to know he cared,
but he seemed to be growing more protective over me with
each day that passed. He no longer liked me going out with
Amelia and even stopped me from visiting Dulcie and Cleo
whenever he could. Through Amelia and Essie I had developed
a circle of friends; they were mostly people leading an alternative

life, involved in putting on parties, festival and events, predominantly men in their mid-twenties. My lack of schooling meant that I never came into contact with girls or boys my own age. I went from having no friends apart from the Harts, to hanging out with a group of older blokes. In some ways I was glad: spotty teenage lads never much appealed to me and I was relieved to bypass first dates and three-thumb fumbles – after everything I'd been through it would have felt rather odd to be learning about kissing and sex all over again. I certainly didn't want to be in a position where I would have to explain my knowledge of the subject to anyone.

I was very slim and toned from all the dancing, with long dark hair and I liked to wear fitted oriental dresses and lots of kohl to emphasise my exotic looks at that time, so I received a fair amount of male attention when we were out. No one really interested me though until Amelia and I started spending time with a man called Nick. Tall, dark and suave, Nick was a friend of a friend at least ten years older than me. He came to the camp from time to time and we often met up with him when we went out. He had a way with words and charmed both Amelia and me off our feet.

One weekend when Amelia went away for a few days, Nick turned up at the camp with an expensive bottle of whisky and a deer he'd been given to cook.

'D'you know how to cook up venison, Rox?' he asked, as he emerged from his car with the carcass.

'Um, I've cooked it once or twice. I can skin it and joint it no problem, if you want.'

I got to work preparing the meat, while Nick sat in the

caravan talking to Dik and Dixey. It was a wet, spring night and the generator was going on and off as the dampness seeped into the sockets. Each time it went off, Perly and I had to run outside in the rain, wrap a plastic bag around the various plugs and restart the genny, in order to get the lights back on. Firing it up involved swinging a handle in circles until the engine kicked in. Once it started the handle would spin at high speed before flying off towards the ground. We had to jump out of the way as soon as we heard the engine start in order to save our ankles from the chunky piece of metal.

Dik has never been a drinker but Nick was working his way through the whisky as I prepared the venison stew. I threw in a handful of juniper berries and some bay leaves, and we were plunged into darkness yet again. Dik ran outside to sort it out. Dixey looked for the candles but couldn't find them, fumbling about in the pitch blackness. Nick approached me in the dark. He put a glass of whisky to my lips. I swallowed the liquor and felt his lips pressing against mine. He lingered for a minute, jumping back as the lights came on and Dik came back in. I was quite surprised but had enjoyed the momentary kiss. The rest of the evening was spent with us hoping the rain would keep falling, so we could steal kisses in the darkness of the caravan. I drank more whisky than I ever had in my life and started to feel quite giddy.

As I stumbled out of the caravan Dixey asked, 'Are you okay, love?'

'I don't feel so good, gonna go to bed,' I muttered trying to disguise my slurring words and shaky legs.

I stood outside, looking up at the stars, pondering the events of the evening. I wondered what Amelia would say about this, she would barely believe the cheekiness of Nick to kiss me in the same room as my parents, let alone dosing me up with whisky right in front of them. I felt excited and confused by his actions. I tried to balance myself on the side of my wagon and struggled to find the steps. Then I felt a warm arm wrap around my waist and pick me up. It was Nick. He kissed me and carried me away. I was so drunk I scarcely registered what was happening.

I awoke with a fuzzy head, relieved to be neatly tucked up in my bed. But as I opened my eyes I realised it wasn't my bed, but Amelia's.

'Mornin' gorgeous. How ya feeling?' said Nick. He was putting on his boots. 'Gotta go to work, my love. You better get off to your own bed and make sure you get the morning-after pill.' He kissed me and left.

I tried to recall what had happened after Nick came to my rescue outside the wagon, but I couldn't recollect what had come next. I got up and snuck into my wagon and my own bed. It was barely light and everyone else was still asleep around the camp. I wasn't sure if I had just been involved in a consensual sexual encounter between two adults or if I had been the uncon-senting object of yet another man's desires. I was attracted to Nick, which was a good start, but I'd had no intention of doing anything more than flirting with him, and if it hadn't been for the whisky there was no way I would have even done that.

I fell asleep and, waking up a few hours later, set about my normal morning. There was no way I could get into town to get the pill, and even if I could find a way I wasn't even registered with a doctor and I was not yet sixteen. I got the post; I had a

letter from Tom. I milked the goats and checked out the damage
the stallion had done to the daffodils during the night. Slowly
the camp woke up around me. We were off to visit Esther and
Peter in Spain that day. I packed my things and checked the time.
We had an hour before we had to leave, so I sat down and replied
to Tom's letter. As usual I told him everything, including all the
details of the night before. I scribbled hearts on the envelope as
I always did and put it on the side, to post on the way to the
airport. I left a note for Amelia.

*Hi Meelie. Hope you had a nice time away, you missed a good week-
end. See you in a week. X Roxy.*

And off we went.

After that first visit to Nerja, Dixey and we children had visited
Esther and Peter in Spain most Easters over the following five
years. They had bought their own house, just across the road
from the place they rented. Each visit I danced with different
tutors and each time we caught up with Harmony and Emily.
Although they sometimes came to stay at the house, Esther and
Peter were still oblivious to the fact that they were our sisters and
Dixey wasn't keen for them to find out. But with each passing
day Harmony looked more like us; Emily, who was still little, had
her mother's blonde hair, but there was no mistaking that
Harmony had the Freeman look.

Harmony and Emily arrived on the third day we were there.
Esther packed us a picnic and gathered up beach towels. We all
scampered down to the beach with Dixey and a friend of Esther
and Peter's. We played for a few hours before Dixey and the
friend decided to go back to the house.

'Watch the little ones, Roxy Riddle,' she said as she walked up the long spiralling staircase towards the house.

'Will do,' I replied.

A couple of hours later the sun started to go down. I gathered up our belongings, dried the little ones and told Perly and Harmony to get ready to leave. We climbed the stairs and turned the corner of the street towards the house. As we approached the house we could hear shouting.

'I just can't believe you've kept this from us all these years! After everything we've done for you, you go and keep secrets from us!' Esther's voice was shrill and anxious. 'We knew that woman, we took her out for dinner and welcomed her into our home. And Dik, he put you through this! It's just too much, deary, it's too much!'

As we opened the door Esther fled the room and headed up the stairs.

'What's going on, Ma?' Perly asked.

'They've found out that Harmony is Dik's daughter,' she replied. She was anxious but hadn't lost her usual calm. 'It's hard for them, the fact that we kept secrets. But even harder knowing that Dik had a child with Roz. I think you'd better go home, girls,' Dixey said to Harmony and Emily. 'I don't want to make the situation any worse for them.'

'How'd they find out?' I asked.

'Oh, Roxy, it's obvious. She looks just like your father. Their friend worked it out just by looking at you all.'

For Esther and Peter this discovery was a serious blow to their relationship with Dik. Now, no matter how Dixey tried to explain the situation, no matter how hard she tried to make them believe it was okay, all they could see was the betrayal and the pain their daughter had been put through. And in a way, the same was true for Dixey. The more she voiced the facts, the more obvious it became to her that it really wasn't okay after all. It was simply something she had decided to put up with rather than make a scene, split up the family and face the reality of having a philandering husband. She knew Dik slept with other women, we all knew, she wasn't any happier about it than we were, but she let him, she agreed to keep the peace.

Esther and Peter were upset for the rest of the week and it affected everyone.

'I'm sorry, Dixey,' Esther told us, 'I will not have those girls or their mother in my house ever again.'

On the plane home Rollin raged about how unfair it was that the children were the ones being penalised for our parents' mistakes. I was just glad to be away from the drama of the situation.

Home at the camp, I walked into my wagon to put my bag down and noticed the letter I'd written to Tom sitting on the table. I'd forgotten to send it. I picked it up and went outside. Dik was standing by the fire. He told me he was off to check the horse.

'Post this on your way, will ya?' I asked, passing him the letter. He looked over it and put it in his pocket.

'Will do,' he replied, walking off.

I looked over my garden and checked the goats before going into the barns to practise for my next dance exam. We'd put a full-length mirror on the wall and raised some sheets of plyboard on the floor, I had a cassette player and my shoes were hanging on the wall in the corner of the crumbling old barn.

I walked back into the camp as it was getting dark. As I came closer to Dik and Dixey's caravan I could hear Dik's voice travelling clearly across the darkness.

'Where is she?' he roared. 'Get her in here.'

Somehow I knew that 'she' meant me. What I could have done wrong? I racked my brains. Maybe I should have cooked dinner before I went to practise my dancing? Had I left the fence open when I checked the goats and let the stallion out?

I walked to the door of the caravan like a lamb to slaughter. Dixey was crying. Dik's eyes were blazing. He had the letter I'd written to Tom in his hand.

'What's this all about?' he asked me, shaking it in the air. 'You little slut, no daughter of mine behaves like that. Dropping your knickers for the first man that winks at you.'

'No, it's not like that,' I said, 'I don't drop my knickers for any man.'

'So he's the first?' Dik asked me, his anger rising to a whole new level. 'I'll kill him. You know this is illegal, don't you?' he turned to me.

'I'm sixteen in a few weeks,' I replied. 'It's not like I'm a child any more.'

We'd had a landline connected a few months before and the phone was in Dik and Dixey's caravan. Dik picked up the phone and called Nick. He screamed down the phone at him, told him he was a lousy, child-abusing fucker, and that he was calling the police.

'Get out of my sight,' he said to me. I left shaking as Dik picked up the phone to call the police. I went into the kitchen caravan and found Amelia peeling some potatoes with tears rushing down her face. Her strong jawline looked even more defined than usual as she clenched her teeth, obviously holding back her emotions. Peter always likened us all to the work of a different artist. I was a Matisse, Amelia was the Mona Lisa – she was far more beautiful than the Mona Lisa, but I could see the resemblance now that she looked sad and full of pent-up emotion.

'How could you do that to me, Rox?' she asked, gulping back sobs.

'Do what?'

'Sleep with Nick. Dixey told me you did. Didn't you know I loved him?' Amelia was a gentle and loving person with a fiery temper. She was the last person I wanted to hurt. I was immediately filled with remorse. I tried to explain myself.

'I'm sorry, A,' I said. 'I had no idea.' I didn't think to tell her how drunk I had been, or that I hadn't known what was going on. Instead I started to wash the floor. Keeping busy seemed like a good idea.

'You had no idea? I've been seeing him for weeks! You of all people should have known that.'

Dixey came in. 'So what's going on, girls?' she asked. 'Are you both in love with the same guy?'

'I'm not in love with him. Don't even remember it happening,' I replied.

'Well I am, Roxy,' Amelia said, as she stomped out of the caravan, kicking the door as she left.

The day got worse and worse. Dik tore through the camp in a fury. First he threw Amelia out, saying she was supposed to be helping out with the children not introducing us to men that took advantage of us. Amelia was understandably mortified but left without a fuss. She moved into a squat a few miles away with some of the people we'd got to know through the parties. I didn't see Nick again. I wondered what happened after Dik called the police. Each time I heard a car I ran outside to see if it was them coming to question me.

But it didn't stop me writing it all down to Tom: I sat down and wrote him a new letter telling him the original story plus the outcome of the letter I had written to him.

CHAPTER 12

Spain

The summer after my sixteenth birthday I was performing at a private event with Dixey and the flamenco group. Up on stage I was completely absorbed, lost in the music, the concentration of giving my best – and the heady feeling of receiving applause. This time as my solo dance came to an end I was showered with red roses. They'd come from within the audience, but because of the lights shining in my face I couldn't see who'd thrown them.

We finished the show and were getting ready to leave when a familiar face came out of the crowd.

'Roxy, that was amazing! Well done.'

'Jeni-Wren! Hello, darling.' I was pleased to see her. She hadn't been around much recently. She was going through a divorce so our gardening days had dwindled as she spent more and more time away from the camp. 'Was it you that threw the roses on stage?' I asked.

'Oh no, it wasn't me, Roxy. It was a beautiful man! Oh, Roxy, he's besotted with you, and very handsome.'

'Really?' I replied cautiously. Since my encounter with Nick I'd steered clear of men. We were still trying to pick up the pieces of that disaster. My friendship with Amelia was all but over and I seemed to have broken the trust that had been growing between Dik and me.

'You've met him before, and he says he's in love with you. That's him, over there, dressed up as a matador. You must go and talk to him.'

Jeni-Wren was about twenty years older than me and was like my second mama. She had more chance to chat than Dixey ever did and from the time she arrived at the camp always took the time to notice how I was feeling. She drove a little Citroën Dolly and together we'd go off swimming, chatting about life, love and men all the way. I liked the way Jeni wanted to introduce me to the world: she loved red wine and would buy bottles and give me sips to taste, explaining the different grapes and regions; and she'd travelled everywhere, so when she gave me advice I listened.

I looked through the crowd for the man dressed as a matador. As I scanned the audience he came up behind me with more roses in his hands.

'For you, da da,' he said, dropping to his knees and holding the flowers out in front of him. He was tall and slim, with short, dark ringletty hair and bright blue eyes. He was very striking in his high-waisted trousers and cummerbund.

I'd seen Dom a few times before the night of the performance but I'd never really got to know him. After that night he came around to the camp once or twice and asked to take me out but nothing happened quickly. I was apprehensive about getting involved with anyone and didn't want to increase the tension between Dik and me. Dik was still very upset and often talked of sending me to live with my grandparents in Spain for a while so I didn't go down the wrong path. Every time I went out partying at weekends he would mention it again, hoping that in Nerja I would pour my energies into dancing rather than parties, alcohol and boyfriends.

Dom was charming and utterly adoring, and very persistent but a good eight years older than me. He sneaked into my wagon and left little heart-shaped messages under my pillow and flowers on the counter. I felt so flattered I could hardly tell whether I actually liked him or just the attention.

Dom and I had been dating for a few months before I started feeling ill. I was dancing or working all the hours that God gave me, living on little more than a lettuce leaf a day and barely sleeping. I was still living in a cold, damp wagon with the icicles hanging off the windows. I'd started getting breathless when I danced and I had an ache in my chest that felt like I'd pulled a muscle whenever I exhaled. I ignored the symptoms for a few months and didn't mention it to anybody. Eventually I talked to Dixey. She suggested I take some homeopathic remedies but they made little or no difference.

After a few more months of discomfort I went to the doctor. I'd never been to the surgery before as I'd always been incredibly healthy. He told me I had chronic wet pleurisy. He prescribed antibiotics and lots of rest. He said that at 5 foot 6 inches, weighing 7 stone was dangerously low and that I should take better care of myself. I'd got very thin due to dancing long hours and avoiding food. When I started dancing I was a healthy size but standing in front of the mirrors in tights and leotards had made me self-conscious. Peer pressure also took its toll. I knew I was never going to be like all the other girls with their perfect outfits, smart cars and suited parents but I could at least be slim.

I lay in bed with my lungs aching for the following month. Dom would appear every day to light the fire and shower me with love and adoration. He worked as a thatcher's apprentice, so was up at the crack of dawn each day and rarely finished before nightfall, but he never came around without a handful of gifts and an armful of logs for the stove.

As I recuperated, the conversation about sending me to Nerja started up again. Dik and Dixey thought that some sunshine and a change of scenery would do me good. Although I loved my little wagon, its dampness was affecting my health. And Dik hoped it would get me away from Dom. Even though our relationship was developing slowly, it was still too intense for his liking. So, as I recovered and got back to my old self, they decided that I should go and spend the autumn and winter with my grandparents in Nerja and take classes with the wonderful flamenco teacher Carmen Juan who was well known in the flamenco world.

Esther and Peter were pleased to have me and I was thrilled to be getting away from Dik's glare. My grandparents' house was a lovely airy villa with an open-plan living/dining room and French windows that led on to a bright, walled patio. Esther was a keen gardener and had brought the place to life with her green fingers; the patio was bursting with blooms and scents, Bougainvillea, geraniums and citrus bushes. I slept in the spare room that looked out onto the street, on the other side of the house from Esther and Peter. The first thing I did was to turn off all the heating and open the windows before going for a walk on the beach.

When I returned I found a little red alarm clock, a black wristwatch and a dressing gown lying on my bed, the first sign that the rules in my grandparents' house would be different from the mostly free and easy ways at the camp. What was Esther trying to say?

On my second morning in the house Esther said to me over breakfast, 'Roxy, I thought we'd take a walk up to the language school and get you enrolled in some Spanish classes, then we'll speak to Carmen about your dancing programme.'

Biddably, I followed Esther to the language school in the centre of town, just a short walk from the house. The receptionist spoke to Esther in Spanish before handing me a written test to see which class I should enter. I tried to wriggle out of doing them as my handwriting was so bad, but they insisted. Thankfully most of the questions were multiple choice, so I only had to scrawl my name and address and tick some boxes. I could read as fast as anyone but as far as writing went, my letters to Tom were all the practice I'd had.

It was decided that I should go into Class Two; I'd picked up some Spanish on my previous trips, but needed to concentrate on grammar and fluency. I agreed and then drifted off while Esther sorted out payment.

As we left the building, Esther passed me a piece of paper

with my timetable on it. I stared in disbelief. I was enrolled on classes that ran from 9.30 a.m. until 5.30 p.m. five days a week.

'Um, when will I dance?' I asked.

'Carmen has a class on Saturday morning for two hours. We'll take you there and see what else she recommends,' Esther said firmly. I was silent. I didn't want to seem ungrateful, as I knew the language school must be expensive, but I had hoped to dance with Carmen Juan most days.

'They say you should be fluent in three months if you go to class every day. It will do you good to have some discipline, deary,' Esther continued.

I nodded miserably. I had pictured myself dancing from dawn till dusk with the stars of flamenco, but that dream seemed to be receding.

I attended the language class every day the following week. My fluency was on a level with most of the others but I struggled to make my writing understood and the verb conjugation completely baffled me. The teachers were encouraging but my heart wasn't in it to catch up. I'd never spent any time in a classroom, let alone eight hours a day. I felt constricted, stupid and I longed to dance.

At the beginning of the first week I raised the subject with Esther over dinner.

'Roxy, we are doing our best to help you make something of your life,' she said, looking wounded. 'I would have thought you could be a little more grateful.' Something in her expression made it hard to argue further. She was a powerful character who was rarely challenged, but easily hurt. But later that evening, I tried my grandfather.

'I know, Roxy,' he said. 'But Esther has gone to a great deal of effort to do what's best for you, and these are the very best classes money can buy. Try and see it through, okay?' He poured me a cup of lapsang souchong tea, and rested his soft, manicured hand on top of mine. I looked at my short nails and weathered hands; years of chopping wood, gardening, and cleaning had left their mark. Peter's skin felt soft in comparison, not a callus or blister in sight, his fingers were long and elegant, but the veins and bones were prominent underneath his loose skin. I caught Peter's eye as he turned my hand over in his. Kind, blue eyes, like my mama's.

'Tiny, tiny little hands, like Dixey's but even smaller,' he said, tracing his fingers around the hard bits of skin on my palms as he spoke. 'They don't look like the hands of a sixteen-year-old lady. I mean they're beautiful, but they tell a story.' His voice drifted off as his mind wandered. He was a gentle, wise man, usually of few words.

The following week I went in to school on Monday but rang Dixey as soon as I got home.

'Is everything okay, love?' she asked.

'Well, not really . . .' my voice tailed off tearfully. 'Esther's enrolled me in school and I really don't want to go. I don't want to seem ungrateful, Mama, but I want to dance.'

'Well, Rox, it's always good to have another language. It will come in handy . . .' Dixey began in a sympathetic tone. But even my mother's gentle persuasion couldn't change my mind or my feelings.

After a fortnight I braced myself to tell Esther that I wouldn't – I couldn't – sit in a classroom all day. Esther took a long deep breath, followed by a sigh.

'Well, Roxy,' she said firmly, 'it's all day every day or not at all; you can't do the course part-time. I won't make you go, but I'll lose my deposit.'

I stopped going all together.

Esther's disappointment in me was palpable. Although we sorted out a couple of other dance lessons, I couldn't help feeling that I had let her down, and we struggled to fit into a routine that suited us. Esther was well meaning but strict and stern. She liked cocktails at 4 p.m. and dinner at 6 p.m., and felt that I should be either at school or in the house with them.

As soon as the sun rose, I would escape for a walk on the beach or a run in the park. Esther couldn't understand why I spent so much time on the patio or out of the house. I didn't understand my emotions either but being indoors made me feel suffocated and sick. I missed the outdoor life, I missed my family. I thought about my sisters every day. For the first time in my life, I truly appreciated the bond we had between us. But my health had never been better: the warm air healed my lungs in just a few weeks, no wheezing or rasping. I could breathe freely for the first time in many months.

Then, during my third week in Spain, Dixey called. We chatted about how I was struggling to settle in and then she said, 'Uncle Tony's here, back from Thailand. He's come to earn some money to send back to his family over there. He's got a driving job and plans to stay for six months or so.'

My heart jumped in terror: I'd just got used to him being away. I put the phone down and ran to the bathroom. I sank to the floor and sobbed hopeless tears of despair. Zeta was eight, around the same age that I was when the abuse first started, or at least around the age that I could clearly recall it happening. I thought of Zeta's beautiful, happy little face, her determined nature and her soft, plump young body that was starting to stretch out as she grew. Wanda, just two years older, was svelte and elegant, her once blonde hair was now light brown, with natural highlights of blonde and caramel. She was a dreamy girl who ambled through life without a care in the world. She struggled to focus on particular subjects, but had the most amazing, colourful imagination and sharp wit. They were both fearless and self-assured. Just as Perly and I probably had been once too.

My nightmares returned but this time they were worse. I was scared to fall asleep at night and woke traumatised. It was Wanda and Zeta I worried about most. I hoped he would have lost interest in Perly by now. I knew Perly worked as hard as I did to keep Wanda and Zeta away from him but she wouldn't be able to keep them both safe on her own. I wished that Amelia was still living at the camp; Perly had confided in her just before Dik threw her out. She could have helped keep the girls safe but she was gone, and poor Perly was alone with what we both knew.

I suddenly felt anxious to go home. I looked at my calendar. Essie and her boyfriend, Sam, were due to visit the following weekend. I thought perhaps I'd go home with them. They were staying for five days.

On their last night we went into town and drank copious amounts of tequila, returning late at night. We sat around the dining table trying to keep the noise down. All week I'd been wrestling whether to say something and the strain was obviously showing.

'You okay, Roxy?' Essie asked me, putting her arm around my shoulder. 'You've seemed really tense all week, and we can hear you shouting out in your sleep.'

'It's Uncle Tony,' I replied. 'He's back. What about the little ones?' I burst into tears. 'I'm coming back with you, I have to come back.'

'No, you're not, Roxy, you're here to dance.' Sam was speaking now. 'We'll sort this out, won't we, Essie?' I looked up and saw Essie's usually calm face filled with fear.

'Yes, we'll sort it out, love,' she replied.

They left the next morning. Nothing more was said about it. I didn't know if I should believe them or not. I was aware of what a massive burden I had laid on Essie but I was hopeful that she would do something to protect them. She loved the little ones just as much as I did.

I waited for the phone to ring all the next day, but it didn't. I dreamt about being an orphan; the same dream I used to have as a child. Other nights Dik's angry face waving his finger in my face and shouting at me for being a liar drifted in and out of my dreams. Dik still had a temper, but his moods were less frequent and extreme now. I worried about how the revelations would affect him. He'd be wracked with guilt, that was for certain. But it wasn't his or anybody's fault. Tony had everyone fooled.

Three days later the phone rang. Esther picked it up on her way out of the door.

'Roxy deary, it's Dixey. She wants to talk to you.'

As I took the receiver, Dixey's voice was shaky on the other end of the line.

'Roxy Riddle, oh my Roxy, what have we done to you?'

Sam had told Dik that Tony had been abusing Perly and me for years. Dixey was distraught, crying and apologising over and over for letting me down. She wanted to know details of the abuse. I said it was true but I didn't want to talk about it.

'Just get rid of him,' I pleaded with her.

'Oh we will, don't worry about a thing. I'm going to call the police.'

Calling the police had never occurred to me. We simply didn't call the police, we never had. The police signalled an eviction or a complaint.

'No, I'm not talking to the police, Dixey. Just get rid of him and keep the girls out of his way.' Perly said the same thing. Dixey pleaded with me to discuss what he'd done to us.

'Talk to me, Roxy. Did he hurt you? How long has this been going on? I mean did he rape you? Tell me he didn't.' I didn't want to upset her any more than she already was.

'Don't worry, Ma, I'm OK. I don't want to go into details though.'

A couple of days later, Dixey and the girls came to see me in Spain. She said Dik was going to get rid of Tony while they were away.

'This will destroy your dad,' she said. 'He trusted him like a brother. He would have trusted him with his babies.' She paused and said, 'Well, we did, didn't we? We trusted him with all of you since the day you were born. After Emma, I should have followed my instincts, but it just seemed so unthinkable that anything like this could have been going on right under my nose. I didn't want to believe it, so I didn't let myself.'

I felt an overwhelming sense of love and protectiveness over my father around this time and I think it was mutual. Dixey handed me an envelope shortly after arriving in Spain. Inside was a small scrap of paper and a £20 note. 'I love you darlin X Dik.' I smiled and tucked it safely into my purse.

Over and over again Dixey said that she'd never heard of such a thing happening when she was growing up. That innocence seemed amazing to me, as so many of the girls I'd grown up with had been abused. It almost seemed like it was just part of everybody's lives. I guess the way we were brought up was ideal for people with such tendencies. Lost souls and disillusioned people flocked to our camp – a warm environment without rules, lights or door locks. Open doors and open hearts, we welcomed everyone in.

Dixey and my sisters headed home, and in theory I should have been free to concentrate on my dancing, happy in the knowledge that Tony was nowhere near the camp. But everything had changed since the past had come to light. To this day I don't know the details of Tony's ejection from the camp but I knew from an unspoken atmosphere between Dik and myself that it was dealt with and best not to ask. Knowing Dik's temperament, I could only imagine what might have happened to Tony and I didn't dwell on it.

Despite the fact that Tony was gone, my nightmares continued. I started having panic attacks and struggled to trust people, even someone as adoring as Dom. He came to visit me in Spain, but things weren't the same as they had been at home, I felt strangely detached emotionally, my mind was a million miles away from him. It was the first time I'd ever felt like that, but it wouldn't be the last.

I didn't talk to Esther and Peter about it, or to anybody else for that matter. Perhaps it would have helped if I had. Esther found me more and more incomprehensible. Everything I did made her concerned. If I picked at one of her rich, creamy meals, preferring just some salad or fruit, she became convinced I had an eating disorder. If I headed out of the house for some air they were convinced I was trying to avoid them and took offence.

One day I overheard Esther say on the phone to my mother: 'How could you send me such a sick child, Dixey?' she said, 'I'm sure she's anorexic if not bulimic. She never eats, she spends more time out running than she does in the house. We never see her. I don't know if her problems are physical or emotional, but I just don't think I can do this.'

I'd never been a problem child before, so hearing myself described as one was quite a shock. I tried to be the grand-daughter Esther and Peter wanted. I was helpful and courteous, I cleaned and shopped and tried to fit in, but their world was so different from anything I'd ever known. I didn't know how to make small talk with their friends, or which pieces of cutlery to use in restaurants. My clothes were unacceptable and my eating habits distasteful. Esther had been a dancer, and had hoped that I would learn from her, but I wasn't even the kind of dancer she approved of – I just couldn't seem to fit her vision of how I should be. I called Tristan and Zeal and spent more and more time with them, escaping the fraught atmosphere at the house by spending weekends at their yard up in the mountains. At least I felt I could be myself with them.

Then, about six weeks after arriving in Spain I got back from dance class to find my bags packed on the doorstep. There was no one in the house but a note sitting on top of my luggage:

I think we'll all be happier if you go and stay with your friends in the mountains. Put your key through the letterbox.

I dragged my bags out onto the street and walked towards the nearest phone box. I rooted through my pockets and found a fifty-peseta coin, just about enough to make a phone call. I dialled Tristan's number.

'All right, Rox?' he said as he picked up the phone.

'They've chucked me out, Tristan, I don't know what to do,' I sobbed. I knew things were bad but I didn't think they were that bad. I was supposed to be in Spain for six months but six weeks after arriving I was homeless.

'Wait where you are,' he said. 'I'll come and get you.'

I spent the next four months living in a caravan in the mountains. Tristan and Zeal were busy, building a workshop on the land, laying concrete and practising their circus skills. They were both workaholics, so I didn't see that much of them. They had a kitchen set up outside, so I made myself useful and cooked for them and their friends most days. Life wasn't much different there to back at the camp, just a bit more relaxed.

The yard, as Tristan and Zeal called it, was a few caravans on top of a mountain overlooking the coast of Malaga, about an hour out of Nerja. They'd got the piece of land cheap as it had no access, amenities or planning consent. To reach it you had to drive up a very steep dirt track, which was impassable after heavy rain.

But once up at the yard the views were incredible. I found a piece of plywood to practise on and placed it under a tree looking across the valley. I had a cassette player, the warmth of the sun, the shade of the tree and I danced every day. Sometimes people would come and sit on a rock and watch, other times I wouldn't see a soul for hours. Getting to dance class was difficult as there weren't many buses but I managed to make it twice a week and made real progress under the watchful eye of Carmen Juan. I also slipped into a relationship with a friend of Tristan and Zeal's. He was ten years older than me and not particularly loving or good for my confidence, but I suppose that reflected how I was feeling about myself at that stage.

Not long after, I received a letter from Dom saying that he'd heard I was seeing someone else, that he was devastated and heartbroken and he'd lost all respect for me, but would always love me. I felt bad for hurting Dom and for not getting in touch directly when I'd known since his visit that our relationship was dead in the water. My new relationship was just a fling and soon fizzled out but in many ways I was glad that Dom and I were officially finished. I didn't feel I could begin to tell him what was going on in my head, and we felt so distant it was a relief to give up the pretence.

As ever, the person I communicated with most was Tom, still locked inside his high security prison. Sometimes months would pass without me managing to get a letter in the post to him but I knew that most of his friends had stopped writing by now and that my letters kept him going, so when I didn't get around to it I felt bad. Our friendship was unusual. He'd been inside for four years and we'd now spent more time writing to each other than we had being friends before he went away. Many people thought it was bizarre that I kept in touch but I'm a loyal person and there was no way I was going to stop writing to him. Each time I wrote a letter, no matter if it had been a day or a month since my last communication, he'd always reply immediately. The postman didn't come up the track to the land, so he'd write to me care of the local bar, at the bottom of the hill. He'd tell me how he was keeping himself busy. He studied endless courses and was working out in the gym every day.

One of his letters said:

'A riot broke out in the canteen today, people were throwing trays and chairs at each other. There's a fair many broken bones in here today but I kept out of it, hen. I locked myself inside my cell so I couldn't get involved. I can't spend 17 years in here and if I get involved in pointless fighting that's what will happen. I'll be an old man with a wee zimmer frame and grey hair before they let me out.'

He told me he was due to be moved out of high security and into Grendon, a category B prison, because he was no longer considered to be a risk. If he kept on with the good behaviour he might be seeing daylight in five or six years.

That still sounded like a long time but it was slowly ticking by. After all the years Tom had been gone, I still missed his warm, brotherly hugs and our friendly chats. It felt ironic that the only man I felt I could be myself with was the one locked behind bars.

CHAPTER 13

Restless Twenties

Books were my alternative existence, my window on a world in which I could be the heroine and find the happy ending I craved. Back from Spain, reabsorbed into the cooking and chores of camp life, and back to caring for the old man Brown, they were my escape. No matter how different a character's life was from mine, whether they were hero or underdog, or both, I'd find a way to identify with them. With Tess of *Tess of the d'Urbervilles*, the connection was instant. There was something about the story of the simple farm girl, with aspirations of a life less humdrum than the one she was born into, that spoke to me. She was born into a working-class family, yet with blood and influences from another world; she didn't fit into the culture of her predecessors, nor that of her birth. Tess was sensitive, but taken advantage of at every turn. I even felt like I looked like her, with her eyes 'neither black nor blue nor grey nor violet; rather all these shades together'.

Rollin used to tease me about my marbled eyes, saying 'They're not brown, like mine and Perly's, or blue like Dixey's, they're not green like Essie's . . .'

Dixey, always keen to defend me, would interrupt, 'Roxy's eyes are gold and brown like the stars, with flecks of green from the grass.'

'No, they're not,' Rollin would retort, 'they're shit brown.'

Like Tess I was growing up into 'an almost standard woman' but it sometimes felt like that was all there was to me.

There are those books that are so important to you, you know exactly where you where when you read them. The spring I read *Tess* was the year that Bob, the landlord, decided he was keen for us to move down the runway a little bit closer to the village. He wanted the use of the hangar and the barns that we were living next to. Dik and Dixey weren't happy about the move, as the new site was next door to a chicken farm that stank when the wind blew in our direction, but we didn't exactly have any other option. That hundred yards down the runway was probably the shortest distance we'd ever moved, but we still had to pack everything up – including all beaten-up old vehicles, wagons to repair and scrap metal to weigh that Dik and Rollin had gathered since we'd moved to the area. We started preparing all the vehicles first, slowly loading things onto the flat-bed and cart.

We moved the first few caravans the day after my eighteenth birthday. Since returning from Spain I no longer lived in the little wooden wagon. We still owned it, but after my illness Dik thought it was too cold for anyone to sleep in, so he was slowly doing it up. Instead I had a small caravan all of my own. It had a toilet and shower room at one end but like most gypsies we never had toilets and showers in our caravans, so instead I put up a rail and used the area to hold the collection of dance costumes I'd been gathering over the past ten years. Hanging side-by-side, the dresses were a rainbow of colours and materials wrapping around each other. Underneath the dresses I kept a wooden box containing all my important papers: the six exam certificates, my driving licence, passport and awards from competitions. Looking at the documents and costumes I was filled with a feeling of pride and completion. I had something to show for my life, and it wasn't a teenage pregnancy.

My caravan hadn't been at the camp long, so its tyres were inflated and ready to go. We moved that down the runway first, followed by Dik's caravan. Dik and Dixey had a caravan they slept in together, but Dik had another one that he kept all his stuff in. He's always been a bit of a hoarder and Dixey didn't like his clutter around her, so they kept it in a separate place. Our friends John and Esta were staying at the time and they camped their bus next to my little caravan.

On exploring the new area we discovered that it had a number of fruit trees growing on it, apples and pears mostly. There was a large area of concrete and a lot more shelter than the camp we'd moved from. If it hadn't been for the chicken factory, it would have been ideal. The smell of the chickens wafted over, filling the air with a sickly, putrid smell. The barns where they were housed were clearly visible, just 20 metres from our camp.

I went back to my caravan. The sun was going down quickly. 'We'll move the rest in the morning!' Dik shouted over.

I went inside and looked for a candle. The generator was still at the old camp along with all the rest of the family. I couldn't find a light to ignite the candle so went outside to see if Dik was still around. He wasn't in sight. I could just get into bed and not worry about the light I thought, but it was early and I was eager to finish *Tess*. I had just one chapter left.

I knocked on the door of John and Esta's bus.

'Have you got a light?' I asked, passing Esta my candle. She lit it and gave it back to me. I sheltered the flame under my shawl and went back into my caravan. I put the candle in its holder and snuggled under the covers with the novel. My heart was filled with warmth as Angel and Tess hid from the police in their final week of freedom, glad that Hardy was providing a happy ending for me. Beside me the candle seemed to be dancing in the light breeze that came down from the skylight. The flame flickered and nearly went out, before springing three inches in the air. The bright light startled me out of my daydreams and back to the pages of my book. The tears were streaming down my cheeks as Tess awakens to see the police surrounding them and tells Angel that she is 'almost glad' because 'now I shall not live for you to despise me'. She is taken away to be executed. Hardy couldn't give me a happy ending after all. But I still believed they existed.

I'd heard nothing of Tony since he'd been thrown out of the camp a year or two before, nor did we talk about the abuse. Nobody mentioned it. Not even Perly and I. We didn't want to dwell on it. Sometimes I'd hear Dixey crying in despair but she didn't say anything to me and neither did Dik. I imagined Tony was probably back in Thailand with his new family. I'd come across the pictures of the little Thai children while tidying the kitchen. Their bright, happy faces filled me with guilt. All we'd done was send him off to uproot a different family on the other side of the world.

The nightmares still came, sometimes I thought they were getting less frequent, and then they'd start again, worse than before. I was going through a bad patch at that time and was scared to fall asleep. I put down the book and watched the flame flicker and dance. Then I got up and decided to go for a walk. I was wearing just a T-shirt so I wrapped a warm towel around my waist and headed out into the evening. The sky was clear with a thousand stars sparkling away. After all the years of living in Norfolk, the skies still never failed to amaze me. Enormous, open skies.

As I walked back through the apple trees, I saw a blue light coming from Dik's caravan. He was sitting up watching television. He'd plugged the small portable TV into the car battery and was watching the news. I went inside and sat down next to him.

'You all right, love?' he asked.

'Can't sleep,' I replied. I leant on his shoulder and thought about the ending of *Tess*. I'd felt a closeness to Dik in recent months. I was no longer scared of him, which seemed to help our relationship. Sometimes he was warm towards me, and slowly the pain of being his scapegoat was healing. I was still needy for the attention of other men though. I did all I could to be noticed and appreciated, constantly running around after people, cooking and cleaning, making tea and doing favours at every opportunity.

I stayed in Dik's caravan for an hour or so watching telly with him before we heard some distant shouting. It sounded like John's voice.

'Fire!' he screamed. We ran from the caravan.

As we rounded the corner towards my caravan, we were greeted by a raging inferno. John was running around in the dark naked, desperately gathering buckets of water to douse the flames licking out of every window.

'Roxy! No, Roxy! Somebody help me get her out!' he shouted across the camp.

'John, John, It's okay, I'm here,' I said, emerging from the trees. He dropped to his knees like he'd seen a ghost.

Esta came over and hugged me. 'We thought you were in there sleeping,' she said in her sing-song Dublin accent.

'No, I was watching a film with Dik,' I replied, looking at my caravan in disbelief.

John suddenly shouted, 'Oh feck, the gas bottles!'

Three gas bottles strapped to the back of his bus were just a few feet away from the blaze.

'They're gonna go up,' Dik said running over to help John get the bus out of the way. They struggled to get the engine to start, so we all pushed it out of the reach of the fire.

Esta put her hand on the bottles. 'They're very hot, we were lucky this time.'

Yes we were lucky, I thought. Perhaps I did have that lucky star guiding me after all. If I'd dozed off it wouldn't just be my possessions disappearing in a puff of smoke. The fire was too far gone for us to put it out, so we stood and watched it burn, there was nothing else we could do. As the front wall of the caravan came crashing down we saw the flames devour the dresses that I'd carefully re-hung that very morning.

The caravan burnt for most of the night. I stayed to watch it. I didn't have that many possessions before the fire, now I had nothing. I watched every single thing I owned go up in a puff of smoke. The feeling of luck was replaced with emotions of loss, sadness and despair as I sat on the ground wrapped in my towel. The heavy cotton towel was warm and comforting. Dulcie had given it to me for my birthday. Now it was the only thing I owned in the world. By the time dawn came the fire was dying out.

Dik hugged me tight, and said, 'Don't worry, love, it's just stuff. Material things are replaceable.' I knew he was right.

The next few days went by in a blur. I had to get my passport replaced so I could enter my exams, I had to borrow costumes and clothes and with nowhere to sleep I dossed with friends in a squat. But the feeling of existing without a single possession in the world was strangely liberating. I felt like I could go anywhere and do anything, and there wasn't a single thing tying me down. I was surprised to find that I actually needed nothing to survive. I still had my family, which was all that really mattered.

The following winter I fell in love for the first time. Rob was a tall, handsome man from the area who I met through his sister Anya, a friend of Dom's. He was gorgeous, strong and athletic with ash blonde hair and blue eyes, and from the moment we met we just clicked. I thought Rob was my destiny and I imagined that we would have children and grow old together. Rob wasn't very open emotionally but that suited me fine, as there were many things I didn't feel a desire to express at that time, and I loved his laid-back nature.

Before meeting Rob, I had been saving up to go to Jerez de la Frontera, the heart of flamenco music and dance in Andalucia, and despite our falling in love, six months later I stuck to my plan and moved to Jerez for the winter. I danced all day every day with some amazingly talented people and I felt like I was truly following my dreams. But I also felt a deep sense of loss leaving Rob behind and I struggled to settle in. I knew a couple of girls from the dance school but I always felt like an outsider. As usual, I hated living in a house, and would fall asleep on the bench under the lemon trees and the stars on the patio. The man who rented me the apartment thought I was some kind of drunk who never quite made it to my bed. He'd wake me up in the morning shaking me and telling me that I was going to catch a cold and I should go inside now.

I completed two dance level exams while I was in Spain and was thrilled to get better marks than most of the other girls in the school, many of whom were Spanish and had been dancing all their lives.

The teacher was forever shouting at them for getting things wrong and exclaiming in despair, 'Look Roxy can do it. She is Irish. Why is the Irish girl doing it better than the Spanish?'

I didn't tell anyone about my upbringing or my family. But then I never did. Apart from the people that I met at the camp or through the family, nobody I met knew where I had come from. Not because I was ashamed of my upbringing but because I knew that most people would struggle to understand it and judge me before they knew me. It was just easier to keep my private life private.

That winter I missed Rob beyond belief. For once I was all alone: no family, no grandparents, no Tristan and Zeal, no Rob – and I was horribly homesick. Three months later I gave up on my Jerez dream and returned to Norfolk, Rob moved into my caravan in Thorpe Abbotts and we made a home together. Rob worked in IT when we first got together but had a knack of being able to pick things up extremely easily, so he changed careers on a regular basis. I got a job working in a nursing home and continued to dance on weekends and during the summer months.

I still went on tour with the flamenco troupe, performing all over England and Ireland and even Amsterdam. Our shows were becoming quite a family affair: Dixey and I had been joined by Zeta and Wanda who were both starting to get quite good. They also played their violins for some of the songs, and Perly and Rollin were learning the guitar, so between us we almost had a full show. When we were offered a gig on the Dutch island of Terschelling – a serious and well-paid event needing an experienced six- to eight-piece performance group – and Steve Homes, our regular guitarist, and Liz Lee couldn't free up a month to come, we put the troupe together ourselves. We hired a new guitarist we'd started working with, a flamenco singer and a clarinet player, and started to make travel plans. As the gig approached, Dik decided to hell with it, we'd take the horse lorry, kit it out as a camper and all go. So that's what we did: just like the old days we packed everything we needed into the back of the lorry, and off we went, with the guitarist, clarinet player and singer and even Rob on board.

I'd never seen Dik in a foreign country before – he'd always made his trips to India alone – but he embraced the experience, particularly being on the road again. He drove the lorry, Rollin and Dixey usually sat up front beside him, while the rest of us sat on the benches, beds or floor in the back. There was a lot of singing and music being played in the truck while we made our way across the waters to the Netherlands. Once on the mainland we took another short ferry ride to the island. Terschelling was beautiful: wide sandy beaches and dunes as far as the eye could see. When we were presented with hotel keys and details of a chauffeur service that we could use to ferry us about, we parked the lorry a short distance from the hotel and gave the musicians the hotel rooms, as we Freemans were used to sleeping rough. We stayed on the island for a week, performing two or three times each day to an incredibly receptive audience. The mood was fun and light-hearted: we were getting paid but also enjoyed free meals in some wonderful restaurants courtesy of the event organisers.

We made for home feeling joyous and relaxed. Dik liked driving at night, so we snuggled down in the back of the truck as we headed for the ferry. Dixey stayed awake and sat beside him. I could hear them chatting in the dark through the thin sliding door that separated the cab from the rear of the truck; it was like being a small child again.

As we dozed off, the truck lurched to one side and I heard Dixey's shrill voice, 'You're going the wrong way.'

'That was close,' came Dik's untroubled reply. I crept down and peeped through the door as Dik manoeuvred the large vehicle onto the other side of the road and down a different road. 'Don't worry, Rox, we just went the wrong way around the roundabout and headed up the wrong road.' Dixey was smiling and unconcerned.

After a while Dik pulled over by the side of the road and

crawled into the back to sleep. The next day we set off again, but before too long a red light lit up on the dashboard.

'We've sprung a leak, water's pissing out all over the road and the truck is overheating,' Rollin announced. It was a Sunday afternoon, so we couldn't get the necessary part for the lorry, so Freeman family ingenuity was required again.

'Lucky we brought the water churns. Give us a hand,' said Dik. We moved the churns as close to the cab of the truck as possible, before passing a long hosepipe out the window to Dik. He positioned the hosepipe so it fed straight into the leaking radiator and secured it tightly with one of Dixey's stockings. For the rest of the journey we took turns pouring water from the churn into a funnel we'd made from a plastic bottle, the water then trickled down the pipe and into the engine, keeping it cool. Most of the water came straight out and landed on the road underneath us, but using this method we crossed the Netherlands, over the sea and safely back to the camp.

Perhaps because my mother had settled down with Dik so young, I somehow thought it was in my DNA. My siblings were all pairing up. Rollin had started going out with Rob's sister Anya, and from the start they seemed set for life. Rollin is a quiet man, extremely loyal and calm, to his family and to his woman. I think he'd found Dik's philandering ways off-putting: he was a one-woman man, as faithful as my dad was roving, who went straight from living at home with all his sisters and family to a stable relationship with Anya. Essie and Sam were married and had their first child on the way.

Two years rolled by, steady and smooth. Rob and I had a nice caravan, worked hard and got on incredibly well. Everyone at the camp loved him, and he seemed to slot right in. I enjoyed cooking for him and looking after him and in return he loved and adored me. I'd been changing nappies and looking after children for much of my life and have a naturally maternal nature; babies seemed like the logical next step. But I was restless. We spent time at Rob's family's cottage in the South of France and holidayed in India together, but it wasn't enough. There was something inside me that was only really happy and relaxed when I was on the move with the unknown adventures of the open road before us. So, in 1999 we decided to save up and go travelling. The following autumn we got working holiday visas and boarded a plane to Australia.

We arrived in Sydney just before Christmas in 1999, watched the fireworks fly over the harbour bridge for the millennium new year and spent six months living in the city. Rob got work with an IT company and I did nannying and danced flamenco in bars. But it wasn't long before I was getting itchy feet again and started agitating to move on, so we saved enough money to buy a van. We drove the depth and width of Australia over the next six months. I loved travelling, I loved driving and I loved being on the road.

We had a campervan with a skylight that stretched the entire length of the roof. I fashioned a mosquito cover out of a piece of net and we slept in the van, under the stars, with the warm breeze blowing on our bodies. We were living in bubble, just us, the road and the skies. We did farm work as we travelled, staying just long enough to fill the fuel tank and stock up on supplies.

Rob was a Norfolk boy, who'd spent his whole life in Diss and always knew the time would come to head back to jobs and a stable life, but I dreaded it coming to an end.

I did a lot of soul-searching that year. I found that driving calmed my mind and put me in a hypnotic kind of state where I subconsciously analysed my life. I had got to a point where everything was going well. Tony was gone, I had a great relationship and a talent but I was far from content. There was an unexplained restlessness burning inside me. I continued to plough through books, and I wrote to Tom religiously on every step of my various journeys, but apart from the written word my brain had very little stimulation. I'd look at job advertisements and wonder where my life was taking me. I had no qualifications. All those dancing certificates and dresses that had gone up in flames now seemed meaningless: apart from dancing I could do precisely nothing. Yet I also knew I wanted more than coming home to raise a family. I wasn't ready for that. Travelling satisfied my thirst for adventure and constant change, but I feared that a part of me would always be discontented if I didn't find a more rooted way of channelling my energy.

But I wasn't quite ready to face real life. When I called Essie during my final week in Australia I told her I wanted to come home for a while, see everyone and then go to South America to learn to dance the salsa.

'What are you running away from, Roxy?' she said. 'How are you going to build a life for yourself if you never settle down?'

I told her I didn't want to settle down and that travelling was all I needed from life. Essie has a stronger personality than me, stronger emotions and stronger aims but she has always had such different aspirations. She and Sam had married shortly after Rob and I met and Essie had got pregnant almost immediately. She told me they were thinking of moving to Ireland so they could get on the property ladder. She wanted a career, a house and children with an education. She has always felt held back by her lack of education and was adamant that she would give her children everything she hadn't had. Essie said that if we were born into the life Dixey was, our opportunities would be endless. 'Rollin would be an engineer, I'd be a famous fashion designer, and you, Roxy, you'd be a goodwill ambassador or a human rights activist. Imagine the lives we could have had if we'd had a proper education,' she enthused.

I thought back to my childhood days when a house seemed like the most coveted thing in the world, all my fantasies of cobbled streets and a settled home. What had happened that had made that fantasy seem like the most boring thing on earth? Perhaps Essie was right. Maybe I was just running away. At age twenty-one I had spent more of adult life on the move than I had at home. I spent my life planning where I wanted to go but when I got there I was already thinking of moving on.

CHAPTER 14

Educating Roxy

While I was away, I was surprised by what I missed. I missed greenery, the fresh air and birdsong, the open skies. I missed my siblings of course; sitting around the fire joking with them, our card games and big meals, their light-hearted ways. And most surprising of all, I missed the camp, the sense of community and camaraderie. I even missed cooking for everyone! We arrived back to open arms and warm smiles from my family, but also a degree of chaos and sadness. On our way home Grandpa Peter had passed away so Dixey and Dik were in America with Esther and her family. They were burying Peter in a few days' time. I didn't have the money to get a flight to America for the funeral but I felt a big loss and deep sadness on hearing that my calm, kind grandfather was no longer breathing the same air as me.

Only a year had passed, but things had moved on at the camp. Zeta seemed to have changed from a child to beautiful young woman in the time we'd been away. She was at secondary school and despite a bit of bullying and teething problems was doing really well academically. Rollin and Anya were living together at the camp and expecting their first child. Perly was at art school in Norwich and had a boyfriend she seemed very fond of.

'Where's Wandy?' I asked, looking around.

'Anya left her at the launderette this morning and we haven't seen her since,' Perly told me, worried. 'We think she might have run away.'

I'd spoken to Wanda a few times while I was in Australia and I knew she wasn't happy at the camp, so it didn't seem out of the question. She and Dik had fallen out over a boy, Rom, who Wanda was smitten with. Dik thought he was a lazy, good-for-nothing so-and-so and had banned Wanda from seeing him. Wanda was completely besotted and pined for him day and night.

'She asked me to take her to the launderette to do her washing. She had a big bag, but I presumed it was her laundry. When I went back to get her she wasn't there,' Anya said. 'What are Dik and Dixey gonna think? They're coming home tomorrow and Wanda's disappeared.'

But a couple of hours later Anya got a message from Wanda. 'Don't worry I'm fine. On the train to Bristol, I'm going to live with Rom. Sorry.'

It wasn't only my siblings' relationships that had developed at Thorpe Abbotts. Electricity and mains water had been connected – so no more generators thumping away or churns to fill – and Dik and Rollin had built a sectional wooden building on the land. It housed a kitchen and day room as well as a bathroom. When Dik and Dixey got home the following day, the first thing

Dixey did was to lead me into the small kitchen and, opening a door off it, reveal her pride and joy: a small room, clad from floor to ceiling in wooden panels, with a long metal bath, like an old-fashioned house bath, and a sink.

'Look, Roxy, I have a bath. I can't believe it, after thirty years, I have a bath.' She clapped her hands together in delight.

It was lovely to see my family again but something had happened before we left Sydney that was playing on my mind. I turned it over and over in my head, trying to make sense of it.

Two nights before our flight home we had organised to go out for some drinks with Dulcie, who moved to Sydney just as we were leaving. We met in a bar in Newtown and spotted Dulcie in the corner with Pat, her on—off boyfriend, and a couple of other people.

'This is Noel,' she said signalling to a man in the corner, as we approached. 'Pat lives with him.'

Noel was older than us, probably in his late forties, with greasy, lank hair and pock-marked skin that gave him an unattractive look. As he said 'Gday' he came up too close to me, breathing down the back of my neck, and when I jumped back in surprise he joked, 'Gees, I say, you could kill a man with your stare.' Something about him made me instantly uneasy.

Later, as I went to the bar to get a drink, I felt someone press up against me from behind.

'You're a right little beauty, I'm gonna screw you,' said a voice close in my ear.

'Get lost!' I said, swinging around. It was Noel. I glared and moved away from him, my blood boiling with irritation.

I got the drinks and went and sat between Rob and Dulcie. 'I don't like that guy at all, he's a sleazebag,' I told them. Rob's eyes glazed over.

'Just relax, Rox, don't be so judgemental.'

'I don't really know him, I think he's all right,' Dulcie said.

We had another drink and moved to a cocktail bar around the corner. I downed a shot of tequila and browsed the cocktail list. Noel approached with a tray of drinks.

'All right, ladies, who's first?' He put the tray on the table. Eight drinks lined up side by side.

'What are they?' I enquired.

'Secret love potion, might help you relax a bit,' Noel said, winking at me.

I eyed the bright blue shots suspiciously, before picking one up and downing it. It was surprisingly nice, a kind of aniseedy taste. Everyone else swallowed their drinks. Two were left on the tray.

'You and me, honey.' Noel put the drink in my hand. I felt myself relax, the alcohol was taking effect. Perhaps Noel wasn't so bad after all.

Then my head started to spin, the heat was getting to me. I got up to go outside for some air and my legs turned to jelly underneath me. I grabbed Dulcie's arm and walked out into the street.

'I feel really wasted. We've only had four or five drinks, what's going on?' I asked her. She giggled and slid to ground beside me. A couple of seconds later Noel emerged from the bar.

'That's our cab!' he shouted, putting his arm out to stop the taxi from driving away. I looked around to find Rob, Pat and he stumbling out of the bar arm-in-arm. I tried to pick Dulcie up off the pavement, and get her in the taxi.

'Let me help you,' Noel said, as he lifted her from the ground. He's very sober, I remember thinking, what's happened to the rest of us?

Hours later – I have no idea how many – I woke to a crack of light peeking through the blind. Where was I? I tried to lift my head, but I couldn't move. I could hear a low buzzing in the background, but couldn't work out what it was or where it was coming from. A figure moved across the room and into my line of vision: Noel, stark naked, dancing around the bed with something in his hand. He came towards me, a broad smile spread across his face, with what I realised was an armful of sex toys. I had to get out of there.

I felt a dull ache between my legs and my head throbbed as I attempted to move for the second time. As I fell off the bed and onto the floor I realised I had no clothes on. My vision slowly cleared up, but my head was foggy and sore. I found my dress discarded on the floor and pulled it over my head. Noel was in the corner of the room assembling his toys as I crawled to the door and out into the corridor. There was a door on my left. I pushed it open, relieved to find it was a bathroom. Once safely inside I locked the door and splashed water onto my face.

'Roxy. Roxy, you in there?' Noel was tapping on the door and whispering. Why was he whispering? Where were we? What had happened after we left the bar?

I looked out of the bathroom window. I recognised the street. Thank God we were still in Sydney. Noel was still knocking on the door, trying to coax me out. I sat on the floor and tried to make sense of events. Where was Rob? And what on earth had I done? I was filled with remorse, though I didn't know what for. After a while the knocking stopped. The flat was silent. I opened the door of the bathroom and let myself out. I was glad to see Noel passed out on the bed.

I gathered the rest of my clothes before finding the front door. I gave it a shove and was shocked to find Rob lying outside the flat on the landing. His foot was blocking the doorway.

'Wake up, Rob, wake up.' I shook him but he didn't stir. Eventually he opened his eyes, looking woozy and confused. 'Wake up, we've got to go,' I urged him. My head was still spinning and my legs were struggling to steady me. There was no way I could get him down the stairs to leave the building. I got Rob by the scruff of his neck and dragged him back into the flat. There was a room on the right hand side with no one in it. I steered Rob towards it. Once inside I pushed a mattress up against the door and fell onto it. Rob wrapped his arms around me and kissed me on the forehead. I hugged him tight and let out a sigh of relief as we both fell into a deep sleep.

Now I went over the events in my head time and time again. I couldn't believe I had gone to bed with obnoxious Noel, an ugly old man. But I had woken up naked on his bed and the day after discovered that I was bruised and injured and I didn't have an explanation. I avoided any personal contact with Rob until the injuries healed, but even then it felt weird to have him touch me. I wanted to talk to him about it but I didn't know what to say and I was worried about how he would react.

Sitting in the kitchen building a couple of days after getting home, the phone rang. It was Dulcie.

'Hi, Roxy, how are you?' She sounded distant and quiet. We chatted for a while, talked about what her plans were, where she was working and what she'd been doing. When Rob and I had woken in the morning we'd found Dulcie in the kitchen making coffee but no signs of Noel. Dulcie couldn't remember anything after the blue tequila. 'Don't understand how we got drunk so quick,' she'd said, confused.

'Pat still renting a room from Noel?' I asked now. There was a long silence.

'Um, yeah, um, I wanted to talk to you about him,' she said, her voice shaking. 'Roxy, do you think he raped you? Well, I think he did. That night when we lost our memories. He's been bragging about it to some of the guys. Apparently he brings different girls back every weekend. He drugs them.'

I wasn't surprised by what I was hearing. In some way I felt relieved to finally have answers, and that I hadn't acted out of character and voluntarily gone to bed with a sleazy creep. We chatted for a while about the night in the bar. With the blue 'love potions' he'd drugged all of us, so he could take me to his room and rape me, with all my friends wiped out around me.

I felt pretty shocked by the implications of what had happened. The idea of Noel doing that to me, while Rob lay unconscious on the landing sickened me but more than anything I was worried about what he'd given me. I'd been worried about pregnancy but if he was doing this to different people every weekend, I could have no end of diseases.

A few days later I called the sexual health clinic in Norwich and went for a full health check. The doctor asked me the reason for my visit.

When I told her what had happened, she looked at me sympa-
thetically and said, 'It's not unusual, more and more people are
getting date-raped every day.'

She told me about a drug called Rohypnol. Originally prescribed
for sleeping problems, a small amount seemed to heighten your
sexual experience, a little more and you'd still respond but would
lose your inhibitions and have no memory of the events. If you
were given a large dose you'd be completely wiped out, like Rob
was. Rohypnol was completely odourless and tasteless, so chemists
had started adding a blue dye to the pill to make it easier for people
to know if it had been added to their drink.

I'd never heard of date-rape, or drug-rape but the pieces of
the puzzle were slowly coming together.

'The next few weeks could be hard, Roxy,' the doctor said
gently, 'you might get flashbacks from that night, some people
have the events slowly come back over time. Look, here's my
number. We can offer you some free counselling.' She gave me
her card. 'Call me if it all gets too much, will you?' The test
results would take ten days.

I felt emotionally and physically numb as I left the clinic and
got in my car to drive home. That night when Rob got home
from work I sat down and slowly explained what had happened,
tears trickling down my face. I apologised, still wracked with
guilt for betraying him, even if it wasn't conscious.

Rob barely spoke. I couldn't tell if he was angry or upset – he
didn't say anything. After a while he reached out and rubbed the
tears off my cheeks, then stood up and walked towards the door.

'I'm sorry for letting you down, Rox. I should have protected
you.'

He went outside and walked up and down in the field. We didn't talk about it further. I was confused by his response but like all the other strange things that life had dealt me, it was buried away, never to be mentioned again.

But just as the doctor had predicted, the following week I started getting flashbacks. The whole night didn't come back to me, but parts of it did. She told me that the drug usually lasted for four to six hours. The idea of Noel using my body like a toy for all that time made me shudder with disgust. I took out the card with the doctor's number and considered counselling but I didn't really have any faith that it would help. So, once again, I decided to keep quiet and keep busy.

That feeling I'd had in Australia, of not having any other talent but dance, had stayed with me. I didn't know what I wanted to be, or what I could achieve, but I wanted to study. Maybe getting an education, a qualification, would ground me and fill the void that I felt whenever I stayed still.

Without discussing it with anyone, I went to Suffolk College and asked about the courses available. At twenty-two years old I was considered a 'mature student' and they recommended an access course. I'd been working in care roles, among other things, since the age of fourteen and got a lot of pleasure from brightening people's days and helping out those in need, so I decided to enrol on an access to health and social science course. I filled in the forms and delivered them to the college a few days later.

Apparently my academic record (or lack of one) made me a high drop-out risk. So, in order to convince them of my abilities, I had to complete what they called a planning period, before I was accepted on the course – two weeks, three assignments and 5000 words of written work. I could understand what they wanted me to do, but I had no idea how to do it.

My handwriting was an abomination and I'd never typed or used a word processor in my life. But Dik picked up a cheap computer from a friend, plugged it in the corner of the kitchen, and I muddled my way through. I can still feel my burning embarrassment when the course teacher handed our 3000 word essays on 'Why I Want to Go into Education' round the class for comment.

'I can't make out what's going on with this paper at all,' said the girl with my paper in her hand.

Nonetheless, I started the course a couple of months later. The course tutor warned me that she didn't think I was up to it, but she couldn't refuse to give me a place on the grounds that I was likely to fail.

'You really should think about GCSEs, Miss Freeman,' she said. 'This course is really very intense, it's not aimed at people with no academic experience whatsoever.' But her dismissive manner and lack of encouragement simply sparked the stubborn side of my personality into life.

The first three months of the access course were some of the hardest months of my life. I was determined to complete the course but, as much as I hated to admit it, I was out of my depth. I stopped work so I could concentrate on it but I still didn't seem to have enough hours to do everything that was expected of me. I enjoyed the classes, but spent most of the time jotting down notes, words and phrases that I didn't understand, and cribbing knowledge I should have had from GCSE textbooks.

The teachers presumed that the students had all studied basic history, biology, maths and various other subjects, which of course I hadn't.

The biology tutor said we were starting at the beginning by talking about mitosis and meiosis but I didn't even know what a cell or an atom was. The research tutor would throw in phrases like: 'Shortly after the end of the Second World War', or 'during the Battle of Hastings era'. I didn't know what an era was, let alone all about 1066. I studied late into the night; I read from the minute I opened my eyes until I could no longer keep them open.

I was relieved to be put in a tutor group that was guided by a warm lady named Gill Lowe. Gill was enthusiastic and encouraging, and never let me doubt my abilities, or myself, by never doubting them herself.

'You're a very bright girl, Roxy. Of course you can do this,' she said whenever I waivered or wobbled. I was used to receiving praise from Dixey and some family members but to get it from a tutor for my academic progress was a completely new experience.

I had received the results from the sexual health clinic and breathed a sigh of relief when they were all negative. Unfortunately my relationship hadn't emerged so scot-free. Rob and I seemed to be growing apart with every passing day. Things had always been so easy between us that we'd kind of floated through the past five years without ever hitting any real problems, but now we were home, with our adventures behind us and me at college, we drifted in different directions. The rape and our inability to talk about it didn't help matters. Up until this point it had suited me quite well not to have to delve into my experiences, but there's only so long that you can carry on without talking.

Mostly the rape struck me as bad luck, but I wondered how at twenty-two years old, I had attracted quite so much unwanted attention from the sexually depraved men of the world. I seemed to have been a magnet for paedophiles and creeps: a pretty, tactile little girl, who craved attention and love from the men around me. They couldn't have hoped for an easier target.

How Rob felt about it I guess I'll never know. He was kind and loving towards me most of the time, but he didn't give much away. It made me feel vulnerable emotionally. I'd told him bits and pieces of my past, always hoping that we could be open and honest with each other, but he just responded with a hug, or a change of subject, so many things went unspoken. He got on well with my family, had a drink and a laugh with Rollin and Dik, was close to Perly and the girls and friendly towards Dixey. He had an open, friendly demeanour and everyone adored him but I didn't feel that I knew him any better than the rest of my family did.

I recall one evening in the kitchen when Dixey, Wanda and I were cooking a curry feast to celebrate Perly's birthday, when we got to chatting about Rob.

'How's things with you, my petal?' Dixey asked.

'Things are good,' I replied, thinking she was talking about college.

'And Rob? Is he kind to you? He is a sweet man.'

'Oh Rob's lovely,' piped up Wanda, 'he's so sweet and kind.'

'He is, Wandy, definitely sweet and kind,' Dixey said. 'He always has a smile on his face and those lovely bright eyes. But, I don't know if it's just me but I never seem to get anything more than that from him. He's always fine, and don't get me wrong he's always friendly, but he gives very little away, and that worries me. I hope he's a bit more expressive with my Roxy Riddle.'

Dixey seemed to have forgotten that Wanda and I were there as she chatted away in her caring way, not wanting a response or an answer, just expressing her observations, half to us and half to herself. But I knew she was right: Rob was no more expressive with me than he was with the local shopkeeper.

Outwardly I was getting on with my life, but the rape, like those years with Tony and Yamir, did have an impact on how I felt about the world and the people around me. I felt a degree of self-loathing, and had little respect for myself, but the main problem was I just felt somehow numb and emotionless. I wasn't introverted or angry, I just couldn't connect with the people around me, including Rob.

I took to shopping. I didn't have the money but banks were giving out loans like peanuts to monkeys at that time, and I was spending them quicker than they could issue them. During the year of the access course I became extremely in debt. My caravan was lined wall-to-wall with shoes – beautiful, elegant, impractical heels I'd have to take off and exchange for my wellies the minute I reached the camp. I'd spend my lunch breaks browsing and shopping for things I'd never had, things I didn't need. I bought expensive kitchen equipment, new baking trays and coffee pots and of course books, piles and piles of books.

And I stopped dancing. Since starting college I'd barely danced a step. I missed it desperately but with each day that went by that I didn't dance, it seemed too hard to get back into. The flashbacks and nightmares gradually receded, to be replaced by vivid dreams of dancing, performing and horse riding. I didn't do these things in my life, but I did them in my dreams.

I kept thinking of what Essie had said when I called her from Australia: 'What are you running away from, Roxy?' When I phoned Essie in Ireland to see how they were doing she was pleased that I was studying and I felt a warm flow of approval from my big sister, but I didn't feel like I'd stopped running. In my mind I was still on the move, but now instead of physically moving, I was fleeing into books. The harder life felt, the more I read.

I worked and worked and completed all the work for the course. I didn't get good marks every time but when I didn't Gill would tell me what I needed to do in order to improve my grade. I'd go home and follow her instructions religiously, so that by the end of the year I passed each and every unit with top marks.

But my relationship with Rob was the casualty. More and more it just seemed like we were going through the motions of life without really feeling any of it, and finally I called it a day. At first, leaving Rob was scarily easy. I felt very little emotion. But Rob was devastated; it was the most upset I'd ever seen him.

One of the things he said to me in those days stuck in my mind: 'You're so closed, Roxy, it's impossible to be close to you. Must be all that crap from your past, it's fucked you up.'

I think a part of me hoped that leaving Rob would fire my feelings back into action, but it didn't. He moved out and I still felt nothing.

Looking back, that year was a strange phase in my life. I had kick-started my brain for the first time ever, but studying had become my whole life. I somehow managed to suppress all of my emotions with study. I felt frozen from the inside out. I saw a few men over the year, but I only connected with them physically, never emotionally. Sometimes I felt like I was going through life as two separate entities, a physical person, and an emotional soul. The soul was looking down at the physical being but could never quite get back in synch with it.

One night, about eight months after Rob and I split up, I lay in bed and thought about the various episodes of abuse and pain I had been through. I realised that each and every one of those events was a physical attack on my body. But that my soul was untouched. Deep inside I was still the same fortunate, happy, and in many ways, privileged person. I decided to stop letting my subconscious mind guide me through life and to consciously accept that the events of the past were all part of my growing and developing. I had to carry on the rest of my life in the same body and mind. From now on I wanted them to work together.

CHAPTER 15

Calling Time

As the year 2002 came to a close, I slowly started to reconnect with the world. Finishing my studies filled me with a sense of achievement. I had a new-found confidence, not just as a pretty face and a dancing girl, but as a person who had been to college and had certificates to prove it. That one year of study somehow made me feel more accepted as part of society. I was no longer terrified of filling in an application form or questionnaire. I had something to put in the boxes that asked for academic background, even if it was just one course. I felt full of potential for the future, and applied to various universities to study physiotherapy.

I was in a good and positive place and no demon from the past was going to wreck it. Dik and Dixey, however, were still suffering from the revelations about Tony Bird.

I heard Mum crying, 'We really let them down, Dik. It makes me sick that he's still out there, probably ruining other people's lives.'

But I didn't think for one minute he had ruined my life. I felt, and still feel, eternally blessed to have the family I was born into. The experiences I have weathered have made me who I am. There were dark days, when I was full of guilt and extremely upset, but I harboured no hatred or anger towards Tony and felt no desire to punish him. But for Dik and Dixey it was different. They had worked together to bring us up in a happy, open and free environment but they had for many years welcomed and nurtured a person who was quietly infiltrating their brood. They wanted vengeance or at least closure. And yet for me, the idea of going to the police just seemed too big a venture to embark on. It was all so long ago, so unspoken and so distressing. I was just glad that he was out of our lives and didn't want to open that confusing chapter ever again.

As I started to defrost, the emotions I'd expected to feel after splitting up with Rob came tumbling in on me. Rob and I had stayed in touch – we couldn't not: his sister Anya, Rollin's wife, had a second daughter, Zanna, shortly after we split up. Our families were entwined. Rob came around to the camp from time to time and sometimes I saw him in town or at a party. Neither of us had got involved with anyone else and gradually I realised that I missed what we'd shared when times were good. It had been true love, a feeling of completeness when we were together. I felt that, with the course out of the way and my regaining a bit of my old confidence, maybe we could go back to how it had been during those first blissful years of our relationship.

So we gave it another go. The first few months were hard. I felt like Rob was punishing me for hurting him and leaving him in the first place. But I'd never stopped loving him and I thought he felt the same. He was still quite cold at times but I trusted that somewhere deep inside was the warm person I'd fallen in love with and decided that I could deal with the cold shoulders and lack of communication as long as we were together. I believed that little by little things would go back to how they had been. I was never going to be the fresh-faced eighteen-year-old he fell in love with. We were never going to travel the world without a care or responsibility again. I thought of the warm nights under the Australian sky and the feeling of completeness that I felt when our love was young and felt deeply nostalgic, but the romantic in me believed we could repair anything – that all we needed was love.

I persevered with my applications but, despite my good grades from college, I wasn't getting a positive response from universities. I was confident that if only I could get to an interview, and show them my determination and spirit, they might give me a place. But one by one, each and every university rejected my application. They gave different reasons or none at all. 'Get work experience and reapply.' 'Lack of knowledge in the field of science.' 'High number of applications, competition was high.'

I wasn't really surprised. I'd spent one year in a classroom in my life so it seemed too good to be true to be able to go straight into university and three years later have a career. Never one to give up easily, I got a job on the physio ward at the Norfolk and Norwich Hospital, went back to college to study A level chemistry and applied again the next year, hoping that more qualifications and work experience would make the difference.

Rob and I moved in together once more, trying with each

day to make it work. We bought a wooden building from a friend – it was basically a large garden shed – and installed it at the camp, gradually turning it into a beautiful home. My family were all around us: Rollin and Anya lived in a mobile home with their two daughters. In fact, Rollin was extending their home as number three was on her way. He'd built a workshop and set up in business as a mechanic.

Tanya, Dik's daughter from before he met Dixey, popped in and out of our lives. Sometimes we wouldn't see her for months or even years, but when we did she had a unique way of always fitting right in. Her bond with Dik was strong from the outset, despite the little amount of time they'd spent together. They spoke the same, looked the same and had the same interests. She had a long-term partner, and two daughters, who, like her, had no qualms with the way we lived. Tanya had another life; one we knew nothing about, another sister, another family, a 'normal' house and a job. But whenever the opportunity arose her and her little family would roll up with their caravan, set up camp and instantly become part of our clan.

Wanda had spent two years in Bristol with Rom, got pregnant, and had a beautiful little daughter named Josie. Then when her relationship failed to stand the test of time, she'd left him and come back to the camp with Josie, who was then just a few months old. I was pleased to have another baby around the place and did all I could to help her out with being a mum at such a young age. Perly was living at the camp with her boyfriend Ben and running a cafe in Diss. I helped her out in my spare time too, baking cakes and working at weekends. Apart from Essie, none of us had left home. Or if we had, we'd returned.

If anything, it was not us kids that were unsettled that year, it was Dik and Dixey. Dik was finding it increasingly difficult to breed horses in the UK, land prices were rising every year and horse prices were dropping. Dik felt like his livelihood was slipping away from him. And although the nest was far from empty, Dixey was for the first time free of child-rearing. Even Zeta, the baby of the family, was at college working towards her A levels. She had finished school with straight As and was looking into studying architecture at university. As the only two without a family to care for, Zeta and I were as thick as thieves in those years, never far from each other's side. She was bright and intelligent, with a keen academic mind.

That spring Dik and Dixey went to visit Uncle Bob and his family in Ireland and came back talking about a piece of land they wanted to buy. It was twelve acres of well-drained meadows and fields in Tipperary, with a run-down cottage and the remains of a second building on it. At first we thought their talk of going back to Ireland was a whim but it seemed they were serious. Dixey spoke to Esther and arranged for her to release some of her inheritance in advance to help finance the purchase. After all their years of struggle to secure a legal home in the UK, I thought it was strange they were going back to live in a field in Tipperary.

'Can't get us to go, so you're leaving home, are you?' Rollin quipped. But with no brood of children to be responsible for at last, Dik and Dixey seemed genuinely happy to be starting something new.

Shortly after Rob and I moved into the wooden building at the camp I fell pregnant. The news hit me with surprise and filled me with confusion. I'd always dreamed of the day that I would find out I was pregnant – the delight in my partner's eyes as I happily announced the news; the euphoric feeling as we planned to bring a new life into the world. I'd got pregnant once before, when Rob and I were trying to work out if we wanted to get back together or not, and it had all seemed too quick and unplanned so I had gone to the clinic and took a pill that brought on a miscarriage. I'd sworn to myself that I'd never put myself through that again.

Now I wasn't sure what Rob's reaction would be, or how I felt about it myself. When we were in our own little world, inside our wooden house surrounded by nature, we were back in our old bubble. We spent nights together, our bodies entangled as if they were one, but when the daylight broke, so did our passion. I'd wake in his arms, and feel a deep contentment.

'Morning, darling, I love you,' I'd whisper in his ear. But he never replied. In leaving Rob, I'd broken his trust: the man I now lived with refused to join in any talk of love or devotion. We didn't speak about our future together and he got irritated if I tried to tell him my feelings.

'It's all a load of crap, Roxy, what does love mean?' he'd ask me, annoyed that I'd uttered the words.

I waited for Rob to get home from work.

'I'm pregnant, Rob,' I announced as he walked through the door.

'You're what?' A look of distress spread across his face. 'How far gone are you?'

I knew he was trying to work out if it was too late for an abortion.

'Not far, just a few weeks. What shall we do?'

'Dunno.' He looked at me blankly.

'What do you want me to do?' I asked him, hoping for some discussion on the subject.

'You're a strong-minded girl, you'll decide what to do,' he replied, leaving the room. He didn't come back until late into the night and didn't mention it when he did. I called my doctor the next morning to book an abortion.

More than a decade after he'd been put away, Tom was finally coming to the end of his sentence. When he'd gone to prison I was a thirteen-year-old girl, now I was a full-grown woman. I'd visited him just twice and hadn't seen him in five years, but I'd written to him for eleven solid years: I still considered him to be my closest ally in life. The day his letter arrived telling me that he was allowed out for the day, I jumped with joy. He was in an open prison and would be slowly re-adapting to society outside of the prison walls. I arranged to meet him on his next day release, in central London.

I got the train to London and walked to Camden. We arranged to meet outside the tube station. It was a wet and windy day. I loitered under the railway bridge to wait for him. I pictured his cheeky smile and bright blue eyes in my mind; I wondered if the years would have taken their toll on his ginger hair.

I took *The Kite Runner* by Khaled Hosseini and was just immersing myself in the unknown world of the boy from Kabul when a familiar voice jolted me out of the book.

'Roxy, hello, hen.' There was Tom, emerging from the tube, grinning from ear to ear. His skin was even paler than I remembered and his ginger hair had dulled slightly, but apart from that he was the same sparkly eyed person I remembered.

We hugged for many minutes before wandering through Camden hand-in-hand for the rest of the afternoon. We'd written to each other continuously but somehow still seemed to have so much to catch up on as we walked, laughing and chatting. The rain started to beat down with vengeance so we took shelter in a small picture house, eating popcorn and giggling like naughty children on a sleepover. The day flew past and it wasn't long before Tom was getting his train back to his prison cell, but with just a few more months until he was released for good.

Dik and Dixey had been in Ireland for a couple of months. Despite trying to embrace a bold new phase in their lives, they had moved over gradually, as if in denial that they were actually going. I hadn't even managed to make it over to see them when Dixey announced she was coming back.

'I've had enough, love,' she told me. 'I can't do it any more.' Dixey said that without the hustle and bustle of the camp, without the children and grandchildren to keep them busy, there was just them – she and Dik, a caravan and a bunch of horses. 'I feel like I'm going back in time, not forwards.'

She came back to the camp shortly afterwards and announced that they were getting a divorce. The news hit us all quite hard. We knew she and Dik had been struggling but none of us knew it was that bad. After all they'd been through, it seemed unbelievable that they could be splitting up at this point in their lives. Dik and Dixey had been our only constant influence; they were the bedrock of our family. I'd long got over wishing they would separate as I had as a child, in fact I'd got to a point where their solidarity and permanence was a benchmark of how people can get through the toughest times and make it work.

They still loved one another, I was sure of that.

'Why are you divorcing, Ma?' I asked her when she returned.

'It's time I focused on myself, love,' Dixey replied, sadly. 'Time I worked through what's happened over the past thirty-five years.' She said she needed time on her own to process everything – the lost babies, the infidelities, the betrayal of her best friend, the revelations that Perly and I had sprung on her about Tony, all the lies and deceit. She seemed overwhelmed by the weight of the past, by the mistakes she had made. It broke my heart to see my mother, who had loved us all so unconditionally, so filled with remorse about her own life.

For me and my brother and sisters, it felt like the heart of our family was being torn in half. Our parents' marriage had been the certainty in our lives. But it brought us even closer as siblings, and there was the next generation to focus on. I was still involved in the upbringing of Wanda's little girl, Josie, and had a great relationship with Rollin and Anya's kids. I was grateful for all that family warmth around me and the amazing sense of community that the camp setting offered.

When I spoke to Dik in Ireland, he sounded low, lower than I'd ever heard him. He'd been softening with age, his warm, caring side was outweighing his sharp, angry side, and Dixey leaving was a blow that left me worried about his mental state. At some points, when he sounded really down, I feared what he might do. He'd brought nine children into the world who were now all grown-up and starting families and careers of their own and I'm sure he felt a little lost. Frida had come calling not long after Mum left, thinking it was her time in the sun at last, but Dik sent her away, so now he was all alone on the bog. I took to calling him at every opportunity, so he didn't feel lonely, so he felt needed and loved. We spoke more on the phone over those months than we had in my whole life, not about anything deep or painful, just about life, family and people, and we found a new closeness.

After many months of waiting, my replies from the universities started to arrive. The first two universities sent me a straight rejection; the third one interviewed me, but said I needed to strengthen my academic experience before I could handle the course. Only my first choice, the University of East Anglia, offered me a place – but not for the course I wanted to do. I turned it down and waited for clearing but when the time came, not a single physiotherapy place became available.

I was back to square one. I thought about travelling and spoke to Rob about going away for a while but he wasn't keen. I think going travelling with me would have been too much of a commitment and he was still punishing me for leaving him three years before.

It wasn't all bad; I'd started having doubts about whether physiotherapy was the right route for me. After nearly ten years in caring roles I had got to the point where the long hours and many thankless patients outweighed the rewarding feeling of helping that I'd originally relished. Instead, a comment from my old tutor, Gill Lowe, that I had 'real talent for researching and writing' made me realise that I wanted to keep studying. It was a compliment that had a deep and lasting effect on my plans and my future.

I decided to apply to the Open University, feeling it was better to keep working as I studied to avoid increasing my already scary debts and enrolled on a course that would lead to an honours degree in European Studies. It included politics, history and governance of the European Union. Quite a U-turn from my caring courses, but I liked the sound of the course description and was eager to know more about the place I had grown up in. So I sent off my application and before I knew it I was working my way through the first modules.

Meanwhile I got a job working for an organic produce company as a wholesale delivery driver and stallholder. My cooking experience and skills also came in handy as I took on seasonal work for various catering companies. I did baking and cooking, as well as general kitchen assistant work. Cooking was something that I enjoyed and could do with my eyes shut but it was never something I considered doing as a long-term career.

One day I'd finished work and was sitting on the grass outside the wooden house studying, when Dixey came to sit next to me. She no longer lived with us in the camp – when she came back from Ireland she said that, as much as she loved to be around us all, she needed her own, warm space where she could paint, relax and think in peace, so she rented a house close by. The camp still bore her mark though – her hanging baskets and flowerbeds were there, if a little overgrown; every vehicle, wagon and cupboard is covered with her scrolling. Our family home was still her family home but I guess she needed a retreat.

As Dixey sat down beside me, I could tell she had something she wanted to say but she didn't come straight out with it. Instead, she talked about Tony for a while. How she felt like someone had come into her life and destroyed all the care and love she'd ploughed into her family. How the thoughts of it haunted her in her sleeping hours as well as throughout the day. How she felt like she'd let us down in the worst way possible. She'd told me on many occasions that she couldn't rest while he was still merrily living his life.

Finally she said, 'We've got to do something about him, Roxy. I called ChildLine and told them everything I knew. I just needed advice, needed to talk about it, and for someone to tell me what to do. They advised me to call the police and have him tracked down, so I did.'

'You called the police?' I looked at her in disbelief.

'Yes, I called the police. But they said they couldn't do anything, not with my statements. Apparently I'm not one of his victims, so I can't take him to court. How can I not be one of his victims? I certainly feel like I am.' I wasn't surprised by her revelation. It had been brewing for a while.

'I spoke to Perly,' Mum went on, 'she didn't say much, just went quiet. But I think if someone got the ball rolling she'd do what she has to do.' Mum was looking at me pointedly. 'I'm just so frustrated that I can't do anything, I should be able to punish him for what he's done to my little girls, what he's done to this family.'

I could tell Mum wanted a response, but I didn't feel ready to give one.

Instead I put my arm around her shoulders. 'We'll sort something out, Ma, don't worry,' I said.

'You're amazing, my Roxy Riddle, amazingly strong. I don't know how you do it, you seem to take it all in your stride, no hang-ups or issues. Always warm and kind. It gives me great strength knowing that you are okay, after all that he put you through.'

She asked for details of the abuse, like she had many times in the past. I'd worked through it all in my mind time after time, I could have told her step-by-step what had happened in the back of that van, but I didn't think that would make her feel any better.

Later though, I thought about what Dixey had said. I thought about the actions of Tony, trying to work out how it had affected my life. I didn't feel like a victim. When I thought about Tony, I was filled with an odd emotion of fondness and love. I didn't feel the anger that I felt I should. So I thought about my family, about my mother's weary face, my father's sad voice. I thought about Perly: she'd met a man and was expecting their first child, she was a kind and loving soul, but she wasn't the free spirit that I'd known as a child. He'd affected her for sure. I knew that on some level he'd affected me too, I was just lucky to have a thick skin and a positive disposition. For the first time, I felt growing up under Dik's critical eye might have been good for me: it had meant I'd learnt from a very young age to find happiness in myself, in my soul and in my own world, and that in its way had protected me from Tony. Time had passed and although the memories became clearer not hazier, as a person I was stronger and more able to deal with them now. Talking to the police didn't feel as out of the question as it once had.

A few days passed. One morning I headed off to work as usual. I reversed the van into the warehouse and loaded the pile of boxes and produce into the back. It was early, just 7 a.m. and no one else was at the yard yet. I had big day ahead of me, a number of drop-offs and collections. Once the van was full, I set off across Norfolk to do my first drop, and by 1 p.m. I was in Suffolk. I unloaded the remaining produce from the van, and reversed over to where a mountain of potato sacks waited to be loaded. It was a warm day and by the time I'd loaded the van I was dripping with sweat and desperate for a drink. I pulled into the local garage and bought a bottle of water. I sat down by the side of the road to drink it. As I did so, I took my mobile phone from my pocket and called Dik in Ireland. We hadn't spoken for a while. I told him about my conversation with Dixey. He didn't sound surprised and didn't say much.

'I guess it is time to do something about it, isn't it?' I said, unsure of what reply I wanted.

'Yes, love,' said Dik, 'it's time.'

We'd never spoken about the abuse, but he had a tender, sad tone in his voice. It gave me all the motivation I needed to make my next move.

I got back in the van and drove back towards the yard. The van handled better with a heavy load. I loved the feeling of being in charge of such a large, powerful vehicle. I wound down the windows and turned up the stereo. I sped across East Anglia, with Elvis singing 'A Devil in Disguise' blasting out of the CD player. I steered the van off the main road and parked in the car park outside Waitrose. The sign outside the building next door read 'Norfolk Constabulary'.

Men in suits and uniformed officers streamed in and out of the building. I looked down at my scruffy trousers and dirty hands and kicked my boots against the tyres of the van in an attempt to free some of potato dust clinging to me. Then I walked up to the reception.

'Hi there,' I said to the man at the desk. 'I'd like to report a man for child abuse.'

CHAPTER 16

Justice Nearly Served

The immaculately uniformed policeman looked at me bemused. I wasn't sure if this was due to the fact that I was covered in mud or because I definitely wasn't a child.

'Okay, miss, come this way.' He ushered me into a small room, and told me to wait for an officer to come and talk to me. I told him in brief about the events that had taken place many years before.

'I am now ready to see justice served,' I confidently announced.

'Unfortunately it's not going to be easy,' said the police officer. 'This is what we call a historical abuse case; I have to tell you that the chances of a conviction are very slight.' I told him I was aware that the time frame hadn't helped but that my memories were clear. The police officer took a few notes and said he would send a detective to my home address within the next few days.

'I don't need anyone to come to my home. I can do it all

now,' I said quickly. The idea of inviting a policeman into our home felt extremely strange, almost unthinkable.

'It's not that simple, miss. We will have to assign someone to the case before we can continue any further.'

'Fine. Well, can you call me when someone has been assigned? Maybe I can come back then?' He agreed to call me and let me know. I shook his hand and said goodbye.

I continued with my day, driving back to the yard, unloading the van and filling in any necessary paperwork. I then jumped into the seat of my car and headed home. I was driving a beaten-up old Mercedes 190. It was cream-coloured with blacked out windows and low suspension. The car was made in 1983, so was just a few years younger than me. But for a twenty-three-year-old vehicle she was a pleasure to drive. Rollin had picked it up for me for just £300, a bargain at twice the price.

When I got back to the camp I told Perly where I'd been. She shook her head and looked at the floor. 'Police coming here, are they? Don't think that's a good idea.'

'Well, I'll see what he says when he calls back, but if they come here, you can talk to them too.'

She shook her head again. 'Well, I don't know, I'm pregnant, aren't I? Depends on when it's going to happen and stuff.'

The next day I received a call from a Detective Sergeant Bloomfield who told me that he had been assigned the case. He hoped to visit me within the next few days so I could discuss it, and if I wanted to proceed, make an official statement. I was still unsure about him coming to the camp. There was no particular reason for them not to come, but the idea didn't sit easily with me. I told Rollin and anyone else who was around that a policeman might be coming to take statements from whoever would talk to him. Nobody seemed particularly comfortable with it, but equally they didn't have a reason to actively object. I wondered if the police would take me less seriously because I lived on a gypsy camp and not in a conventional home.

When Rob got home, I told him about going to the police and how a detective would be coming round in a day or two. After all these years he didn't know much about what had happened with Tony, but he knew enough to realise this was a big step for me, and gave me a hug. His strong, athletic body made me feel safe and secure for the moment that he held me, but things weren't any better between us. Nearly four years after we'd got back together we still had major communication problems. I didn't doubt the love we felt for each other but I'd been counting the days since we'd got back together, the days that went by without him telling me he loved me. The first night we spent together after the ten-month separation he had declared undying love, but since that day, 1450 days had passed. My logical mind knew they were just three little words, but to me they had turned into something much bigger. As time drifted by, his warmth towards me never really returned. Slowly I had begun to put less effort into trying to make things good again; instead I sought refuge in work, study and my friends.

Detective Gary Bloomfield and a colleague arrived at the camp one damp Saturday morning. I made them tea and chattered nervously about everything and anything, avoiding the subject that I should have been discussing for as long as possible.

'So, Roxy, let's talk about your memories then, shall we?'

Gary said finally. He was settled on the sofa with his cup of tea and a notepad. His colleague sat on the armchair next to him. I knew I couldn't avoid the topic any longer. I walked over and sat on the floor in front of them. I've always felt more relaxed and comfortable sitting cross-legged on the floor than upright in a chair.

Over the next couple of hours I told two complete strangers, from totally different backgrounds to mine, about the experiences and emotions I had endured at the hands of Anthony Bird. I'd never verbalised them before, and was worried that I wouldn't express myself clearly. The feeling of trying to turn memories into words was surreal and far more difficult than I'd imagined it would be.

When I came to the end, Gary said to me, 'I have two questions, Roxy. Why do you want to do this? And why now?'

I told him that I wanted my parents to be able to sleep at night, that I wanted Perly to be freed from her shackles and that I wanted to protect the little Thai children from his grip.

I was surprised by Gary's response. I thought I'd given a good and well-thought-out reply so I was taken aback when he said, 'You can't put yourself through this for other people, Roxy. It's too much to go through to benefit other people only.'

I told him that I didn't have a deep personal desire to punish Tony, but that my family meant the world to me and if I could give anyone of them some release it was worth going through.

Gary had big, soft, brown eyes, with a sad look to them – probably from all the rough stuff he'd had to hear through the years of his career. I was glad he had such kind eyes. It made me feel calm and relaxed in his company. I knew from the moment he walked through the door that I could trust him and that he would do his best to see justice served. He asked for details about Tony, where he might be living and what he did. I told him to call Dik in Ireland, who might know more or less where he was in the world. When we'd finished talking I went and got Perly so she could talk to him. I was quite surprised and relieved that she agreed so readily.

Before he left, I gave him some names and details of other girls and people he might want to speak to in the course of his investigations. He told us that we had a long journey ahead of us. That it would probably be at least a year before we saw any real progress. He would gather evidence over the following months and then he would try to track Tony down to get his statement. Only then would he present the information to the legal team to find out if we had enough to go ahead with a court case. He repeated the warning that the officer at the police station had given me the previous week: 'Historical abuse cases such as this very rarely lead to a prosecution.'

The months passed. I got the odd update from Gary on his progress, but apart from going into the station to sign my statement, I had little involvement or control over the investigation. Gary spoke to three or four different girls, some gave statements, others didn't but they'd all had similar experiences to Perly and me. Tony had abused most of the girls many years before and in different countries, so their statements could only be used as character evidence. Nobody came forward in the UK. Apparently Tony had focused his attention solely on Perly and me in recent years.

After a few months of investigating possible victims, Gary said he was now concentrating his efforts on finding Tony. He'd been to the various addresses in Kent that Dik had suggested, but he was nowhere to be seen. Rumour had it that he was in Thailand.

'Don't worry, Roxy, I'll get him. As soon as he swipes his passport to return to England I will be alerted. It's just a matter of time.'

I was nearing the end of my studies, with less than a year to go before graduation. My life had changed so much since I started my OU degree. With no time to dance, I'd put on weight and lost my confidence in performing. I was working fifty hours a week between two different jobs and studying evenings and weekends. I got up at 5 a.m. and to bed at midnight every night for that entire year. I was running on empty physically and emotionally. My only aim was to get my precious degree. But for what? To prove myself? But to whom? My dad? My family? Rob? Myself or the world? A degree seemed like a formal recognition of my intelligence, a formal acceptance into society. But with no plan for when it ended, I was running out of motivation. I counted the days until I reached the finishing post.

Rob and I still lived together but spent less and less time with each other. I went out with my friends and visited people abroad, a pile of study in tow; he worked long hours and then went to the pub. Some days I'd make the effort to cook a nice meal, but he'd rarely come home to eat it. It wasn't that we hadn't noticed we were drifting apart, we'd even talked of splitting up, but the task of separating seemed just as hard as rescuing our fated relationship. Then one day he announced that he was leaving. He said that he couldn't offer me what I wanted and that he could never go back to how things had been in the past. He found my friendships with other men difficult to deal with; he didn't trust me, and he wanted out. I had many male friends, most of the people I was close to apart from my sisters were men, but Rob had never been jealous in the past and I'd never cheated on him. I just liked male company.

I was sad to hear the words coming from his lips but I knew that our relationship was stagnant and, as much as it hurt to admit it, I wanted out as much as he did. I didn't understand some of the things he said that day, most of his explanations were drowned in my sobs of despair about failing in the face of love. I realised why the novelists of the world found it so hard to write a happy ending: happy endings were rarer in real life than they were in literature.

One thing Rob said struck a chord and made me aware of the way he felt I conducted my life.

'You say you want me to declare my love to you, Roxy. But if I did, it wouldn't be enough for you. You don't want my love; you want the love and adoration of every man you meet, everywhere you go and everyone that sees you. Well, you already have that. I can't compete with them.'

I looked into his tearful eyes, admired his strong handsome features. He was the most handsome man I had ever met. He said he could never give me what I wanted, so it was better we parted. He was right, I have always wanted the love and affection of the men I meet, but I didn't want to love them all back. He was my one and only true love, my future, my destiny. Our relationship had consumed me and there was nothing I wanted more than to rewind the clock to the days when it was easy again. But like him, I knew only too well that our end was fated.

He got a trunk and put it in the middle of our home. Each day over the next couple of months he added one or two items to the box. Every day I'd pray that he'd change his mind, or that he'd fill it and leave. But the torture of existing in limbo continued. Some days the trunk looked nearly full and I thought he must be ready to go, but then the next day he would take things out of it again, throwing my mind back into doubt.

Eventually he did leave; he filled the trunk when I was in Ireland for a mass family get-together – everyone but Dixey, which still felt all wrong – for Dik's birthday. I came back to find him and the trunk gone. But he still kept coming back; late at night he'd appear in my bed. During those nights of morose, sweaty confusion, he'd utter the words I'd longed to hear for so very long. But he'd disappear before dawn broke, before the meaning became real or required any kind of action.

I called Dik shortly after Rob moved out.

'He's gone, Dad. Rob's gone, we've split up.' I told him Rob's parting words. I wanted to be reassured that I didn't need to compete for other men's love any more, because I had the love of my father. Dik's reply was gruff and uncomforting.

'Get him back, he's a good man and good men are hard to find. Get him back or you'll regret it forever. You're not going to get any better than him, Roxy.'

His tone was judgemental and critical. It immediately threw me into a state. I felt tears rolling down my cheeks and was tempted to put the phone down.

Instead I took a deep breath and replied, 'Don't say that to me,

Dik. I know he's a good man, but I was unhappy and so was he. We tried, God only knows we tried, for the past nine years but we weren't happy. And there's no point in flogging a dead horse.'

Dik's voice was still tough as he talked to me about what a poor guy Rob was, ending up with me.

'Poor lad, I bet you've put him through hell and back,' he said.

Dik always found a way of taking the man's side when there was any upheaval; he did it half in jest, and half as a way to avoid showing any real emotion. Again I wanted to hang up but I knew if I did it would be another thing that I regretted, another thing that went unspoken. So I told Dik to stop misguiding his affections and offer me the support I needed.

'He's not a poor lad, Dad. We are both going through a hard time. But I'm your daughter and I need your support and love to help me get through the next few months.' I paused. 'I need it to help me get through the rest of my life, so stop telling me that I'm making a mistake and be a real dad to me for a change.'

He was silent on the end of the phone. When his reply finally came, his voice had softened.

'You do what you've gotta do, love. You know where I am if you need me.'

He told me to be strong and to keep him updated on the progress of the trial. I agreed and hung up, relieved to have expressed my thoughts for once in my life.

Then, one day, the call from Gary Bloomfield came.

'I've got him. He flew into Heathrow early this morning. I drove up and arrested him as he came into the country. I've been interviewing him most of the day.'

'Oh right, okay. What did he say?' I hoped he'd confessed it all and we could avoid a court case.

'He denied everything, said you'd made it all up. But that's what we'd expect.'

Gary told me they were setting a date for court. It wouldn't be long to wait. Gary applied to have him remanded in custody, but the judge deemed that he wasn't a big enough risk to society and should be released on bail, until the court date was set for September 2007.

The day of being called to bare our pasts to a room full of strangers sped towards us all too quickly. On the morning of the hearing, we arrived at court and were ushered into a small, stuffy room. The temperature and lack of windows didn't help with the already panicky tension that was rising through my body. I hadn't seen Tony for thirteen years and I didn't know how seeing him after such a long time was going to feel. I couldn't shift the uncomfortable feeling of guilt that was hanging over me. It didn't matter how logically it made sense to punish a paedophile for his actions, the idea just didn't sit well in my soul. A few minutes after arriving, a woman came in to talk to us. She warned us that we might not get the verdict we were hoping for and she reeled off statistics on abuse convictions. They were very low. The historical element didn't help matters, she said. Before she left the room, she gave us contact details for the victim support officer, in case we wanted to undergo therapy after the case came to a close.

Shortly after she left, Gary Bloomfield entered the room. It was nice to see a friendly face, but he had none of his usual calm demeanour. Perhaps the pressure was affecting him too.

'I have some news,' he announced in a sombre tone. 'Bird is not here. He turned up at the police station in Kent to sign according to his bail conditions a few days ago but since then he hasn't been seen. He missed one of his appointments and hasn't turned up at court this morning.'

Perly and I had been psyching ourselves up to face him for weeks. We had never considered the idea that he might not actually turn up, that this might not be the day of reckoning. It hit us like a body blow.

'So what happens now?' Perly asked.

'Well, if he isn't here within the next half an hour, which I doubt he will be, then we will proceed with the case in his absence.'

Perly looked at the clock. I could feel her anxiety increasing, and she had already been tense when I'd picked her up earlier that morning. She'd left her critically ill baby son, Logan, with her boyfriend, Ben, for the day. Logan was six months old and had been born with a rare bone condition. He had spent much of his life in and out of hospital and that very morning had been fitted with a tracheostomy tube to aid his breathing. He still has it now, four years later, and they are rebuilding his windpipe. With the birth of Perly's little boy, I was now the proud aunty to fourteen children – eleven girls and three boys.

We waited patiently for ten o'clock. At five minutes past, Gary reappeared.

'As we expected, Bird hasn't shown up at court this morning. There is now a warrant out for his arrest. He has skipped bail and failed to appear at court. Hopefully by the end of the week that's not all he'll be guilty of.' He told us that we would be called to give evidence shortly.

Perly was called in first.

'Wanna come in with me, Rox?' she asked as she stood up. I sat near the door of the courtroom and listened to my little sister give her evidence. Dixey stayed outside in the foyer waiting, looking at the floor. It wasn't that she couldn't face it; more that we agreed it would be easier for us if our parents weren't in the courtroom. I looked at the twelve faces opposite me, the jury who would be judging the honesty of our statements and influencing the fate of one old man, if he was ever seen again.

Perly spoke slowly and calmly. She talked of years of abuse at the hands of Tony Bird, similar experiences to mine but they somehow sounded more real, more serious coming from someone else's mouth. Hearing her say the words made my blood boil with anger that someone could do such things to my little sister and anger that I had failed to protect her for so many years. The jury looked serious and thoughtful as she spoke. Tears trickled down the faces of one or two, as Perly's voice quivered near the end of her statement.

'Basically he abused me a few times every week for years. I can't give details of every time, it would take weeks.'

We left the courtroom and went back to our small stuffy space.

'I need some air,' I said, standing up to leave the room. But as I walked towards the door the usher came to get me.

'The court would like to hear your evidence now, Miss Freeman.'

I took a deep breath and re-entered the room. I was even more aware of the sea of faces than I had been when Perly was speaking – not just the jury, but the two legal teams, the judge, even a few members of the press, all staring at me. The heat was unbearable as I entered the witness box. I felt my head spinning and my vision blurred. I tried to focus on the wall to steady myself but had somehow lost my vision. I sat on the bench and put my head in my hands.

'Please stand, Miss Freeman.' The judge spoke sternly; he was seated just a few feet away from me, and his voice shook me back into my senses. I stood up and apologised to the room. I looked around for a friendly face. I focused on Gary Bloomfield. He was standing in the row with the legal team. He gave me a warm smile and a nod.

The next hour passed in a blur. The barrister asked me to tell the court my memories of the abuse. I tried to go into as much detail as I could, but my nerves and the heat made me rush through my evidence. I was desperate to get out of the court-room. Thankfully the defence team weren't particularly rigorous in their cross-examination, as their client wasn't there to direct them. I looked at the empty dock and was filled with a sense of failure.

Arriving back at the camp, we found Dik and Essie waiting for us. They'd stayed at home while we were giving our evidence to make it easier for us to speak openly. The case was in court for a few more days, with various people giving evidence. I attended on a couple of occasions but mostly tried to concentrate on work and study. On the final day of the hearing we were all summoned to hear the judge summarise the week's events and for the jury to reach their decision.

I sat on the benches next to Perly, Dik and Dixey as the judge detailed everything that had been said. I saw the jury stare at Dik; I was aware of his pain and discomfort as the court absorbed his appearance. At sixty, Dik still had a head of thick dark hair which he wore twisted into a topknot. His previously slim figure was now that of a comfortable elderly gentleman, his round tummy stretching the smart shirt he wore under his black suit. The judge discussed the errors of judgement he'd made letting Tony Bird infiltrate his family, his failure to protect us. By the end of the day I'm sure I wasn't the only person that felt like Dik was the one being judged. In the absence of the real criminal the members of the court needed somebody to blame. Unfortunately for Dik, he seemed to get the brunt of it that day.

As we came out of the courtroom we ran into Emma, all grown-up but still recognisable, and hopeful of seeing justice done at last.

'You!' she yelled when she saw Dik, and launched herself at him in a flail of fists, 'You told them I was a bloody liar! All these years I've lived with what that man did to me and you told them I was bloody lying!' Her family pulled her off him, but I could see Dik was shaken.

We went for coffee with Gary and waited for the jury to reach a decision. The day had a surreal feel. It seemed almost pointless to be going through the motions when there was no one there to sentence at the end of it. Dik and Dixey both looked like rabbits caught in the headlights, startled and speechless. After what seemed like eternity, but I'm told was less than an hour, the voice came over the speakers.

'Will all members in the case of Bird, please return to Courtroom Two, where the case is commencing.'

We made our way back to the courtroom. Barely a word was spoken amongst our party. It was like we were all under a spell of silence as we took our seats, again opposite the jury.

'Have the jury reached a unanimous decision on all counts?' the judge addressed the jury.

'Yes, we have,' said the representative.

'How does the jury find the defendant on count one, guilty or not guilty?'

The judge was an elderly man; he had a serious voice and a curved spine. I looked at his wig and couldn't help but find the archaic attire amusing. I let out a nervous giggle as the representative looked at his notes.

Eventually he replied, 'Guilty.' The following counts all followed in exactly the same fashion.

I think we all sighed with relief, but after that there was nothing, just a large empty pile of nothingness. Gary assured us that they would start looking for Tony immediately and that he would be in touch if and when they tracked him down. 'If' seemed like the operative word.

CHAPTER 17

Reflection

With Tony on the run, the trial had come to a standstill. We had a guilty verdict but no one to stand in the dock and be sentenced. All our hard work, pain and determination had essentially resulted in nothing. I received regular updates from Gary Bloomfield, but basically they had no idea where to find Tony. The police were holding his passport and driving licence so he couldn't leave the country by plane but he had emptied his bank account and the police had reason to believe he had bought a campervan. They started a media campaign and his profile appeared on *Crimestoppers*. The newspapers ran headlines such as 'Britain's Most Wanted Paedophile on the Run'.

My thoughts went back to my early years and I realised how easy it was for people such as him to disappear out of the system and into the inviting warmth of families such as ours to live out their fantasies. In my heart I didn't expect him to ever be found. I think half of me hoped he wouldn't be. I still had a strange kind of guilt over the situation. I had been through the whole process, gone to the police, given my statements, stood up in court and spoken the truth but had never felt like I wanted vengeance. When I thought about him it wasn't the nightmares or fear that filled my emotions, it was his kindness to me as a little girl, giving me time and attention when no one else had, and I felt bad about repaying him with a prison sentence. But the biggest problem I had with punishing him was the strange feeling that now I was fine, so why should someone be punished for doing things that had, in the long run, made me a strong and positive person? Overwhelmed with the ambivalence of my feelings, I tried to shut the case away in a box in my mind and not think about it.

The situation between Rob and I was still tortuous. We couldn't make each other happy but neither could we leave each other alone. When we were together we tormented one another, but when we tried to be apart we were drawn back again. My family gave me much strength and confidence during that time. Rollin, although still a joker and a tease, was a strong and protective influence in my life. His stability and calm nature was inspiring. Essie and Sam were in Ireland with their two daughters but we kept in touch, speaking on the phone most weeks.

All of the family around me had beautiful, intelligent children and babies. Rollin and Anya had three between them, plus the older daughter, Lily, that Anya had from a previous relationship. Wanda had two daughters and was living at the camp with them both. It was nice to be surrounded by children again, as life had felt empty without a gaggle of cheeky faces around the place. But living amongst the noise and chaos wasn't always constructive to my studies. During my years with the Open University I went through times where I had to lock the door and put in earplugs to be able to engage with the work at hand. And the distractions of family life often won over the necessity to work. Feeding babies and chatting with siblings always felt more appealing than knuckling down to the finer points of EU policy. So although I was getting to the end of the degree, and had done well in my first three years, it had been far from a walk in the park. Sometimes it felt like a battle.

As the pressure of my studies mounted up, and although Rob had moved out, the situation remained largely unresolved, and the familiar feeling of suffocation mounted up. I felt like I couldn't breathe and I longed to get away. Apart from my childhood, this was the longest time I'd ever spent at home without a trip or journey. To say I had itchy feet would be an understatement.

One evening, as my siblings all settled down with their partners and children for the night, I got in my car, drove to Portsmouth and boarded a ferry to France.

I came out of the port at Dieppe at 6 a.m. I'd been travelling all night. I drove through France with a feeling of freedom and happiness in my soul and Elvis on the stereo. I had very little money and not much of a plan but just being alone and out of England raised my spirits. Putting the miles between Rob and I would truly help our wounds to heal. I was single for the first time in years, I had no commitments, other than submitting my essays to the Open University, and the sun was shining

The Harts had all moved to the South of France a few years before, so I decided to head to Dulcie's house. I hadn't seen her for some time, but I thought she'd be pleased to see me. I looked at the map. It was a good 550 miles, nearly the entire length of France, to her address and I'd barely slept. As I got out of the port and onto the main road I could feel my eyelids getting heavier with every minute that passed. Eventually I approached an exit onto a minor road, swung the car in and looked for a quiet place to stop and rest. Turning up a lane I discovered a wooded area. I climbed into the back of my car, locked the doors and tried to make myself comfortable. The windows quickly steamed up and I couldn't stretch my legs so I got out and laid my duvet down on the ground. It was a warm spring morning. I wondered how safe it was to fall asleep lying outside but before I could really engage with the thought, I drifted off.

My kip *en plein air* was just what I needed. When I awoke, I did the drive to Dulcie's in one journey, stopping once to fill my tank with fuel. As I reached the South of France and the temperature increased considerably, I wound open the sun roof and peeled off some layers and kept going. I closed in on Dulcie's house as evening fell and felt a sense of regret as I switched off the engine. I had such a deep desire to keep moving.

It was, however, lovely to see Dulcie. She was in the process of rebuilding a wonderful old house; she had a one-year-old son and was engaged to a French man. She seemed happy despite some health issues. Her doctor had discovered that the radiotherapy she'd had in her youth had damaged some of the valves and arteries around her heart. She was preparing to go into hospital for an operation.

I spent a week with her. We baked cakes and talked about the past, as usual the years and distance of recent times was soon forgotten. It occurred to me during that stay just how special a childhood friend is. Growing up in the way I did, I never had a ton of schoolfriends to accompany me through life. My first friend, my cousin Ome, spent her entire upbringing on the Loony Line, and still lives in the same area now. We wanted to stay close and spoke occasionally but as time went on our horizons felt irreconcilably different, and our past so long ago. Tom had been out of prison for a few years now, and was working for a Kurdish human rights charity, as well as pursuing other photographic projects; we spoke on the phone as regularly as we could. Dulcie was the one and only female friend that had stayed with me. Oddly I've never felt a lack of female company in my life, perhaps because my horde of sisters is so large and constant, but Dulcie was and always will be a treasure to me. We're like chalk and cheese in many ways: she's shy and quiet in her spirit, not massively ambitious, she doesn't share my eternal need for change and action. Dulcie had been taken out of school at a young age due to her illness, so she was a bit of a loner like me. During that visit I admired her air of calm positivity, despite the looming stay in hospital.

As my stay came to a close, I reloaded my car and prepared to leave. I had two suitcases, one full of clothes and one full of books and I had nothing else apart from lots of pairs of shoes stuffed into every nook and cranny. We said our goodbyes and I headed for Spain. As dawn broke I drove through the mountains and across the border into northern Spain. Eventually the road opened up in front of me as I entered the flat planes of central Spain.

The expansiveness of the views and big skies reminded me of Norfolk, but unlike the Norfolk scenery the land here was dry and deserty and the wind was hot. As I drove past Valladolid the clear blue skies darkened, giving way to ferocious black clouds. After a short time I was in the thick of the heaviest rain I'd ever seen. I ploughed through the storm, expecting it to pass and for the sun to return, but the further south I got the more persistent it became.

I approached a truck crawling along in the slow lane and indicated to overtake. As I pulled out into the fast lane my windscreen wipers came to a standstill, making visibility almost impossible. I hit the brakes and looked for a safe place to stop. I crawled along, leaning out of the window until the bright lights of a service station beckoned ahead. A few coffees later, when the rain was just as relentless, I approached a man driving a breakdown truck and asked if he'd drive me to the nearest town or service centre. Four hours and three garages later I had a quote of £480 and a possible wait of three or four days.

I didn't have the money or inclination to hang around that long, and I certainly wasn't going to spend more than the car was worth on one little motor. So I camped out and waited for the rain to pass. I called a friend, Rachel, in the south of Spain and told her about my problem.

'What's the weather like there?' I asked.

'Lovely, hot, very hot, we haven't had a drop of rain for weeks.' I looked at the map. I was 65 miles north of Madrid. Often the temperature changed drastically once you passed Madrid. So I started preparing to continue my journey without any wipers. Then the phone rang again.

'Rox, get a potato, cut it in half and wipe the windscreen with it. Someone here reckons that will keep the water off.'

'A potato, Rach? Why would that help? And where am I going to get a potato from? I'm in the arse end of nowhere.' The potato idea may have been a no-go, but it got me thinking.

I rooted through my car, looking for something, anything, that might stop the water from sticking to the windscreen. I came across a bottle of baby oil and decided to give it a try. I found that if I polished the windscreen with baby oil and kept my speed above 70 mph the rain and sleet bounced off. The next 100 miles were a little hairy to say the least, but I got there. By the time I reached Granada, the sun was shining.

Rachel and her daughter lived in a sweet little detached cottage on the edge of a mountain. It had idyllic sea views and pretty terraced outside areas bordered with citrus and fruit trees, and before I knew it I had stayed a few dreamy months with them, sitting in the sun, walking on the beach and making pancakes. Rachel and I would talk endlessly about the past and I would try to be upbeat about the future. I suppose I was licking my wounds from the previous few years. I was pleased to have finally broken away from Rob, pleased that he could get on with his life and I could get on with mine, but it didn't stop me missing him. I was excited and happy to be in a country I loved, and around people I adored, but my emotions were all over the place. I'd hoped that a change of scenery would help me concentrate, but I couldn't seem to get back into the studying frame of mind. Nearly five years after my first day at college, I only had to submit all the remaining units at a satisfactory level before I would get a date for my final exams, but I'd sit down to work and my mind would drift off – raking over the past, day after day, hour after hour.

Slowly though, my life in England receded and felt less significant. I kept in touch with my siblings and parents on the phone, but my contact with them was much less than it had ever been in the past. A few months after I arrived in Spain I was sitting on the roof terrace finally getting down to my coursework when the phone rang. It was Essie in Ireland.

'Roxy, I just had the shock of my life. I was in the newsagent's with my girls, just popped in to buy some stationery. I was walking towards the door when I saw the front page of the *Irish Daily Mail*. He's on the front cover, Roxy, a big picture of Tony on the front cover.'

'What did it say? How does he look? Have they found him?'

I'd almost forgotten all about Tony, and the case. It seemed like a different life, a different person. Even hearing his name was surreal.

Essie paused. 'Well, I was in a bit of a daze to be honest, took me by such surprise. They haven't found him. The headline said: "UK's Most Wanted Sex Offender Thought to be in Ireland".'

'Why would he be in Ireland?'

'I didn't read it all, Roxy. I had my girls with me. I didn't want them reading it and realising what was happening. I struggled enough as it was, just to get out of the shop without totally breaking down in front of them both.'

She told me that the police had followed links Tony had in southern Ireland and they thought he might be hiding out over there. Over the next few days I got further reports of the media coverage of the case. He was on *Crimestoppers* and *Most Wanted in the UK*, but most of the newspapers that featured him were the Kent dailies and the Irish nationals. It seemed like the hunt for Tony Bird was closing in.

*   *   *

I changed and grew as a person in the time I spent with Rachel, living in the little stone house on the hill. We set the world to rights with our debates and discussions. I started to get used to being on my own and even began to feel liberated by it. The idea of finding a lifelong love and having children became less appealing. I wanted to experience life without my family or a boyfriend to consider every time I made a move. I thought about staying in Spain permanently.

It wasn't many weeks after I left England that I heard that Rob was expecting a child with a new girlfriend. The news didn't surprise me; he'd always jumped from one relationship to the next without taking a moment to recover. I felt a pang of pain – a part of me will always love him. But more than pain I felt relief – relief that I was single, relief that I hadn't had a baby, relief that I was free.

As the summer came to a close and autumn set in, I focused at last on working for my final exams. I had a lot to cram in: the year had been so full and eventful that I could barely recall the subjects let alone the detail. Then one bright afternoon in January, I turned on my mobile to check my messages and was surprised to hear Gary Bloomfield's voice.

'Hi, Roxy, It's Gary Bloomfield here. Can you give me a call please? I have some news on Anthony Bird.'

I sat for a few moments contemplating the message. I had a feeling of sadness and loss in my soul. As I tried to explore my emotions I came to the decision that Tony was dead. I couldn't imagine any other reason why I felt so strangely sad but also lighter. I imagined that he could no longer live with himself and the knowledge of what he'd done, so he'd taken his own life. It was such a strong intuition I felt sure I was right, but thought I'd better call Gary to confirm. He answered his mobile on the second ring.

His warm voice greeted me, 'Hi, Roxy, how are you?'

I told him I was still in Spain and that life was good.

'I got your message. What's the news?'

'I'm pleased to tell you, we have Tony Bird in custody. He was picked up by my officers this morning on the Isle of Skye.'

I gasped.

'Are you okay? I know it's taken a while, but I told you we'd get him.'

'Yes, I'm fine. I just didn't expect ever to receive this call.'

He told me that Tony had been living in a hostel on the Isle of Skye for many months. He'd talked to the owner of the hostel about wanting to buy a boat, but hadn't pursued the idea when they offered him points of contact. Eventually the owner became suspicious of his hermit lifestyle and odd behaviour. Tony had checked in using his real name, so a quick search on the Internet revealed a mass of results, including contact numbers for the police dealing with the case. Within hours of receiving the call, the police had Tony detained in custody.

Gary told me that they would now go about setting a date for Tony to be sentenced. They would wait for a suitable date so that he could be sentenced by the judge who had initially heard the case.

'It won't take long, just a few weeks, Roxy. Whether you decide to attend or not is your choice. Many people find that the sentencing process results in a degree of closure though. It might be good for you all to come along.'

So, a few days later I packed up my car and said my goodbyes. It felt wrong for most of my family to sit in the courtroom without me.

'Be strong, beautiful girl,' Rachel said as she hugged me tightly.

'Come back soon, Aunty Rox, thanks for all the pancakes and yummy food!' shouted Rachel's daughter, Lila, as I drove down the mountain to commence my journey home.

I left Rachel's on a Friday morning. I drove all day and half of the night. I'd picked up a second-hand motor for the windscreen wipers during my time in Spain, so the rain didn't faze me as I passed through the Pyrenees. As usual I enjoyed being behind the wheel, but I didn't have the carefree emotions I'd had when I'd driven the same journey in the opposite direction a few months before. A year had passed since we'd gone to court, a year since I'd worked myself up to face the man that had filled me with such confusing emotions for most of my life. It's strange what can change in twelve months. I no longer felt the fear or anxiety of seeing him. I knew now it was the right thing to do. I felt grimly prepared.

I arrived in Thorpe Abbotts on Sunday morning. Life at the camp was much the same as when I'd left. People came and went, babies were born, and the piles of scrap cars and half-built wagons built up. Dik arrived over from Ireland the day after I got back from Spain. It was nice to see him and his warm loving hug was more than welcome. He'd grown his beard again, but apart from that there was little sign of change. He still had a head of black hair, but I sensed a sorrowful look in what had previously been such steely cold eyes. Tom came to stay too; he wanted to offer me any support I might need. His bright ginger hair was giving way to strands of white now and his face had aged. London life was taking its toll. He was involved in various charity projects and had his usual contagious energy and open nature.

Arriving at court a couple of days later, we were each searched before being directed to the courtroom. We were seated on the public benches alongside the members of the press.

'I have deliberated over this sentence for many days . . .' intoned the judge in his authoritative voice. In reaching his decision, he said, he'd taken into consideration that Tony was an elderly man (seventy-two at this point) and a man with a clean record. (Emma's accusations had been quashed on appeal so could not be considered to be a mark against his name.)

I was aware, as if by electrical current, that Tony was standing in the dock but I hadn't looked at him directly. I steeled myself to glance over at the frail figure standing before us. He had his head tilted as he looked at the floor. There was no jury present on this day. They'd done their job a year ago and were no longer required. It was all down to the judge. As the judge read out the way the abuse had affected me in my adult life, the details of the nightmares and panic attacks, I felt a childish pang of fear run through me. All Tony's threats over the years before rushed through my mind. I took a deep breath and looked up to see the expression on Tony's face. I had anticipated this moment for many years. I expected to see him looking back at me with empathy and remorse, his eyes full of sadness and regret for not denying his urges.

I looked Tony straight in the eye but the face I expected did not meet mine. A grey-haired man, with a bitter face and cold eyes, glared back at me from the dock. He stared at me with an expression of thunder and shook his head in disagreement. I froze to the spot, like a naughty child caught telling a lie. But the fear that he had held me in for so many years was gone. My family were not disgusted by me, nor was anybody else. I hadn't been thrown out on the street or become a social outcast. I looked at my parents sitting beside me, and was filled with a sense of security and safety. Squeezing Dik's hand I looked up again and caught Tony's eye once more, sending his hard glare right back at him. I kept his stare until he could look at me no longer.

I had nothing to be ashamed of. I realised in that moment that the guilt I was carrying around for punishing a man I thought cared about me could finally be put to rest. He didn't care about me. He was a deluded man with no remorse or regret for what he'd put my family through. He was completely in denial about what he'd done. But despite all this, I still don't think of him as a baddie, and I don't think I ever will. I grew up with him as 'good old Uncle Tony'. He was so liked, loved even, by everyone that met him, that I've never managed to see him as inherently evil.

The judge read out each of the counts of sexual abuse of which he had been found guilty before announcing his sentence. He gave him six years for each of the crimes, the minimum sentence possible. They would run concurrently so effectively he was charged with six years minus the year that he had previously spent in prison for the sentence that was quashed on appeal.

Tony was taken away in handcuffs and we all left the court-room. We went for a drink with Gary Bloomfield and discussed the events. He said he was disappointed with the sentence but that he thought the judge was playing it safe. By giving a light sentence, he had no grounds for appeal this time.

'He won't come out of there alive, I'm pretty sure of that. He's already old and frail, his sort don't do well in prison,' Gary confidently announced. I could sense the disappointment emanating in waves from my family, but I was just glad it was all done and dusted.

Speaking to Perly a short while afterwards, she said to me, 'Five years! I have to live with the nightmares and memories of what he did to me for the rest of my life and he'll be free to fuck up more people's lives in just a few years' time. How's that for justice?'

I knew she was right, but we'd done all we could do. We'd voiced the events of the past, dispelling the guilt and shame.

CHAPTER 18

Happily Ever After?

I sat my exams a few weeks later. As soon as they were done, I got back in my car and drove the 1500 miles back to the south of Spain. I did the drive quicker than the previous time, no stops to take in the scenery or visit friends. Just me and the Merc on the *péage*. I wanted to get away but I wasn't sure what from. Or what I was going to. It was just the familiar emotion of needing to be on the move. Rachel's house was too small for me to live there permanently and I was even more broke than when I'd left home a few weeks before but I knew that I didn't want to be in Britain. I felt such a desire to get far away and keep moving, I would have happily gone on a road trip for the rest of my life.

I stayed with Rachel for a few weeks, before heading up into the mountains to stay with some other friends. I spent the next six months living in the hills between Granada and Malaga. I had a strong network of people around me, musicians and friends, some old some new. John and Esta lived there now, as well as

Maxine. They played in a band together along with other musicians. I went to lots of their gigs and enjoyed late-night swimming in the ocean on the way home. I longed to dance again. Surrounded by Spanish music and culture, I felt the flamenco fire burning inside me once more, but I'd lost my dancer's body through years of sitting at a desk. I still had the rhythms and movements vibrating through my soul, but the confidence to perform them was gone.

But I had a different confidence now, that of an educated and independent woman. I'd made a pact with myself to have at least a year on my own, no boyfriends or family around me. I missed my family but being away from them made me look at life in a different way. It also made people respond to me differently. I was Roxy rather than 'one of the Freeman girls'.

During the next few months, I did various bits of work, including cooking and shopping in exchange for accommodation. I also did admin work for a music festival. I booked DJs and formatted spreadsheets. I didn't have a permanent base in Spain but drifted between different people's places, always trying to make myself more of a help than a hindrance. One of the many things my parents taught me was how to be a good guest. I cooked and cleaned wherever I stayed, and left before anyone got fed up with having me around.

The time in Spain was a respite from the intense emotional turmoil of the last few years. As I slowly emerged back into the real world, I started to make plans for the future. I'd passed all the units for my degree and was due to graduate officially in the autumn. Now I was considering furthering my education with an MA or a vocational course in journalism or creative writing.

The Open University sent me a list of places where I could graduate. I browsed the list and decided not to make a decision until I'd worked out where I wanted to be. I had six months to go.

Leading up to the festival, the admin work came to a close and I agreed to do some promotional work for the festival at various nightclubs. The directors of the event sent me out with the IT technician from the festival office, Arnaud, a debonair French man. He spoke perfect English, with just the tiniest hint of an accent, and was witty and charming. We got on well and laughed our way through the night. Arnaud had a knack of fixing everything he came into contact with. He quickly sorted out my lack of suitable attire by gluing flyers together to create an eye-catching fan and hairpiece.

Halfway through the night I left the nightclub and went outside to get some air and rest my feet. The four-inch heels were taking their toll on my toes. I sat on the wall, my shoes placed carefully beside me, and watched the youngsters stream in and out of the door.

'Why have you taken the shoes off?' Arnaud's dismayed voice came from behind me.

'My feet ache,' I told him rubbing them in my hands.

'Put them back on. You wear them so well. It's unusual to find a lady that can walk elegantly in heels.' He went on to tell me of his memories of being brought up in Paris, surrounded by stylish women in classy shoes. 'English girls can't wear heels, they don't have the poise to pull it off, but you do – such elegant posture.' He placed the shoes back on my feet and took my hand to help me down off the wall. 'Me lady,' he said, miming a courtly bow as I descended.

We spent the following few weekends together, distributing flyers, chatting carelessly and laughing. He was open and warm, with no pretensions or expectations. One night our talk turned to romance.

'I'm not looking for a relationship, just enjoying being on my own for the first time ever,' I told him, confident that I was in no danger of getting involved in anything more than a friendship.

'Me neither, I've only just come out of a relationship myself, definitely time to be single for a while.' But as the nights got longer, our friendship intensified.

'One night will be okay, won't it? We both know where we stand,' I said as we fell into bed after a long night out.

'One night, no expectations,' he said in reply.

One night turned into two, and two into three. Before we knew what was happening, the festival had been and gone and we hadn't spent a day or night apart. I looked at my calendar, twelve months since Rob and I had finally separated, and I was still single. Or was I? Arnaud and I had never discussed what was happening between us since the 'one night' pact over a month before.

The deadline for graduation enrolments was quickly approaching. I found the letter from the Open University and logged on to the website. I hovered over Norwich Cathedral; it was the closest one to the camp. Just before I submitted my choice Arnaud came up behind me.

'Brighton Dome's nice and would make a lovely setting for a graduation.'

'Brighton?' I asked. 'Why would I go to Brighton?' I'd been

there once or twice as a teenager but only for the odd day or night.

'I have to go back to England in a week or two, I have work in Brighton. Come with me.'

'I could do, I guess, but what would I do in Brighton?' I scanned through the list of courses I was considering doing, one of them was in Brighton, but it was the most expensive one. I'd ruled it out.

'Well, I'm not going back without you, Roxy,' he said in a sombre tone that I hadn't heard him use before. 'You know I love you, don't you?' He kissed me on the forehead and hugged me tightly. The words didn't scare me like I expected them to and my reply didn't shock me like I'd thought it would.

'I love you too,' I said.

I clicked the 'Brighton Dome' button and clicked Submit. 'How many guests?' another selection appeared. I entered zero and put in my contact details.

'What are you talking about, zero?' Arnaud said as he looked over my shoulder. 'I'm coming, and what about your parents? They'll want to be there.' I hadn't thought of bringing anyone with me. The graduation seemed more like a formality than anything else. I didn't want a fuss to be made.

'You don't want a fuss?' He looked at me in disbelief. 'Do you realise what an achievement this is? For anybody, let alone you. People don't just graduate and not have a fuss made. You're amazing, Roxy, you've done all this work, having never gone to school and you don't want a fuss to be made. Well, I'm going to be making a fuss and you should give your parents the opportunity to do the same.'

I'd never considered what I'd done to be amazing in any way but hearing someone say it was a good feeling. Dixey was always singing my praises and telling me I amazed her, but she'd done this all my life. I just presumed she was easily impressed.

I enrolled on a journalism course at Brighton Journalist Works. The fees were high and I only had a few weeks to earn them. I returned to the camp and took a live-in care job for a month but with only a couple of weeks before the deadline for payments, I was still only halfway there. So I set about hunting for grants or loans that I might be eligible for. Finally I wrote to a small charity that offered one-off payments for people from Norfolk and Suffolk who were in need of financial help to pursue their dreams. I was amazed to receive a reply that read:

Dear Roxy, thank you for sharing your inspirational story with us. You have clearly worked very hard to reach this, your final academic hurdle. We hope that a contribution of £1000 from the Foundation will assist you in reaching your full potential. We are sorry that we cannot offer the full amount you require, but applications have already closed for the year. This is a goodwill gesture from the trust, issued in recognition of your hard work. The funds will be released directly to your place of education as soon as you let us know that you have secured the full amount to undertake the course. We would like to congratulate you again for getting this far and wish you all the best for the future.

I was shocked and delighted to receive the letter, but I still had to find a substantial amount of money, and I had just a week to do so. Neither of my parents was in a position to help: Dixey was living very simply, and Dik helped us all out financially as often as he could but being the father of nine children his resources were stretched.

Reluctantly, as I liked to be self-reliant, I turned to Esther. Our relationship had been bumpy for a good few years after my disastrous teenage stay in Spain but we were quite close again. Her reply warmed my heart.

'Writing is in your genes,' she wrote.

Dixey's brother Anthony is a journalist and Peter left no end of diaries, short stories and even an autobiography found hidden away in his study after his death. It made her very happy to think of me pursuing a career in writing and of course she would help.

Arnaud and I found a first-floor flat to rent just outside Brighton city centre. The idea of living in a city excited and terrified me at the same time. Apart from a few months in Sydney I'd never lived in a city. The flat had a spacious and bright lounge and a beautiful kitchen, but it was a bit further away from the beach than we hoped. I moved most of my things from the camp, but I didn't have room for my extensive book collection or half of my shoes. They stayed in my shack at the camp.

There was one more worry: the rent per month was more than I could imagine earning working full-time let alone part-time while I studied.

'Don't worry about it, Roxy, concentrate on your studies. I can support us while you do the course,' Arnaud reassured me. He had a way of always surprising me and saying the exact thing to ease my mind.

I'd only known Arnaud for a few months when we moved in together but neither of us questioned the decision. In Arnaud I'd found the love and support I'd spent my life unconsciously seeking. He had no hang-ups, and no problem expressing his feelings or emotions. And yet everything about us was different. He was a home-loving city boy, I was a country girl with a perpetually restless spirit. He was an only child, brought up by just his mother, with few other family members. My siblings were scattered around Europe, some in houses, others in caravans and wagons and seemed to be set on taking over the world with their offspring.

I often wonder what would have happened if I'd had children young. I haven't ruled out motherhood but as the years pass, having children has become less of a priority for me. Other things always seem to take precedence. I love my large chaotic family and the more time I spend away from them the more I miss the company of children, but I love my calm, independent life too.

Some parts of me are scared of bringing a little person into the world. Scared that I wouldn't be able to trust anyone else around them, scared that I couldn't give them what they needed in life. But most of all I don't know how I'd bring them up. I can see the pros and cons of school. I don't feel held back by my lack of schooling, but some of my siblings do, some of them hold anger over the way we've had to struggle to become part of a society that will never really accept us.

Living in a flat in the city centre, I encounter hurdles every day, hurdles that most people can't even begin to understand. I struggle to fall asleep at night because I can't feel the fresh air blowing on my face. If I open a window the traffic passing by keeps me awake. Living on the first floor and looking down at the street makes me feel cut off from the soil and the earth. Rooms with no natural light give me the familiar feeling of panic and despair. The city is never dark and never quiet. There's no birdsong, no sound of the trees blowing in the wind or scent of rain in the air.

I find that I can fit into most circles and groups. I don't look any different to the people around me. I don't sound any different to the people around me. But I don't feel a sense of belonging here or anywhere else in the world. The only times I feel really settled and calm are when I'm on the move, or when I'm surrounded by my family. Not a day goes by when I don't feel a deep longing to be near them all – to rewind the clock to the careless days of child-hood, when we were all going through life as one. When we children tumbled over moss mounds, without a care in the world.

People talk about security – job security, and financial secu-rity. I'm not sure that I'll ever know what those things really feel like. But I have some security now with a man who loves me. I think back to the days in the wagon with the warmth and sense of belonging I had being with my family and I think I had it then too. I lost my path somewhere along the way, but I seem to have found my feet again. I'm glad my parents brought me up the way they did. They made mistakes but they did their best and they've given me one hell of a life.

I don't want to live in a caravan and move from place to place, day after day. But neither do I want to feel like a prisoner within these walls for the rest of my life. Growing up on the road makes it hard to settle, but I know that if I want to shackle my wander-ing spirit I will have to put down roots.

★   ★   ★

As the day of my graduation drew closer, the idea of all the people looking at me started to scare me. Despite my years of performing in front of large crowds, for some reason the idea of walking up on stage and accepting a certificate that I'd spent four years working for seemed like an insurmountable hurdle. Arnaud had to go abroad for work the week before, so couldn't come after all. I considered cancelling the event and getting my certificate sent to me in the post. I phoned Arnaud.

'I'm not going to the graduation. I can't face it. I don't like the idea of all that attention.'

He replied in his calm, reassuring tone, 'You are going, Roxy, you've done a lot of much harder things than this in your life. Stop being modest, and let your family celebrate your success.'

I called Dixey. 'Hi, Mama. Wanna come to my graduation next month?'

'Roxy! Do I want to come? Of course I want to come, nothing would make me happier! Just tell me when and where and I'll be there. What about Dik? I'm sure he'll want to be there too.'

She and Dik seemed to have got through the difficult early days of their divorce and were getting on much better. Their divorce saddened me beyond belief. I secretly lived in hope that Dixey would work through the difficulties of their past and reconcile with him. The father that had once terrified me with a glare had become an extremely strong and loving force in my life, someone I could turn to with any worry or doubt.

Dik has never been one for formalities and such like, so I wasn't sure how he'd feel celebrating my graduation, sitting in the hall surrounded by robed people and a brass band, but I called and asked him if he wanted to join us.

'All over, is it? Well done, love. Yes, I'll be there. It might be a flying visit. I'm busy on the land, getting some more concrete laid and a roof on the cottage, but I will be there.'

I woke early on the day of graduation. I got ready and went for a walk on the beach to clear my head. Arriving at the Dome I couldn't see either of my parents. I got ready and sat in the row of other students. I looked around me but none of my family seemed to have arrived. As I waited to cross the stage and accept my certificate, it occurred to me that I was one of fourteen Freemans in my generation, but the only one to get a degree. For the first time, I felt proud of what I'd achieved. As I came out from behind the curtain I heard an almighty racket coming from the balcony above.

'Go, Roxy! We love you!'

I looked up and saw five figures clapping and shouting. Essie was making the most noise, jumping up and down on the spot, holding her daughter's hand. Beside her were Zeta, Dixey and Dik.

It was a glorious, bright day. We took photos in the gardens and Dik took us out for lunch. We chatted about the ceremony and about the fast-approaching graduation of Zeta. We lifted our glasses.

'To Roxy and her fabulousness,' said Essie, beaming from ear to ear.

Dik put his arm around my shoulders and Dixey squeezed my hand.

'To family,' I replied.

Acknowledgements

Special thanks to Angela Herlihy for noticing me and helping get this project off the ground; to Mike Jones for believing in me and taking a chance; to Kerri Sharp for her continued support and invaluable expertise; and to Victoria Millar for her patience and amazing insight.

I couldn't have written this book without the love and support of my family and friends, so thank you all, but particularly Arnaud for loving me, despite my erratic moods and the endless sleepless nights; Perly for being amazing and offering constant enthusiasm; Dixey for her unconditional love and for passing on her sunny disposition; all my siblings for cheering me on and inspiring me; and last but not least Dik for his emotional and practical help and for making me the strong and resilient person I am today.